GW01466450

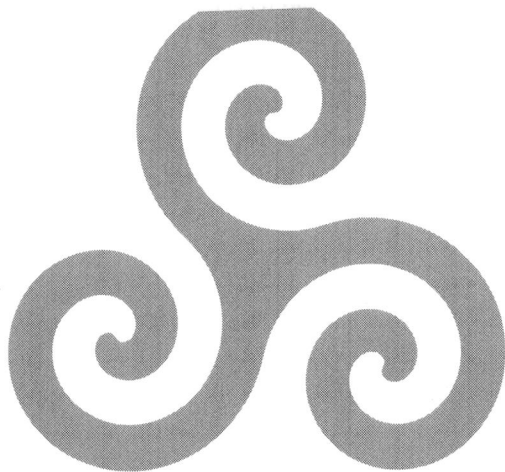

BACK *to*
LIFE
...finding the dream

clodaghwhelanone.com

COPYRIGHT

ISBN: 978-0-9957169-8-8

First Print Edition 2017

Published by clodaghwhelanone.com

Cover design & interior formatting: Mark Thomas / Coverness.com

TABLE OF CONTENTS

~

To my Dad
Eamon A. Whelan
(14 February 1936 – 6 April 1994)
With Love and Thanks…
For sharing a love of books,
Nurturing a love of learning,
Encouraging a sense of adventure
And an inquiring mind.

~

Chapter 1

IT'S BEEN A LONG TIME

Dublin

January '98

Dear Dad,

It's a long time since we've spoken – and almost as long since I've written to you. I think my last letter was written about a week before the funeral. So I guess this one is long overdue.

But I have to tell you that it was the best funeral that I was ever at! You would have really enjoyed it – meeting all those people again. It was a pity that you had to miss it, but I guess that is the way of life… and death.

There were <u>so</u> many people there. You know how big the parish church is? Well, I don't think that I have ever seen it so full (except maybe for Christmas). I think that everyone there was struck by the size of the crowd that turned out to remember you. You certainly made an impact!

One of the aunts was so amazed that she asked Mum, 'How do you know all these people?' Well the obvious answer was, 'Through Eamon – and the rest of the family.' Mum just told her, 'We rent-a-crowd!' But the question did set me thinking: How did we know all these people? How many people do you meet and connect with over fifty-eight years of life?

Each of them had their own particular memories of you. If you put all their memories together it would make up something like the photo-collage that Niall made for Mum. But it would never tell the full story of your life, and the life under the surface in that agile mind and that sensitive heart.

Many of the people there shared the same view of you – and they all had good things to say about you: 'He was a gentle man.' 'He was great fun.' 'He had a great sense of humour.' 'He was a great man for the books – and thinking. He did a lot of thinking.'

One old friend of yours said that he thought that you were cut out for the academic life with your love of reading and thinking and passing on knowledge. He said that you were an honourable man and, in business, you expected everyone else to be honourable too. But they weren't all as you expected.

Sensitive was another word they used, in the sense that you took things to heart and felt deeply. You took the business to heart – a bit too much at times. Most of the people who knew the full story knew it was that that killed you. Or at least, it was the stress over the years from when your business folded. That was what triggered the cancer, wasn't it, Dad?

It was freezing cold outside the church, but with so many people around, it really warmed the heart – even though I was shivering in the cutting April wind.

It was such a close call on the Monday night. The doctor said that you wouldn't last much longer. So I went shopping for a dress for the funeral on the Tuesday before you died. I asked my friend, Aine, to come with me as I needed a second opinion and I couldn't think straight myself. I don't think that I could have faced the shops without her. But I wanted to look well at the service and do you proud.

It was a nice dress, but the fabric was a bit thin for the weather on the day. My teeth started to chatter as we stood around outside the church waiting for the cars. Although I don't know if that was from the cold outside, or the cold on the inside that was running down my spine.

It rained at the graveyard – that heavy miserable rain. But was it *that* kind of rain or did it just feel like it? I remember the priest saying something about, 'Blessed is the man who has the sun shine on his wedding day and rain on his burial day.' Sounded like a pretty feeble excuse for the weather to me!

But then, all of a sudden, the rain stopped and the sun came out. It was beautiful. The umbrellas came down and people started to look up and see what a beautiful place you have to rest, with a view of the mountains and the sea.

Afterwards, it felt as if half of the huge crowd from the church had come back to the house. There were people packed into every corner. There must have been fifty people in the kitchen alone. Funny, I always thought it seemed so full when there were just the six of us.

It was really great to see so many friends there – some of them I hadn't seen since school days. Then there were other people whom I hadn't even met before – friends of yours from work or wherever, but I recognised their names and remembered some of the stories you used to tell.

But eventually the house became too crowded. Everywhere I turned there was another face – but not *yours*. So I had to go out to the garden for a while so I could remember *yours*.

When I thought of my last visit to you in the hospital

mortuary, I could feel the tightness in my chest move up to my throat. Then the tears started to fall, but I felt that I had to stop them or I wouldn't be able to carry on for the rest of the day. So I pictured your face in happier times in the garden.

I sat by the barbecue that you built a few years back. It was your pride and joy, but the ivy is starting to climb up the red brick now. I guess with the Irish climate, it never got the use that it deserved. Your pear tree is thriving; there'll be a bumper crop this year.

When I went back into the house, they had just started on the food. Anyone who found a seat for their meal was lucky. Most were doing the standing shuffle with their plates, as the circulation of people with plates increased.

Two of your old work buddies found a prime spot. They pulled up a chair at each end of the narrow table in the hall. There was a huge bunch of tulips on the table between them – they were comical dining 'a deux'! Somebody suggested that perhaps they could do with less tulips and 'maybe a candle or two' instead… for the 'ambience'!

Mum got the camera out to take a photo of them. I guess a funeral is not really a day for photos, but this shot was just too good to miss. You would have loved it.

A lot of relations came back too, after the graveyard. So many faces from the past. They remembered me from visits to the country twenty years ago or more. I would have been about ten then. But I only had a vague recollection of some of them. I guess ten-year-old kids tend to remember the Cidona and the crisps, and the stomach somersaults of the long drive in the car more than the tall people they visit in the country.

Anyway, more recent memories were stronger in my mind, like the weeks in the hospital.

Some of the relations from the country hadn't made it to the hospital in time to see you. Time was so short, with only three weeks from the tests to the end. How were any of us to know what the timescale would be? All we knew was that it wouldn't be long.

There were lots of 'hospital stories' told after the funeral too. About your sense of humour right to the end. And there was talk of the intensity of living over those weeks for all of us. I think we all got a strong appreciation of life and priorities during that time.

While I'm on the subject of humour, Dad, you'll be glad to know that your funeral was held on the day that our Bren was supposed to have his twenty-first birthday party. So it was a fancy-dress event after all! Did you plan that? It wouldn't surprise me, knowing your sense of irony.

The other irony, which I'm sure you planned, is that you left right at the start of the new tax year. You always blamed the anonymous 'tax man' and 'the banking system' for the failure of your business. But it wasn't their fault. It wasn't anybody's fault, really. Business is a risk – sometimes it works out, and sometimes it doesn't.

They say hindsight is 20/20 vision and, looking back, we could all see the resentment and bitterness eating away at you before it became the cancer. I know that setting up the business was your dream, Dad, and we should all follow our dreams. But you didn't see that it was time to let that particular dream go and find another one.

So, your business failed, but you were never a failure, Dad. You learned from the experience and you passed on that learning to all those people setting up their own businesses. You put so much work into those training courses. I'm sure you'll be glad to know that a lot of your former trainees came to the funeral to pay their respects to you.

Your mother was at the funeral too. It was a hard day for her. She was so proud of you and it was a comfort to her to see how well regarded you were by so many people. I think Granny was still in shock. I guess that you never really expect that your children will go before you, especially when you are on the plus side of eighty years!

But children do put themselves under their own pressures and stresses, at any age – teenage or middle-age. She just couldn't understand how the cancer had hit so quickly; that there was no warning! But we didn't have the words then to explain to her what we felt to be true – that it was the stress that you had put yourself under over the years that eventually took its toll.

There were a lot of your former business colleagues at the funeral as well, especially from the motor industry. One of them mentioned the book that you wrote on the motor industry. I never realised that you had written a book. I reckon that I must have been too wrapped up in my own teenage stuff at that time.

And there's a lot more that I didn't get to know about you, Dad. You were here for twenty-eight years before I came along. So much happens in that many years. I'm sure there are some great stories to be told. But memories fade with time…

If only you had let the memory of the business fade. Maybe we would have had more time with you. But maybe not… Who knows?

I know my memories of the good times won't fade: the good times in the hospital and the thirty years before. But, eventually, my memories of the funeral will fade. So I just thought that I'd write to tell you what a great day it was before I let it go.

I guess memories are a bit like dreams, in that respect. There's a time to hold on tight and there's a time to just… let go.

But, being the philosopher that you were, I'm sure you know.

All my love

Your daughter,

Clodagh

Chapter 2

SWIMMING IN INFORMATION

The Waterside
Dublin 4

Saturday, 21ˢᵗ February '98

Dear Dad,

Sorry I'm a bit late with the greetings this year, but I just wanted to write to say...

Happy Birthday, Dad.

We really missed you at dinner last week. Although Valentine's Day will always be your birthday, it's not a day for happy celebration anymore. It just stands as a reminder that you're gone.

We still celebrate your birthday, and we all meet up at Mum's for dinner. But she doesn't make the heart-shaped cake with the pink icing anymore. I think that it would be too painful for her now, remembering all those other happy birthdays... until the oven timer 'pings' her back to reality. How many candles would there have been this year – sixty-two? I guess that she would probably have needed a bigger cake tin anyway.

I'm sorry that I didn't write sooner to wish you a Happy Birthday.

But, I think that I have been pretty angry with you for leaving us so soon.

Is that what you call early retirement, Dad?

I've been throwing myself into work as well, maybe a bit too much. So sometimes I don't have the energy or the inclination to write. But I will make more time for you Dad, I promise. I'll write more often, and fill you in on what's been happening.

Love,

Clodagh

Saturday, 21ˢᵗ March '98

Don't worry, Dad, I'm not forgetting my promise to keep in touch. But this has been such a busy month. First, I had a friend from England visiting for a week, then we went down to Kerry for a weekend, then there was the Paddy's Day Festival in Dublin, and the Natural Health Exhibition, and the new course I've started... All on top of the day job. Woah! Life has been busy and my head's in a tizzy!

But I think that I should start this letter again before it starts to sound like the ramblings of a lunatic. So I'm going for a walk to clear my head. I've so much to tell you that I really don't know where to start! I'll try again later...

Saturday afternoon, 21ˢᵗ March '98

Well, I guess that I should start where we left off. The world is a very different place to the one that you left, Dad. It's hard to believe that it has been four years already. So much has changed – as is the way of the world. Yet some things haven't changed at all.

As for me, well I've had loads of changes in my life since you've been gone. I started a new job the year after you died, and I've gone back to studying too. But I'll fill you in on the job first.

It's funny the way things work out. Although most of my working experience was in big multinational companies, I started to feel drawn to working with small businesses. Then I saw a job advertised by one of the semi-state agencies for a company development executive in the small business division. As soon as I saw the ad, I said, 'That's the one for me!'

As you can imagine, Mum thought that I was mad, chucking a 'permanent pensionable' job for a five-year contract. I don't think that she really understood that I needed to be learning again – and that need was stronger than my need for job security. But I can understand that, especially after all the financial juggling that she had to do to keep the house running while your business was going through its ups and downs.

It was a bit scary changing jobs after eight years in the same company. It took me a good six months to get past the occasional crisis of confidence and to feel that I was making any progress.

I kept asking myself, 'Am I qualified for this? Have I enough experience to do this?'

But, gradually, I stopped asking those questions as I started to build up my confidence. I'm enjoying the job now, even though the workload can really pile up at times.

I've been learning a lot too, about various different aspects of running a small business. The management principles are pretty much the same as for big businesses, but the reality of life can be very different from the textbook theory. I don't think

I've been to a meeting yet that hasn't been interrupted by the phone or some other 'crisis'. But then small businesses don't always have the luxury of enough staff. The owner or manager is usually juggling a million different things all at the one time. I can see the stress etched on their faces.

The companies that I am dealing with are in the furniture sector, but that covers everything from picture frames to filing cabinets. Even though they are all very different types of businesses, the pressures and stresses on the owner-managers are pretty much the same across the board. So I've been getting a good insight into the pressure and stress that you faced in your business. I remember I was still in college learning the theory of marketing when you set up the business, and knew precious little about the reality of the marketplace and the risks involved.

It's funny the way your perspective can change over the years. Back in '86, after four years of studying for the degree, I vowed that it would be a long time before I went back to studying again. But I think that I must have inherited your love of learning, as I have been doing a lot of work-related courses over the years. Last year I finished a course in finance, and now I have just started a new course for a diploma in business strategy. The lectures only started last month but I'm getting a real buzz out of it already, Dad. It's fascinating to step back from the day-to-day stuff and see the bigger picture of how the world is changing – not just in business, but in everything!

There are huge changes happening, Dad. They're calling this the Information Age now, with all the advances in technology and communications. You would be amazed by all the developments.

Do you remember when I was frantically searching for a topic for my final project for the marketing course? Gosh, it is hard to believe that is twelve years ago now! You had been thinking of getting involved with interactive video for training courses at the time, and wanted to find out more about the market.

It was a handy project for me. You had loads of books and reports on the technology so the background research for the project was done for me already. All I had to do was carry out a survey to find out whether businesses would be open to using the technology for training staff. Or so I thought! But I discovered that there was a bit more to it than that when I got into writing up the research and the findings of the survey. Writing that report felt like pulling teeth!

I remember that you were so excited about the potential for interactive video. At that stage, I didn't even know what the 'interactive' bit meant! But I discovered that I wasn't the only one, as I had to explain it to practically every training manager that I interviewed for the survey. I had the explanation off by heart: 'It is a training course, on video, that allows the user to progress through the course at their own pace of learning.' There was very little awareness of the technology back then in '86, certainly of its use in training.

But I have to admit, Dad, when I was doing those interviews, I sometimes felt like a bit of a fraud as I didn't fully understand all the benefits of the technology myself.

My, how things have changed! Interactive technology certainly seems to be the buzz-word these days. But videotapes are starting to become a bit out-dated now, Dad. CDs are the latest technology, and DVDs.

I know the boom in music CDs had started before you died because I remember that someone gave you a classical CD for a Christmas present one year. But the laugh was that you couldn't listen to it as you had no CD player! No offence, Dad, but your precious hi-fi stereo was a bit out-dated, even then.

I came across some photos recently of that last Christmas Day. It struck me how pale and thin you looked compared to photos of previous Christmases. Funny, I didn't notice that at the time. Perhaps I should have noticed. Maybe if I had, things might have worked out differently or… maybe not. Granny hit that sensitive spot in the hospital when she asked, 'Would it have made any difference if he had gone into hospital sooner?' Would it? Maybe, maybe not. I think, perhaps, we have all had those thoughts at some stage since. Is it guilt or remorse or just wishful thinking? But then, who could insist that you go to the doctor when you insisted that you were fine? We can't change the past, only the future.

So, where was I before I went off on that tangent? What was I telling you about? Oh, yeah… CDs!

Yes, I reckon that the videotapes will be on the downhill slide soon, now that they have developed these new DVDs. That is Digital Versatile Disc to you, Dad!

They are much the same as CDs, only they can hold a lot more information. You can even play a movie on them. Just imagine, no more tape rewind! They are also using them for what you would call computer games. Coming up to Christmas, you see loads of ads on the telly for PlayStation and Nintendo games, among others. That's a boom that is relatively new too, but I don't know too much about it myself. I think that it is some sort of system that you link up to the TV or a computer screen to play the video games. More interactive stuff; but on discs, not tapes!

It's a far cry from the old Space Invader machines, eh, Dad? Though, from what I hear, these new games are just as addictive.

There are some games on the computer system in work, but I don't get much time to use them. I have access to the Internet in work too. That is the big buzz at the moment. And it wasn't even heard of when you died. It's like millions and millions of computers around the world all connected. So once your computer is connected to the Net you can talk to any other computer that is connected.

It is amazing, Dad! There is so much information out there!

In some ways, it is a bit like a library. You can spend a lot of time flicking through books before you find the one you want.

But if you are looking for information on a particular subject or a particular book and you don't know how to look it up, or have a librarian to ask, you can spend a long time looking. And then you can waste a lot of time reading interesting stuff along the way and forget what you were looking for in the first place!

I've gone browsing (or 'surfing' as they call it now) on the Internet a few times. But I really need to learn how to find my way around it a bit better. It's not like a book where you can just check the index for where to find something. It's kind of trial-and-error. Sometimes I feel totally inept and get very frustrated with it. But I am learning; it just takes time.

The other thing about the Internet that really cuts down on time is the electronic mail. It's brilliant, Dad! It's like sending a letter to someone that arrives in an instant! I can send an email to my friend down the corridor to ask her what she is doing for lunch. Or I can send an email to Trish in Australia and it takes the same amount of time to get there, whether it is to the other side of the office or the other side of the world!

You remember Trish, don't you? She's still living out in Brisbane. Sometimes I miss the chats that we used to have in college days. But we still keep in touch. We used to have a 'natter on paper' every six months or so. Although it took about two weeks for a letter to get to the other side of the world, so the news was a bit out of date by the time it arrived. Now we can keep totally up to date using email, and there are no colossal phone bills either, as it only costs the price of a short local call.

Speaking of phones, the mobile phone craze has really taken off too. When you were here last, it was a really 'yuppie' thing to have a mobile phone. But now the prices have come down so much that everyone seems to have them. I haven't got one myself yet, as I can manage with just the phone at home and the answering machine. And sometimes I like to get away from the phone.

But there is just no getting away from ringing phones anymore. You can hear phones ringing everywhere now – in the street, in the pub, in the supermarket, even on the beach! Sometimes it is just so hard to find peace and quiet.

The world seems to be shrinking too, with all this communications technology. They say that we are now living in a global village. It definitely is a small world. But, there is a downside to this Information Age. Sometimes there is just too much information coming at you.

I only have to look at my desk in work to know that the paperless office is a myth. Sometimes I feel like I am swimming in paper! As soon as I start to make progress on clearing the desk, another wave of paper lands on it. And then I switch on the computer to find yet another wave of information coming in through the email.

Some days there is just too too much information, Dad. My brain goes into a tizzy trying to cope with it all. I start to feel as if I am in some sort of whirlpool – going down. Then I find that I can't focus on doing just one thing because my mind is juggling so many other things at the same time. On those days, I can't even absorb what I am reading. When it gets to that stage, it's not so much like I'm swimming in information, it feels more like I am drowning! Those are the days that I would love to just get away from it all, find a quiet place in the country and immerse myself in a good book.

I still love books and reading. I got that from you, didn't I? Well, you will be glad to know that, despite all this new technology, books will still be around for a long time to come. They are so much easier on the eyes than a computer screen, and they fit into your pocket too!

But that brings me to another new invention, Dad. They have brought out pocket-sized computers now! Can you imagine? Going out for a walk and finding a quiet spot to sit down to rest and read for a while. Then you put your hand into your pocket and take out… a pocket-sized computer!! No, I can't imagine it either. I'd miss the furry feel of the paper and twiddling with the corner of the page as I read the last few lines. I'd miss the surprise of opening the book at random and finding out what it has to tell me today.

I'm still as bad as you were for the bookshops. I can lose myself in a bookshop. The sheer volume and range of books available never ceases to amaze me. When I get over my initial disorientation and find my way to the section that I want, I start dipping in between the covers. And I can lose track of time completely!

That happened to me just last week, Dad. I went into the shop for a particular book and I found myself beachcombing the shelves. Two hours later (yikes!) I surfaced with two carefully chosen titles... And a list as long as my arm for when the budget is in a healthier state!

We used to have some really good conversations about books. Do you remember those, Dad? I used to feel very close to you then. At that stage, I was still going through my teenage angst and insecurity, but you made me feel very grown-up by talking to me as an adult, discussing books and ideas. But then there were less and less of those conversations as the years passed.

Looking back, I guess that I just got out of the habit of reading for enjoyment. I think that it started when I was in college. Somehow, I began to feel guilty about reading just for fun. In some warped kind of thinking I reckoned that if I had time for reading then I should be reading textbooks. In the end, I'd do neither. Instead, I'd just veg out in front of the telly for the evening. And you were so absorbed in setting up your business then that you didn't have the time or the energy for reading much, or for chatting about books. I missed those conversations, Dad. I think that I am only now starting to realise just how important they were to me. Sometimes I feel that they were the closest connection that I had with you.

What got me on to this rambling about books anyway? Oh yeah! Technology! On the positive side of things, you'd be amazed by some of the stuff that you can do on the Internet, Dad. You can even use your computer to go shopping! You can order a book and have it delivered to your door a couple of days later. I tried my hand at buying some books on the Internet, and it is a really nifty service. But I still do enjoy a good browse in a bookshop, and computers can never replace that.

Oh dear, I am still on the subject of books. Which reminds me… I've got a test looming next Friday for the new course. Aaargh! Even the word 'test' makes me feel like I'm back to school! Anyway, I'd better go and do some reading for it. There is so much to take in, Dad. But I'll get back to finish this letter at the weekend…

Sunday 22nd March, 1998

Well, Dad, the test went better than expected. I guess that it is a bit like riding a bicycle – it just comes back to you. But learning information is easy compared to learning new ways of doing things and adapting to life changes.

I think that Mum is still finding it hard, adapting to life without you. But after thirty-five years together, that is hardly surprising. She misses you so much. Her gammy knee is still acting up and it seems that arthritis has set in too. The doctors say she may need a knee replacement operation soon. And, as if that wasn't bad enough, she was mugged recently, and the house was burgled one night while she was in bed. So she hasn't been sleeping too well lately. It really has been one trauma after another for her over the last few years.

Our Fiona was pretty cut up about your death too; in more ways than one. She had a bad accident shortly after the funeral and she was a bit like the Bionic Woman for a while, with metal pins and plates holding her arm together. She couldn't do any dress designing work for a long time after as her arm was so bad. So she has had a very difficult few years.

But I'm sure that you know all about that, and you've been helping her through the tough times. Anyway, life seems to be turning around for her now, and she seems to enjoy her new work in the movie business. She works very long hours, as the wardrobe department are always on call. But it's a good opportunity and it may help her to get more work in costume design.

You'd be so proud of Bren, Dad. He got his master's degree with flying colours! But then he has been tinkering around with computers and wires for as long as I can remember, so he probably had a head start on the rest of the class. Sorry, Dad, but there are no prizes for guessing where he is working now… Yes, you got it in one – in a computer business, of course!

Niall is working in a high-tech business now too; in the place where they make those little pocket computers that I was telling you about. But it is all the way across the other side of the city, so it is a bit too far for him to cycle every day. I think he misses the cycling. Anyway, he has taken up driving, and he passed his driving test with no bother.

I remember when I took up driving… Five tests later, I finally passed! And do you remember the first and only time you gave Fiona a driving lesson? You forgot to tell her where to find the brake pedal! I never did get the full story of how she avoided the tree, but I still remember the two white faces that arrived home after that particular lesson. Funny the way you never volunteered to give any more driving lessons after that!

Well, Dad, that's enough of this reminiscing for the moment. It's getting late. And I've an early start in the morning and a busy day ahead. I'm not sure what tomorrow holds – whether I'll be swimming or drowning at the office. But I am sure that it will be one or the other!

I'll write again soon.

Love,

Clodagh

Chapter 3

CRYSTAL BALL

The Waterside
Dublin 4

Thursday, 26th March '98

Dear Dad,

Is the world going mad? Or is it just me? Life just seems to be work, work; busy, busy; rush, rush. In the newspapers, I've been reading about all these big companies laying off staff and moving to countries with lower labour costs. Yet, for the small companies I'm dealing with, business seems to be booming here. Whether they are getting new computer systems set up or expanding into overseas markets, they all seem to be looking for help adapting to change in one form or another. It has been getting busier and busier at work over the last few months. But over the last few days, things have really started to snowball! Maybe it is spring in the air that has them all looking at growth.

I'm getting back out on the road a bit this week, visiting companies that I haven't seen in quite a while. Some of them remind me of your business, Dad. They see the opportunities and they have the will to grow, but they don't have the systems and finance in place just yet.

I really admire the bravery of people who set up their own

business, taking control of their own destiny. Yet they also take on responsibility and risks too. That must be scary. You had the courage to do it, Dad. It must have been a big step for you – to step out of the security of 'the job', especially with a family to support and kids still in school and college. You must have had a dream, a vision of what you could make of the business. I bet you enjoyed the independence at first, being your own boss. If only you'd had a crystal ball to see when things were not working out the way you had envisaged. But I guess you got too attached to your vision to step back and see things objectively.

That's the part of the job that I love, Dad; talking with the men and women who have had the courage to set up a business. Sometimes I can empathise with them from my own experiences and from my experience of your business. Other times, I can be of more use to them by 'holding up a mirror' and asking the hard questions of where the business is going – the questions that you can't ask yourself when you're too close to it. I feel that I am of some help to them, even by just asking those thought-provoking questions.

But fathers always know better than daughters, don't they?! So I could never ask you the challenging questions about your business. You gave me an education, Dad, but you never let me use it to help you. Was it just stubborn male pride that you didn't want any help? Or perhaps it was me? Maybe I just didn't have the experience or the confidence then to say what I could see from the outside. Would you have listened? I felt that you never really asked my opinion about your business – your baby. Then again, I guess that I never really offered it, either!

Anyway, I've got the confidence now, from experience, to

offer my opinion and ask the hard questions about business. I've noticed that some people take challenging questions as food for thought. They're open to different possibilities and different ways of thinking and doing things. Other people see a challenging question as a threat and they close their minds to any variation on their vision. Which would you have been, if I'd asked?

Yes, I enjoy meeting such brave people, Dad. And it has been an education for me. I have so much to learn from them. It's the bloody paperwork and administration that I don't enjoy so much. I'll be on the road for two days next week, and that will generate at least four days' paperwork! Oh, the trials of life! It's a necessary evil, I suppose. But does there have to be so much of it?

Speaking of paperwork, I still have a lorry-load of reading to catch up on for the business strategy course. So I'd better take a break from writing and focus on that for a while.

Saturday, 28ᵗʰ March '98

Well, I've cleared some of my quota of course reading for this weekend. This strategy stuff is really fascinating, Dad. It' all about looking at what's happening in the business environment, seeing where the opportunities and threats are, and identifying the strengths and weaknesses of the business. Then the tricky bit is to come up with a strategy that will keep the business competitive in a fast-changing environment.

There used to be a time when change was predictable; not anymore. That's one of the things that really struck me: the amount of change happening these days. And the pace of change seems to be accelerating too. Things are moving faster and faster. And, boy, is that causing people to be stressed out!

We're going through a Strategic Change Programme at work too, to shape up the organisation for the new millennium. But we're still working to the old systems while they are introducing the new way of doing things. So, for the moment, a lot of people seem to have double the paperwork while the two systems are running together. And pretty much everyone seems to be under more stress than they were this time last year.

One of the girls in work got a promotion this week, and she's moving to another department from Monday. So there were a few from the office going to the pub after work for the proverbial one or two to celebrate. I wasn't really in form for going out last night as I felt a bit brain-drained. But I went anyway. I hadn't had a good natter with the girls for a couple of weeks as we've all been so busy lately. I was hoping for a bit of light relief, with an update on the social lives and potential romances! Only the conversation was all about office politics and stress levels! Has nobody got a life outside work anymore?

Rhetorical question, Dad! But, I'm sure you can relate to it. I remember the time, just before your business folded, when you had meetings in the office on Sundays! It was the only time that you had to get together with you partners to find out what had been happening in the office during the week while you had all been out on business.

We knew that you were under a lot of pressure then. But, even so, I used to get a bit annoyed when you disappeared after Sunday dinner. It really bugged me that you preferred to spend Sunday afternoons with your business partners instead of your family. And I resented it; that the business seemed more important to you than us, your family. But I understand now how easy it is to get sucked into work. So much so that you lose the balance of life.

I'm trying to keep some sense of balance in my own life, but it's not always easy. Exercise helps. I was pretty good about getting down to the gym regularly when I first joined. The only trouble was the boom-boom-boom music was starting to make me hyper. There was an antidote though – the peace and quiet of the steam room. But then other people would come in and start talking about their work stresses. Back to square one again!

I haven't been to the gym in a week now. The energy levels are flagging a bit. I've just realised where all my energy is going – work! Maybe I should look at getting back into a yoga routine at home. That worked for me before, at a time when I needed to get more balance in my life. At least it worked until I started going to classes! It was the drive to the yoga class at the tail end of rush-hour traffic that was a bit counterproductive. After six weeks of that, I'm afraid the class went by the wayside… There just didn't seem much point in getting wound up in heavy traffic in order to chill out with yoga stretches and relaxation.

Perhaps I should just get out and walk in the fresh air a bit more. I remember when we were kids, you used to bring us out walking on Saturday afternoons. You had time then. They were some wonderful walks – up the mountains, through the Pine Forest, along the strand at Sandymount and down the South Wall of the Liffey and right out to the lighthouse in the middle of Dublin Bay.

Come to think of it, Dad, why am I paying to go to the gym

– or not as the case may be! – when the South Wall is only a few minutes from home with good fresh sea air and wonderful views across Dublin Bay? And there's no booming music or sweaty stuffy atmosphere either.

Well, strike while the iron is hot!

I think that I'll go for that walk now and see if the South Wall is still as long as I remember it.

Tell you about it later…

Sunday, 29th March '98

I don't think that the South Wall has shrunk in the last twenty years or so, Dad. So it must be that my legs have got a bit longer since I was last there. It only took me about twenty minutes to walk all the way down to the lighthouse. As I recall, the last time I did that walk with you it took the best part of an afternoon. Was that because you had to cajole all those little legs to keep moving? Or was it just that Saturday afternoons seemed to go on forever then?

The lighthouse has had a new coat of red paint and the walls around it have been whitewashed recently. Though it seems that was just too much temptation for a few graffiti artists! The sea has taken its toll too. On the first stretch of the wall, it looks like the sea has been battling with the river Liffey to pull the blocks apart. It takes some concentration to avoid twisting an ankle. But they seem to have done some sort of repair job further along and the surface is more even there. By that stage, I could lift my eyes to take in the view across the bay from Howth to Dun Laoghaire. I love that sun-shimmer on the water. It makes the whole world seem brighter.

At the lighthouse, I sat down on the rocks for a rest. You know, Dad, if I had no other demands on my time, I think that I could quite happily spend hours just watching the waves. But thoughts of all the reading I have to do for the course brought me back from my daydreaming.

Back at base this morning, I tried to get into reading up on my notes, to no avail! So I put on some relaxing music and did some yoga breathing and stretches to try to clear my head of all the clutter that's been whizzing round my mind this week. That worked, but not as I had intended! I came to the realisation that there is more to life than reading notes on business strategy on a sunny Sunday. So I picked up *The Tibetan Book of Living and Dying*. That book has been such a comfort to me since you died, Dad. I just wish that I had discovered it before you died so it may have been a comfort to you too.

It helped me to get things back in perspective again. And today I have declared a work-free, study-free day! I've decided that I deserve a totally indulgent day doing whatever takes my fancy at each moment. First, I planted some seeds in the flower box on the balcony. All growing well, it should be a riot of colour in the summer. Don't ask me what I did with the rest of the day. I can't remember. But, I know that I had a thoroughly enjoyable time just pottering around.

And so another weekend bites the dust, Dad. I've got a paperwork day in the office tomorrow. But then I'm back on the road for Tuesday and Wednesday, which I'm looking forward to. I'll write you an update next weekend.

The Lighthouse
South Wall
Dublin Bay

Monday, 30ᵗʰ March, '98

Well despite the sun shining outside on a glorious sunny day, it was a <u>bad</u> day indoors! Although I got clear of a lot of the paperwork that I'd planned to do, the old bureaucratic system really kicked in today with a vengeance! The more work I did, the more work that came in to be done. I really felt that I was treading water (or drowning!) in another high tide of paper! My frustration level rose well into the red. Danger zone! I could feel myself getting really tetchy with work colleagues as well.

So at lunchtime, I escaped from the office and went for a very pleasant walk by the river to calm myself. That helped – temporarily. Even so, when I got back to work, I could feel the frustration turning to anger at the management 'system', that unfeeling system. How futile is anger? And that thought only added fuel to my own frustration.

By mid-afternoon, I could feel myself turning into the Antichrist! So to avoid inflicting myself on others in that state, I bailed out early. I went straight home and changed into my civvies. Then, as the sun was still shining, I headed for the South Wall – I needed to burn off some negative energy! I belted down the wall at a blistering pace. As I walked, I could feel all the anger and frustration rising. I let it rise and walked faster and faster. I was pretty burnt out by the time I got down to the lighthouse, so I sat on the rocks to rest for a while and let all the thoughts and emotions flow.

I found myself watching all these little puff-ball clouds scooting across a clear blue sky and the choppy little waves hopping up out of a relatively calm sea. It reminded me of a passage in the book I was reading last night on meditation: 'Be like the ocean looking at its own waves, or the sky gazing down on the clouds that pass through it.'

Suddenly I felt a great sense of calm and I was able to observe all the dark clouds floating through my mind. I got some good insights into the nature of the negative emotions that I'd been feeling all day – and their source! Some of which I had been conscious of and some of which had been unconscious, until now.

First of all, Dad, work and the 'system' were only the trigger. I know that I do have a tendency to put pressures on myself as well. But, underlying that, I came to realise that I'm going through some sort of crisis-of-career at the moment. I don't enjoy the job I'm doing, just now – or find it as rewarding as I used to. Perhaps it is the way I'm doing it. Perhaps it is the organisation that I'm working for. The nature of the job has changed a lot since the organisation structure changed last year. I've come to realise that it is not the same job that I signed up for three years ago.

So what do I do about it, Dad? An old adage springs to mind: 'What you can't change you have to accept… and what you can't accept you have to change.'

Since I can't accept this ongoing frustration, it seems that I need to make some changes in my life. I think that I need to take a long hard look at what I'm doing and determine which parts of the job I really enjoy and find rewarding and which parts I don't. And then I need to start thinking about my options to do more of what I find rewarding and less of the things that I don't find rewarding… And still earn a living! I've realised that this has been brewing for quite a while, Dad. But I need to start making decisions soon before it starts doing my head in!!

Insight No. 2 – Nature really helps to put things into perspective.

To hell with the gym for a while. I need to get out and walk down here to the lighthouse much more often for more walking insights and direction. For me, walking here is a bit like a form of meditation. I need to focus on my feet at first. But by the time my feet go on automatic pilot, my mind goes into free flow.

Then I can watch my thoughts as they pop up and get some insight into what's happening below the surface of my mind. Or I can just watch the sea and realise how insignificant my turmoil is in the grand scheme of things.

Insight No. 3 – When the pressure and stresses seem to be overwhelming, put them in a time warp to get a more realistic perspective on them.

My mind wandered back to this time four years ago in the cancer ward at St Vincent's Hospital. You were still conscious then and in good form, but you only had a week of life left. Though we didn't know the exact timescale then, we knew it was short.

That thought put my work frustrations in perspective. And it also brought me to two more realisations, Dad.

One: I've been pretty impatient with Mum lately. But I see now that her current moaning mode probably comes from her grief rising again – coming up to your anniversary – and not just from her gammy knee. I've been a bit unfair on her lately. Truth be known, I've probably been doing a bit of the burning martyr myself!

Two: Part of my own frustration and anger today has probably come from my own grief bubbling under the surface. Grief after bereavement is a funny thing, Dad. As time passes, you think that you are over it, but it pops up again when you least expect it. And I've been so busy lately, keeping myself occupied with too many distractions. I haven't given myself time to acknowledge what's going on under the surface and feel the sadness.

Final insight of this afternoon: negative emotions are natural too.

But I put so much energy into positivity that I don't allow the negative emotions to flow when they need to, so they tend to erupt. As they did this afternoon! On reflection, I haven't felt so frustrated and angry in a long, long time.

By this stage, Dad, you may be starting to think that I am totally neurotic. But, I'm glad that I took some time out today to discover these insights. And writing to you does help me to clarify these flashes of insight into my thoughts and feelings.

Well, we can't be happy all the time, Dad. So when I get home, I think that I'll put on the tape I made of your old favourite, the Red Army Choir – powerful music! Then I'm going to just sit and listen, and spend some time thinking about you… and shed a few tears. I feel that I need to work through these feelings – the anger, the frustration and the sense of loss. It's Brendan's birthday tomorrow, and Mum is doing dinner. I need to get my strength back for then. If I don't, I'm afraid that I might start getting tetchy again tomorrow. And it's really not a very good time of year for that for any of us.

So, to sum it all up, I found another little gem of wisdom from that book on living and dying: 'What we have to learn, in both meditation and life, is to be free of attachment to the good experiences, and free of aversion to the negative ones.'

I think I learned a lot today, Dad!

But I'm not really in a letter-writing frame of mind anymore. I'm probably a bit burned out – emotionally and physically. So I need to get home to refuel with some nourishing food. I'll write some more later in the week. I may be in better form then, or maybe not… What does it matter? as Anthony De Mello would say.

Thursday, 2nd April '98

Well, I'm back in form again! But it's a funny old world, Dad! On Tuesday (after my crisis-of-career day) the boss called me into his office to tell me that I had been made permanent in the job. How ironic! Just as I decide that I need a change, I'm made permanent! So that means that I can now join the pension fund. But what state will my head be in when I'm sixty-five? On the positive side, and of more immediate benefit, it also means that I may be eligible to apply for a career break. That would give me a sort of safety net to take time out and consider my options.

My friend, Jacqueline, was also made permanent. After the good news had been announced, we adjourned to one of the meeting rooms for a private natter. One of the lads stuck his head in the door to remind us of a meeting later in the week. I'm sure he thought that this was the mutual congratulation society.

Little did he know! Jacqueline had called me aside because she was concerned about my emotional well-being after noticing my mega-frustration day on Monday. That is one of the good things about the job. There is a great support network among a small group of friends, which comes into play when needed, no matter how heavy the workloads. I really appreciated her concern. And it is so important to me to have an objective sounding board, especially when I'm finding it hard to see the wood for the trees.

But I got to see more of the wood on Wednesday, Dad, as I was out of the office to visit a couple of companies in County Meath. It was wonderful to be out on the country roads, away from city traffic. Driving can be a great meditation in itself when you're out in the country, off the beaten track. And it was a good opportunity to remind myself of what the job is all about, in the real world – away from the 'system'. Both companies are doing well, and that's what it's all about.

On the drive back to Dublin, I got another flash of insight into my motivation for doing this job and working with small business in particular.

In a way, it's like I'm trying to help other businesses avoid the pitfalls that yours went through. And maybe I'm trying to prevent other families from going through the situation ours went through when your business became higher priority than your family… and your health. Or maybe I'm trying to help the business owners to reduce their stress levels by helping them to get better management systems set up and so avoid crisis management situations. The only problem is, Dad, the more companies that I deal with, the more stress I'm putting onto myself. So, for the sake of my own health and well-being, it's definitely time for a rethink!

But, for now, it's late and I need some sleep. So I'm going to hit the sack and listen to the pitter-patter of the rain outside. It's such a lovely restful sound.

Goodnight, Dad.

Sunday, 5th April '98

I drove out to the graveyard at Shanganagh this morning to leave some forget-me-nots on your grave for your anniversary on Tuesday. The grass had been cut recently. It felt like velvet under my hand; a far cry from the soggy clay of my first visit. I sat by your feet for a long time, wishing you were here so I could ask your advice. What to do? Which way to go? What if, what if… I'm so unsure of where my life is going and where I want it to go.

And then I saw clearly that the only thing we can all be certain of in life is that we will all die at some stage – and we'll be a long time in the grave! So life is for living, and if I lose that perspective, I might as well be in the grave already. Thanks, Dad, for the advice.

I felt better after that and I decided to get busy living. So I drove down to Dun Laoghaire to join the Sunday strollers on the pier and savour an ice cream on the walk. The sea air was bracing and I had a real good-to-be-alive feeling by the time I got back to the car to drive over to Clonskea.

Mum had organised an Anniversary Mass for you, and she had invited all the family – she still never misses an opportunity to get us into a church! I went to the Mass to remember you. But

I was a bit switched off from the ceremony so I used the time for reflection.

We all adjourned back to the house after the Mass. It was really good to see all the aunts, uncles and cousins again. It must be Christmas since I last saw them all together. We talked about you a lot. Mum was in great form doing 'mother hen', feeding a house full of people. It was good to see her so cheerful, as she's been feeling down for so long.

Friday, 10th April '98

Happy Easter, Dad! A time for new beginnings.

It's Good Friday today and it's been a good day in more ways than one.

There was very good news on the TV this evening. The politicians have finally reached an agreement on the Peace Process talks in Northern Ireland. An historic day! Although the agreement still has to go to referendum to be ratified next month. Hopefully, the diehards won't use that day as an excuse to justify their existence. And hopefully, Granny will sleep more peacefully at night up in Fermanagh.

She still doesn't talk about you much, but she has photos of you all over the living room. I reckon she must miss you dreadfully. I think she deserves a bit of peace at her age.

It was a good Friday for me in Dublin too. I met Karyn, Michael and Andrew this morning in town, as we were all off work today (a four-day weekend! Yippee!!). It was so nice to meet up with friends for a late breakfast and then just ramble around town for a while. Time flies! It must be at least six weeks since the four of us last got together. But from the sound of things, work is pretty hectic for all of them too. It seems to be the same story across the board.

After we all went our separate ways, I had a really pleasant walk home by the canal. Then I settled in to some reading for the afternoon. When my concentration started to wane, I did a bit of yoga to get the circulation going. That put me in the humour for some fresh air, so I wrapped up and headed for the South Wall.

So much for spring! We've had a polar airflow over the last few days – the forecast for this evening is minus three! It's been pretty windy too. So it was a very refreshing walk, to say the least – but not so cold and windy that it stings your face.

There was a storm last night, and loads of driftwood had been washed up onto the South Wall today. I felt a bit like Dorothy in *The Wizard of Oz* when the twister hits Kansas! All these little bits of driftwood were skipping around my feet, spiralling in the wind eddies.

There was an awesome view across the bay towards the mountains with wonderful light. That sort of watery winter sunshine was coming from the west over the city, in total contrast to the dark rainclouds to the east over the Irish Sea. In between, there were loads of white horses on the waves, galloping in to the strand against a backdrop of snow-capped mountains down in Wicklow. When I see a view like that, Dad, I think what a gift it must be to be able to paint.

With the strength of the wind, I was forced to take the Buddhist approach to the walk – the middle way! It was too dodgy walking near the edge of the wall as there were some seriously strong gusts of wind. And I didn't fancy a swim in the

Liffey today!

Very few people were out braving the elements. I only passed about five or six people, but every one of them was smiling. So was I. That kind of weather makes me feel very alive. I felt good for the rest of the day and I know I'll sleep well tonight.

Sunday, 19ᵗʰ April '98

The bonus to a bank holiday weekend is that it's a short working week afterwards. And this week has really flown by. I had a great day on Tuesday (with no phones ringing!) and got a lot of the paper backlog cleared up. I also have a better mental perspective on the work situation this week, Dad. I can only do what I can do during working hours. And I've stopped letting the fretting about it overlap into after-hours…Well, I'm trying! My new walking routine has helped a lot in that regard. I've made it a priority to get out for a walk after work every day, whatever the weather.

I was expecting a quiet weekend and I'd no plans for Friday evening apart from chilling out. Then Karyn phoned for a natter. She had no plans for the evening either. So I called over to her apartment and we did a demolition job on a couple of bottles of wine. It seems that she has reached the same crisis point as me in that work has become her life, and there has to be more to life than just work, eat, sleep. But she has decided what she's going to do about it. She's planning on quitting her job and taking a year off to travel on one of those round-the-world tickets to Australia and back.

I admire her courage and I envy her sense of direction. I suppose it's an option I could consider too. What's to stop me?

Lack of funds and the mortgage for a start!

Niall called over on Saturday afternoon to put up a mirror for me. It's handy having an engineer in the family. Although he's probably a bit overqualified for my odd jobs.

I would have tackled the job myself, but the metal frame was quite heavy and there were two holes at the top that had to be lined up straight.

My big decision was where to hang it? In the hallway or the living room? With the weight of the frame, Niall advised against hanging it on a plasterboard wall if I didn't want to be looking at a gaping hole in the weeks to come. So that narrowed down the options to one wall in the living room.

It's a very different style to the little wooden-framed mirror that was there before, and it may take a bit of getting used to. But it does seem to bring more light into the room.

Hanging mirrors can be thirsty work, so when the work was done we adjourned to the local where I paid the 'engineering consultancy' fees in Guinness!

I enjoyed chatting with Niall over a couple of pints and there was a really cosy, relaxed atmosphere in the pub.

The only problem for Niall was that they didn't have Sky Sports. So he was missing the football or Formula 1, or whatever other sports fixture that was on that afternoon. Well, after all his hard work, I couldn't see him deprived of his Saturday fix of sports! So I headed back to base and he headed up to Toners Pub to meet his buddy and talk sport.

I finally got my head back into studying this afternoon, Dad, and I felt a great sense of satisfaction after putting in about three hours of concentrated reading.

Just as well I did. We're back to lectures next Friday and Saturday. That means another pile of reading material for next week.

It wasn't hard to concentrate today as the topic was so interesting – Future Scenarios. That's all about painting a word-picture of possible futures.

What will the world be like in five years; in ten years; in thirty years or more?

There are even companies that make a business out of identifying trends and extending the current trends to try to predict what the future will be like for life, work and business.

It makes fascinating reading and I'm starting to get a vision of what the future world will be like. But I can't see where I fit into it. I wish that I could see what *my* future looks like.

I suppose it's a bit like the old interview question: 'Where do you see yourself in five years' time?'

Hell, I can't even see beyond next month, Dad!

Well, maybe my new mirror will bring a bit more light into my vision of my own future. Mirror, mirror on the wall… I wish you were a crystal ball.

I know that I need a change. Not just change for the sake of change. I need a new direction. I need to see where my life is going.

But, right now, Dad, I feel trapped – trapped in my job, trapped in my social life, even trapped in my home. I feel like a hamster in a cage running round and round in a wheel. Running to stand still. I long to escape from that feeling. But what do hamsters do when they escape the cage? They burrow! No, I don't want that. I don't want to hide underground. It may be safe and secure, but it's another trap. I want to be free – like a bird flying from a cage. I want a wide, wide view of many roads and places… And a chance to see all that the world has to offer.

But, it's dark now, Dad, and reality calls me back from my flight of fancy. I've an early start for work tomorrow, so it's time I got some sleep.

'To sleep, perchance to dream.'

Maybe tonight I'll dream of a crystal ball, or spreading my wings and flying around the world.

Goodnight, Dad.

All my love,

Clodagh

Chapter 4

SEA CHANGE

South Wall,
Dublin Bay

Thursday, 23rd April '98

Dear Dad,

I've been doing a lot of thinking this week about change. I need to change my life. And that scares me a lot, because I don't know how or where to start.

But I can't just sit around waiting for life to happen. I have to make it happen.

I have to invite change into my cosy little life – big change – before the cosiness starts to smother me.

I don't know what started me thinking this way. Maybe it was getting out from the four walls and walking by the sea. Maybe it was the work frustrations, or reading about strategic change. Maybe it was seeing the sea changing from winter to spring. And now summer is coming... Next week! (Where does the time go to?)

Whatever the reason, I feel that it is time for me to invite a new season into my life.

I've made the decision – even though I haven't a clue of the direction as yet.

I've been putting too much of my energy into work projects. Now it's time I started putting more energy into my own projects.

What are they? You might well ask, Dad!

I'm not quite sure myself yet. But I'll let the thought simmer for a while, and I know an answer will come to me.

Meanwhile, I'm back to lectures again tomorrow for more learning about Change Management. So maybe that'll give me some ideas.

The Waterside Apts
Dublin 4

Sunday, 26th April '98

A funny thing happened in the library on Friday, Dad. I only went down there to use the photocopier, but I found the woman using the copier ahead of me was battling with a paper jam. So I had some time to kill while the librarian fixed the machine. I went over to the index to check if they had any books by Deepak Chopra (my most recent discovery). But all they had listed were a couple of magazine articles. So I just went for a ramble around, aimlessly scanning the shelves. Then, one word jumped out at me from the spine of a book – *Synchronicity*.

The author was an American lawyer, Joseph Jaworski, who used to work with Royal Dutch Shell Co. I remembered that he was mentioned at one of the last lectures in the context of scenario planning. But this was no theory book. It was the story of his own individual journey from being a highly ambitious, highly stressed lawyer to opening up to other possibilities.

Creating a new vision for his future and making it happen. For me, it was one of those rare inspirational stories that fire up the imagination.

Strange thing, Dad! Synchronicity is that phenomenon where significant coincidences start happening to support you in achieving your desires if they are in keeping with your purpose in life. I still don't know where my life is going yet. But, by coincidence, this book has presented me with a sort of roadmap of what to expect along the way – the ups and downs, and especially the pitfalls.

Energy is a funny thing too, Dad. It's amazing how energy becomes available to you when your attention is focused. I had no problem paying full attention through four hours of lectures on Saturday morning – even though I had stayed up till 2 a.m. the night before reading about synchronicity. But that may have been because the topic was so relevant to me – more change management! This time, the talk was about putting resources in place to give the company more flexibility to deal with a 'surpriseful' future.

I'm starting to get the impression that my own future is going to be pretty surpriseful. So maybe I should start putting some of this theory into practice for my own personal change management programme. Perhaps it's time that I took stock of my own resources too – especially the cash reserves – or rather the lack of them!

Friday, 1st May '98

This has been an extraordinary week, Dad. I don't know if it's synchronicity or just plain old coincidence, but some more relevant books have been finding their way to me this week.

A few weeks ago, I met Denise Moroney for lunch. She set up her own marketing consultancy business a few years ago. Brave move! Anyway, after we got the business talk out of the way, the conversation veered on to life changes. I was curious about how she came to the decision to leave a good job and set up on her own. By way of follow-up to our conversation, I found a book in the post from her last Monday – *Mindstore* by a guy called Jack Black.

Well, if *Synchronicity* gave me a roadmap, I think that *Mindstore* has given me the wheels. It's a very practical book. He starts off talking about stress and the impact of negative thinking – I can relate to that! But then he goes on to explain how to think yourself into a deep relaxation to counteract stress. I tried it… It really works! And there's a bonus too, Dad. Apparently, when you are in that deeply relaxed state, it helps the creative side of the brain to kick in. Good! I could do with some creative thinking, especially about my finances!!

There was another coincidence the next day. Just as I'm starting to recognise some of my fears and insecurities about change, Jacqueline, my friend at work, brought me in a copy of Susan Jeffers' book, *Feel The Fear And Do It Anyway* – very apt. More reading to absorb me.

I'm now starting to see some of the boxes that I've been thinking in and how I've been limiting myself with my own negative thinking. So it's time for me to start 'thinking outside the boxes', and be a bit more creative about what I might want to do with my future.

Money is one of those boxes, Dad.

When I start to think: 'I could do this!' or 'I could do that!', a little voice pops up inside my head and says: 'But how will you pay the mortgage?'

The money flows in, and the money flows out… every month. Isn't that why they call it currency? Like a current, it's supposed to flow.

So why do I find myself worrying about it, Dad? I'm starting to realise that I have a huge insecurity about money. Maybe I picked that up at the time your business was in trouble. I don't remember being like that when I was waitressing through college.

They say that ninety per cent of what we worry about never happens. So why am I wasting energy on it?

Then another coincidence happened, Dad. Just as I decide that I need to let go of my insecurity about money, I get a letter from the bank telling me that they owe me £60 in overcharges! Synchronicity at work, maybe?

Sunday, 3rd May '98

Well, summer is really here at last. After an extraordinary week, I've had an extraordinary weekend! I woke at 6 a.m. on Saturday full of energy! It seems that the more positive I get, the more energy I get. As I wasn't going to loll in bed while the sun was shining outside, I decided to start the day with a walk on the South Wall. It was a beautiful morning and I had the wall to myself. Am I the only person in Dublin who goes for a walk at 7 a.m. on a Saturday? But there were a few other walkers and runners starting to appear as I was heading back around 8 a.m.

Then I treated Betsy to a car wash and she is positively

gleaming. She got the full treatment – jet wash, vacuum and inside windows cleaned too. I didn't get as far as giving her the anti-rust treatment. That can wait until next week. They're only small patches of rust anyway! But for sixteen years of age, she's lookin' good!

It seemed a shame to waste the sunshine, so I took to the balcony with my new books to work on my non-existent tan. Mum still jokes about calling over for 'lunch on the balcony'. I'd be hard pushed to get a chair onto it, never mind a table! But if I sit on a cushion in the doorway, I can get comfortable for an hour or so before I need to move back indoors to stretch.

The neighbours came over for dinner last night.

Maureen is selling her apartment next month and heading off to Greece for the summer. And Karyn is renting out her apartment for a year, and packing her bags for Australia next month. So it will probably be the last evening that the three of us will spend together for a long time.

There was no sadness, though. It was a sort of 'new beginnings' celebration, which we christened with a few bottles of wine and half a bottle of sambuca. No wonder my head was a little bit tender this morning.

But, even though it was after 3 a.m. when I got to bed, I still woke early and full of energy. I tell you, Dad, this positivity is powerful stuff!

Thursday, 7ᵗʰ May '98

Is today the feast day of some ancient mariner, or is it the start of the sailboat racing season? When I went down to the South Wall for my walk this evening, there was a fleet of sailboats out from Dun Laoghaire Harbour. At least ninety of the little white sails and thirty or forty of the big multi-coloured spinnakers. (No, Dad, I didn't count them all. The numbers are estimated on the basis of multiples of ten counted. My curiosity got the better of me.)

I'm starting to develop a fascination with sailboats. Sometimes I think that I might like to try sailing. There must be a great sense of freedom being out on the open sea. But then, when I see the sea in one of its angry moods, I'm not so sure.

Anyway, the big racing sails didn't hang about for long. They headed straight out into the Irish Sea, and seemed to be sailing almost in line formation. But they must have really had the wind behind them as they had all vanished by the time I got to the end of the wall. Perhaps there is a second Bermuda Triangle just outside Dublin Bay?!

Behind the white sails that were left on the bay, a big grey-blue raincloud started to form. Then the sun came out above the mountains and a rainbow emerged at the edge of the cloud. It was over in the direction of Shanganagh Cemetery. So I fancied that it may have been your spirit, and I got into some 'soul talk' with you.

Next thing, the sun beamed over the mountains. The visibility was so good that I felt I could have touched the heather on the hills if I'd reached out. And then a second really sharp rainbow formed further out on the bay, above Dalkey Island. The space between the two rainbows was lit with a vivid wedge of white light. A truly awesome sight! Maybe my 'soul talk' got some 'soul answers', eh, Dad?

Perhaps we can have another chat at the weekend when I'm

up in the Wicklow Mountains. There are a few people from work organising a hill-walking expedition. I'm really looking forward to it. It's been months since I've been out walking on the hills.

But before then, I need to do some work on an essay. It has to be handed in at the next session of lectures. We've been given a task to 'be creative' and invent a business and work out its growth strategy to the year 2008! Ten years! And the world is changing so fast!

I've been doing some thinking about all this change in technology and work practices and how it's causing so much more stress. There must be a way to use the same technology to relieve some of that stress. Maybe I should use some of the *Mindstore* techniques to see what creative ideas I can come up with.

Well, apart from my walks, this week has been pretty uneventful. Although I am enjoying that. I've been spending a lot of time reading. My latest find is *Emotional Intelligence*, which is helping me to understand my anger and frustration on my recent crisis-of-career day. I'm starting to see just how much I've been bottling up my feelings… Family trait, eh, Dad!

I've only just realised today that I haven't turned the telly on this week. Or, if I have, I've turned it off again just as quick! And I don't miss it one little bit – not even *Coronation Street*!

Perhaps it's been my reading about positive thinking that makes me realise just how much negativity there is on the telly. The news just seems to report bad news – is there so little good news in the world that it doesn't merit reporting?

Or is it just that we've grown accustomed to expecting the worst?

It's time I took a break from this letter, Dad. I need to put on my positive thinking cap and put some writing energy into my creative essay so it won't be hanging over me for the weekend.

Back to the future… again!

Sunday, 10th May '98

What a wonderful weekend it has been, Dad! I woke to glorious sunshine on Saturday – another early morning, as I had to meet the hill-walking group in Glendalough at ten o'clock. I thought the drive would take about an hour. But I wasn't quite sure. So I left myself plenty of time to enjoy the journey. It was a beautiful morning for driving through Wicklow. The gorse is in bloom and the roads were lined with super-sunny yellow. I found myself singing along to the radio at full volume – if a bit out of tune.

The walk was thoroughly enjoyable and, as usual, I have since found muscles which I didn't know I had. Hardly surprising since we were out stretching the legs for a good five hours. There were mixed levels of walking experience within the group – and very mixed experiences of the weather over the course of the day.

Good old unpredictable Irish weather!

I started off the day wearing shorts and ended up in full rain gear.

We didn't run into too many other walkers on the route that we took along the ridge above the valley, but we did see several herds of deer at a distance, and a herd of goats. The deer are definitely the more elegant creatures.

The route covered all sorts of terrain – from an almost vertical climb at the start, to knee-high, trudge-through heather, and then on to squelchy marsh near the stream at the head of the valley. The heather patches looked innocent enough, but they were deceptive and dangerous, as the heather covered some large boulders with deep crevasses between them.

I stepped into one clump, but there was nothing solid to meet my feet. My leg went down and down into the gap in the rocks underneath. Just as my thigh was being swallowed up, I managed to grab some heather to break the fall. I was lucky with the angle and flexibility that I went down or it could have easily resulted in a break.

Plaster of Paris for six weeks! Perish the thought!

One of the lads from head office wasn't so lucky. He slipped on a wet rock and injured his wrist as he fell. Fortunately, one of the girls had done a first aid course and she fixed up a sling for his arm. They were calling it a sprain. But I've seen swelling like that before when I broke my thumb that time, and he was holding his hand at an odd angle, so I reckon it was more likely a break than a sprain. His pain was evident as the colour drained from his face.

Then the rain became more persistent. Nobody was in the humour for tackling the ridge on the other side of the valley. So we took the path back down by the lakes and adjourned to the Glendalough Hotel for warmth and 'refreshments'.

On my way back to Dublin, I took a wrong turn at the junction just after Roundwood. That led to a surreal experience, Dad!

About a mile further on, bright primary colours jumped out from the green hedges – vivid blue, red and yellow. I slowed down and saw they were signposts for 'Victor's Way'.

From the road, I caught a glimpse over the hedge. There in a field, in the middle of nowhere, stood this big Japanese-style temple gate – and not a temple in sight! My curiosity got the better of me!

There was a car park, but no other cars. No people in sight either, only several gigantic statues spread out across the field beyond the Japanese gate. I felt kind of uneasy leaving the car – it was so quiet. The silence was almost eerie until it was broken by bird song and my feet crunching the gravel of the car park.

When I got closer to the temple gate, I saw a sign, saying: 'Pass through the Gate of Happiness… an Irish upgrade of a Japanese Shinto Gate. If you go through one way it's the Gate of Happiness; if you go through the other way it's the Gate of Freedom.'

Beside the gate was a bell: 'Ring the Bell. Her name is Amnesia. She sounds to remind you to forget the world outside.'

Zany! And intriguing!

Then I found some leaflets. 'Welcome to Victor's Way contemplation space. Pass through with a smile and gracious detachment… and lots of disbelief.'

Disbelief indeed! I had to pinch myself to be sure that I wasn't dreaming. Here in the middle of County Wicklow, scattered across the field, were 10-feet-tall stone statues of mythical gods from the East, but with a modern flavour. Ganesh, Lord of Knowledge (with an elephant head) was reading a Bill Gates Computer Manual! Tabla Ganesh (the 'musical' elephant head) was playing the drums accompanied by a trendy rat listening to the Spice Girls on his Walkman!

A 'strange and magical place' for sure! You'd love it, Dad.

It was so peaceful, walking around these zany statues, trying to figure out what they mean – to the sculptor and to me. The leaflet did help to explain some of the symbolism, and it certainly gave food for thought!

On the way back to the car park, I saw signs for a photo exhibition in a barn. The photos show how the statues were made in India and then shipped to Ireland. A 'complex and difficult task'. And expensive too, I'd say. I couldn't even guess at how much it might cost to ship this stone art over from the village on the other side of the world.

I met Victor as I was leaving the photo exhibition. He strikes me as one of those misunderstood geniuses. His plan for the 'contemplation space' is a full complement of fourteen stone carvings – seven Indian and seven Irish. It's definitely a third millennium project, as he reckons that it will take about forty years to complete. As he said himself, he'll be long gone by then. But he knows what he's trying to achieve.

I think that he may be a man ahead of his time, although I admire his determination and his vision. He's definitely a man with a mission in life. Perhaps the world will catch up with his vision of the need for 'contemplation space' in the third millennium.

I was certainly glad of the time I spent contemplating his creation. Maybe it will help me to be more open-minded when it comes to creating my own vision for my future.

But, back to coincidences, Dad. Another funny thing happened today.

For some reason, I bought a copy of *The Sunday Times*, for

a change from the *Sunday Business Post*. Why? I don't know. I usually don't get finished reading the *Business Post* until Wednesday at the earliest – and *The Sunday Times* is twice the size.

Maybe I'll get through it before next Sunday!

Anyway, as I was sorting through the various sections, the front page of the Sports Section caught my eye just as I was about to discard it.

An 'exclusive offer' for <u>free</u> sailing lessons with <u>two</u> vouchers from the newspaper (naturally!). The list of participating centres included the Surfdock, on the Grand Canal Basin – just behind my apartment block.

Now there's an incentive for me – my first sailing lesson for free in my own back yard.

I had been half thinking about learning to sail, but I'd been dithering about making the commitment to do a full course. I'm not going to have much spare time on my hands until the start of June when the Business Strategy course breaks up for the summer. Before then, there's a group project to be completed and I still haven't finished that darned essay. I have made some progress on the idea, but not much progress on the writing, I'm afraid. I keep putting off the writing for some reason or other. And time is running out.

Got to go now, Dad, to stare at a blank page… or scribble down some ideas… do something… anything… Aargh!

Wednesday, 13th May '98

Well, the emotional turbulence seems to have settled down a lot this week, Dad. I've adopted a new habit – getting out of the office for lunch every day. In the canteen, the conversation usually revolves around work anyway so it's hardly a break from it. Since I've started getting away from all that for my lunch break, I'm beginning to realise just how much negativity there is in those conversations. At the moment, everyone seems to be moaning about something or other. And then that mindset gets carried back to the desk and on into the afternoon.

So now I go home for lunch. I put on some relaxing music and make a sandwich. Then I do about fifteen minutes of deep relaxation. And then – ping! – I'm fresh as a daisy again and ready to face the trials and tribulations of the office for the afternoon. I'm learning to be more aware of my thinking too, Dad. And, somehow, hassles don't bother me as much as they used to. I'm starting to see them as 'challenges' instead of 'problems'.

Sometimes, it's a real challenge just to keep thinking in positive mode. There are times when I can feel other people pulling me down with their negative thinking. And it's not always possible to get away from the conversation or the situation, especially when it happens at work.

But I found a great tool in the *Mindstore* book to help me protect my positive outlook. He calls it his 'bell-jar technique'. I'm learning to use it anytime I begin to feel negativity from other people starting to affect me – whether it's their anger, antagonism or just plain old moaning about the woes of the world. It's so simple really. And, it works… when I remember to use it. All I have to do is imagine a big bell-shaped glass around me with special glass that deflects negative energy from outside, but lets positive energy flow through.

It's easy to imagine when the book describes what to visualise. But with some of the other tools in the book you have to create images from your own imagination. I find those creative visualisations more challenging. My imagination seems to have gone a bit rusty over the years, Dad. I think it's time for a 'tune up'!

I heard that Jack Black will be in Dublin next month running a two-day course on the Mindstore techniques and how to use them to best effect. And I want to learn more about developing my imagination and creativity. So maybe I'll ask the boss if the training budget will fund me to go on the course.

'Feel the fear and do it anyway!' What's the worst that could happen? He'll say no!

But, nothing ventured, nothing gained, so I guess there's no harm in asking.

Though I really do hope that he says yes. So I'll just visualise him saying yes before I ask.

Speaking of creativity… This last week has been bizarre! While I've been out walking by the sea after work, I've had lots of poems popping into my head – almost every other day. It must be years since I've written a poem. I wasn't even trying to think of any. But then I seem to catch an idea or an observation from thin air. And by the time I get back from the walk, there's a fully formed poem in my mind waiting for paper.

I've started to remember my dreams too, Dad. Some of them are zany and so vivid. They do say that 'The mind works in mysterious ways'… Ain't it the truth! I guess my subconscious mind is trying to tell me something. I'm listening! I've started writing down what I can remember of my dreams as soon as I wake. The memory tends to evaporate if I don't write it down straightaway. But I don't understand the language of dreams. I should get myself a book on dream interpretation to find out what my subconscious is saying to me – what 'I' am saying to 'me'.

Wait a minute! I have a vague recollection… Didn't you have a book by Carl Jung at one stage? Something about dreams and the subconscious? I must ask Mum if it's still around the house somewhere. It must be. She'd hardly have cleared out any of your books. It was heartbreaking enough for her when the time came for her to clear out your wardrobe. And I know that she still holds on to some of your clothes.

Major achievement this week, Dad! I finally finished my creative essay.

And I made a bloody good job of it too (if I say so myself!). There was a great sense of satisfaction in seeing the final product typed up. So why, oh why, was it like pulling teeth trying to motivate myself to start writing it? Laziness? Procrastination?

Or maybe I just needed to put in some thinking time before I actually put pen to paper and fingers to keyboard.

Once I let the ideas flow, I came up with a humdinger of an idea for a new business for the new millennium. I started thinking about technology and how it is affecting business and work practices, and the accelerating pace of change. And people are so stressed coping with change that it's causing them illness – physical, mental and emotional.

So then I thought: 'How can you use technology to relieve stress?'

Brainwave! The Internet!

Not everyone has the luxury of living near the office, or getting out at lunchtime to find quiet space for deep relaxation. But the Internet will be available at most desks over the next few years. So why not use it to provide stress-relief at the desk?

But how?

Well there are lots of natural stress-relief solutions – from deep breathing and stretches, to mental affirmations and visualisations. Though, when you are caught up in a stressful day, it's difficult to remember any of them.

But if the information was there on the Internet, at your fingertips…

There's definitely a need for it, Dad. I thought it was a good idea for the essay, though I haven't worked out the details of how to do it… yet. It's only an idea just now. But the more I think about it… Hey, it could work! I could do it! But I'd need to learn a lot more about the technology and natural remedies that help relieve stress. And I'd need to figure out how to make a business of the idea – i.e. how to make money out of the website to cover the cost. We have another big project to do after the final exams, so I may use that as a tool to develop the idea a bit more.

Meanwhile, I have to put some thought into the group project and my part of the presentation. Each of the groups has to make a presentation on their project to the whole class. I'm dreading it. Even though I know most of the people in the class by now, the thought of standing up and speaking in front of them all…

Oops! Change that thinking! It's a 'challenge'! An opportunity to practice.

⌐ Fear and do it anyway!

, practice makes perfect so I'd better sign off now, and
⊦   ⊃me practice into what I'm going to say for my part of the
presentation.

Goodnight, Dad.

Thursday, 14th May '98

Thursday, 14ᵗʰ May '98

Talk about last minute deadlines! Eight p.m. and I'm <u>still</u> in the
office watching presentation slides printing off. It's literally like
watching paint dry.

One hundred and seventy-five seconds per slide (I timed it)
and thirty-five of them to print!

It would have been much quicker if they weren't in colour…
As if the audience would even notice the difference.

Why, oh why did I volunteer to co-ordinate the slides for
the presentation tomorrow? Because I totally underestimated
the time it would take to standardise the text that the other
members of the group were to send me, and print it.

I'll know better next time! Next time? What next time?

I don't think that I have ever been in the office this late before.
It feels kind of eerie when there's nobody around. It's a totally
different feel to early morning when there's nobody around.
Funny that. It's probably just the dark outside that's making
me feel a bit jittery. Well, partly that and partly the boredom of
watching paint dry! So I thought that I'd write to you, Dad, to
take my mind off it.

Speaking of being in the dark, my holiday plans for next
month are sort of up in the air. British Airways are doing a
promotional offer on their new Dublin–Southampton flights.

So I thought that I'd go to visit my friend who came over to Dublin last March.

But technology confounds and I haven't been able to get an answer from his mobile phone. The flight was such a good deal though, I decided to book it anyway.

I've never been to Hampshire before, and I don't know much about the area. So I bought a guidebook last week. There seems to be some really nice places to visit along the coast, and inland too.

Don't they say a change is as good as a rest, Dad? While I'm really looking forward to a rest from work, I'll be glad of a complete change of scenery too.

I sure hope that I can get a connection on the mobile soon. Or I may end up doing tour guide for the week for myself! What fun!

But… positive thinking! There's a whole four weeks to go before my flight.

And only three slides left to print. The end is in sight, at last!

So I'd better sign off and start packing up.

I'm so looking forward to getting home to sleep. It's been a very long day. And I need to recharge the batteries for the presentation in the morning.

Our group is first on the list to present our project. Aargh!

Why did I have to think of that? Now I'll be having nightmares… if I sleep at all. Anyway, Dad, I'll fill you in on the presentations when I get back from the weekend and I'll have no projects or homework hanging over me.

Our instructor was a young guy called Neil. What you might call a trainee trainer. I think that it was his first lesson too. Though I'm sure he didn't know what to make of us. He must have thought that we were off the rails. Right from the start, the three of us were in silly humour – joking and laughing. But that was probably just a cover for the nervousness about getting out on the water.

For the first hour of the lesson, Neil showed us the ropes on dry land: how to rig the boat, catch the wind, operate the main sail, and steer with the tiller. It was when he got on to explaining how to upright the Topper after capsizing that the realisation slowly began to dawn that there was a high probability we were going to get wet at some stage of the afternoon.

Well, I guess that's why they kitted us out with the wetsuits in the first place!

I've discovered that sailing is a bit like driving a car.

Someone can explain all the theory to you about how to operate the gears, but, it's only when you cut out on the clutch a few times that you start to understand how to make the car move – or not, as the case may be!

After the theory lesson, Neil loaded the three of us into the inflatable boat with the outboard motor and brought us down to the pontoon at the far end of the Canal Basin for the acid test!

Yours truly was the first to walk the plank – metaphorically speaking, of course.

Neil did offer to come out on the Topper with me for my first attempt. But, I couldn't quite figure out how two of us were going to fit in that little boat (maybe 'boat' is a bit of an overstatement!). So I said that I'd try it out on my own first.

Then I learned the value of the theoretical lesson on uprighting a capsized Topper!

Perhaps my subconscious told me that I should master the art of uprighting before moving on to more mundane things… like manoeuvring the boat on the surface. I was barely three yards from the pontoon when the wind caught the sail and over she went. And in I went. Splash!

When I'd recovered from the shock of hitting the water, my first priority was find air!

Then I put the uprighting theory into practice, and dragged myself back into the Topper. But the rope for the mainsail was tangled in the tiller and… Over she went again!

Oh, I know they say practice makes perfect, but after three (!!!) dunkings in a row, I reckoned that I'd had enough of this capsizing lark.

By this stage, Aine and Karyn were splitting their sides laughing at my amateur antics. So at least I provided them with good entertainment value for their money.

I think that Neil was a bit more concerned with the survival of his student. By my third splash, he was out on the water with the outboard motor to talk me through the tiller tangle.

With a bit of expert advice, I managed to avoid another capsize and I was even starting to get the knack of manoeuvring – on the surface this time!

Then it was Aine's turn to go out on the water.

Neil went out with her, sitting at the front of the Topper astride the mast.

He also learned a valuable lesson yesterday: To avoid chattering teeth <u>always</u> zip up your wetsuit when bringing

Saturday, 30th May '98

Sorry it's taken me two weeks to put pen to paper again, Dad. It's been an eventful couple of weeks. Things at work have really started to snowball again. And I've been out quite a lot in the evenings too; catching up with friends before they start to think that I have fallen off the face of the planet. Thank God it's a bank holiday this weekend… Time to step off the merry-go-round for a few days.

Well, after all the anxiety and the sweaty-palm syndrome, our group presentation went quite well. On the day, it wasn't half as nerve-wracking as I'd expected. Though I have to say, it was a relief to get it over with. Being first up meant that we could relax for the rest of the day and listen to the others giving their presentations without a sense of dread. At this stage, I know most of the twenty people on the course. They were all in the same boat, having to speak in front of the whole group as well. With hindsight, I don't know why I was so wound up about it.

But, back to the present… It's time for action! I've managed to persuade Aine and Karyn to join me in 'taking the plunge' this afternoon on the first sailing lesson for all of us. Got to go now, or I'll be late.

Fill you in later…

Sunday, 31st May '98

I don't know if you had ever tried it, Dad, but sailing is certainly an interesting experience and I've got the bruises to prove it!

We took the plunge all right – a bit more literally than we had expected!

ticket and our summer savings, the only plan we had was to get to Greece before the sun ran out – and get back home before the train tickets ran out.

What an adventure that was. Two weeks of bread and cheese and train stations for two carefree weeks in the sun.

I remember setting out on that journey – the excitement, tinged with apprehension. Catherine seemed totally fearless. I was more cautious, even then.

What happened over the years?

When did holidays become something to be planned to the last detail?

No surprises please!

What happened to that sense of adventure and independence?

Jacqueline thinks I'm mad, Dad, travelling on my own. Ironic, really, since it was her that gave me the book *Feel The Fear And Do It Anyway*. I reckon this holiday is a good opportunity for me to put it into practice. A practice run for my next big change – whatever that may be. It's not like I'm going to be backpacking and sleeping in train stations, or travelling to Outer Mongolia. I think that would be stretching the current 'comfort zone' a bit too far.

I might hire a car. I've never done that before. And, being mobile would give me more flexibility. I'm sure there are plenty of B&Bs in Hampshire and, if the worst comes to the worst, I could always sleep in the car.

It'll probably stretch the budget a bit more than I had expected, but so what!

My holiday resolution is: 'I shall not worry about money!' There'll be plenty of time for that when my Visa bill arrives next month. All the same, thank heavens for Mr Visa!

My arms are starting to ache again after all that sailing exertion this afternoon, so it's time to light a few candles, pour a glass of wine and go for a long soak in a hot bath with a good book.

My favourite pastime!

Goodnight, Dad.

Love,

Clodagh

Chapter 5

FREEDOM CALLS

Victoria Park Guest House
Netley, Hampshire

Saturday, 13ᵗʰ June '98

Dear Dad,

Greetings from Hampshire!

Pushing the 'fear boundaries' was certainly the order of the day today.

It started at the airport. So here I am… Now how do I hire a car?

Aah… Avis! They try harder! (So the slogan says.)

I felt like that teenager with the Interrail card again. Only this time I was armed with driving licence and credit card and a big question: 'Where do I go from here?'

Within twenty minutes I was sitting in a brand new Polo and nervous as hell about driving. My legs were like quivering jelly – as if I was about to face the ordeal of the driving test again.

Three deep breaths, and I got back to basics.

Where's the ignition? Brake? Accelerator? Gears? Indicator? Oh, no! It's on the wrong side. That'll take a bit of getting used to.

I drove around the car park three times before I plucked up

the courage to drive out onto the road. Figuring out the road on the map is not quite the same as being on it with other cars. I could feel the tension across my shoulders and hear my pulse beating in my neck. It seemed to pump up a few gears at the approach to every junction. (Please, don't beep at me. I'm a tourist!)

But once I got familiar with the car, I began to enjoy driving. The power of freedom – and power steering. The Polo is really nifty. I'm going to be so spoiled driving it. Poor Betsy! It's going to feel like driving a tank when I get home to her next week. The roads here are brilliant too, Dad. They're well signposted. You can actually read the signposts because you don't have to keep your eyes down to look out for potholes on the road. I'm starting to relax and enjoy the driving now that the initial nerves have passed.

This afternoon I found my way to the river Hamble and the boatyard where I'd been sending letters. I called in to the office to ask after my friend. It seems he's working overseas for a few months. My last letters were still in the mail tray. So he wouldn't have known that I was coming over.

No one could tell me when he might be back, so I just left a note on his boat to say I'd called and I may swing by later in the week. Maybe he'll be back by then. Maybe not. Maybe it's just as well. Maybe I wouldn't feel such a sense of freedom if I had company for the week.

I moved on to Netley then, to do some sightseeing – ancient abbeys and country parks. Then I spotted this really nice guest house with flowers in hanging baskets, car parking – and a Visa sign! My energy was running low, so after I'd booked a room for the night, I thought I'd rest for a while. But my mind wouldn't settle. I suddenly felt the need to walk and stretch my 'jelly legs'.

The walk did me good. On the way back from the park, I came across a pub with a good selection on the food menu. Hunger pangs hit. How could I have forgotten to eat? I must have been too busy taking in my new surroundings. Well, they do say hunger is the best sauce. The meal was excellent. The pub was called the Prince Regent, or the Prince Albert, or something like that. Something Victorian. There's a lot of Victoriana around here, Dad – Victoria Country Park, Victoria Guest House, etc. I got a sense that there were some Victorian attitudes about too, judging by the looks I got from some of the pub clientele. What is so odd about a woman dining alone and enjoying her own company? Or perhaps it was just my paranoia.

Anyway, I reckoned that I'd feel more comfortable back at the resident's bar in the guest house. It's much quieter here than in the pub. Easier to think and write with no noisy pub machines. There's a match on the telly, but the volume is low. Scotland are playing, so the landlord is engrossed. There's a very homely lilt to his accent. Earlier on, I was chatting with his wife for a while. She asked about my holiday plans. I told her they were totally flexible and took the opportunity to ask her for recommendations on sightseeing options. She told me that she envies my freedom. I'm only just beginning to appreciate it myself.

But back to the sightseeing, Dad... There are so many options to choose from. It's time I got stuck into the books and brochures, to draft a plan of action for tomorrow.

Perhaps Portsmouth, or the New Forest. Decisions,

decisions…

Maybe I'll just flip a coin.

Angel Inn Coach House
Lymington

Monday, 15th June '98

If it's Monday, then it must be Lymington.

I've covered so much ground over the last couple of days, Dad, that I have to remind myself where I am!

The first coin landed heads for Portsmouth. So yesterday I spent the afternoon rambling around maritime museums and historic ships. It would have taken me two days to see everything so I just did the tour of one of the ships.

More Victoriana! Back in 1860, the ironclad *Warrior* was the atomic bomb of its day – the 'ultimate deterrent'. From the maze of rigging, I'd say she was fast and an awesome sight under full sail. But she also packed an extra punch when the coal burners fired up a boost of steam. A whole 5mph on top of her speed at full sail. It seems insignificant in this fast world. But it gave her that extra edge in her day.

Our Niall would have been fascinated by the engine room and her construction – a real feat of engineering. I was more struck by the sense of human presence on board. A full crew was 655 men. That's a hell of a lot of testosterone for the one place! I'm getting an appreciation of the need for navy discipline. But I'm sure their energy was kept well focused. It took the strength of 176 men just to raise the anchor! (What strength will I need to 'raise anchor' when the time comes?)

My energy seems to be drawn to ships and the sea on this holiday. People had told me that I should visit the New Forest. They said it's very beautiful. I drove through it today. It is beautiful, and mystical in places. But it struck me as 'tended' or managed by man. Plenty of ponies, but not a sheep in sight. It's not as wild as the West of Ireland. I think that I prefer natural nature – unmanaged and free. Perhaps that's why I'm drawn to the sea.

Even in the New Forest, I managed to find a sea theme at Buckler's Hard. The village was famous for shipbuilding in the days of sail before the river silted up. The reconstruction of life in the shipbuilders' houses was so realistic. As if in a time warp, I felt I had been transported back through the centuries. The tourists seemed oddly out of place among the ducks on the village green. I was starting to feel out of place too spending so much time in the past. So I moved on to Lepe Country Park for a walk by the sea to ponder my own place in history and let my thoughts flow free. But even the seashore seemed 'managed', with groynes holding the pebbles in place. I noticed then that my energy was low and my eyes were turning critical. So I drove on to Lymington, to find a comfortable place to recharge the batteries.

Lymington is a pretty town. I had scanned the accommodation guide for a budget B&B. Then, armed with my map, I drove around the town on reconnaissance of those in my price range. But none of them looked particularly appealing from the outside. Oh, I know that appearances can be deceptive, Dad, but I've had three eventful days and I felt that I deserved to give myself the treat of a slight upgrade.

At £35, my treat is a room at the Angel Inn – a seventeenth-century coaching inn on the High Street. I arrived just in time to get the last vacant room at the top of the house. Carrying my bags up three floors and along the low, narrow corridors, I had initial qualms that I was being consigned to the box room. They were soon put to rest when I walked into a spacious room in crisp powder blue overlooking the town, the water and Yarmouth beyond.

My extravagance has been well rewarded. There's even space to stretch out and start the day with some energising yoga tomorrow. But for this evening, energising is far from my mind. Quite the opposite.

First priority is to soak away my anxieties in a hot bath. The bathroom is luxurious. I could throw a party in there if I had the notion.

And there's a bonus – a power shower!

I've been having a few power showers in my mind over the last few days – imagining myself under a cascade of fresh spring water, washing all my negative thoughts away.

I picked up that trick from the *Mindstore* book too. And it's true what Jack Black says: 'It only works!'

But it works better for me when my energy levels aren't so depleted. I think I've been expending too much energy over the last few days packing so much into such a short space of time. Old habits die hard!

I'm still just learning how to balance my energy levels, Dad.

Even on holidays, I can see that I spend too much time 'doing', and not enough time just 'being'.

So tonight will be my night for just 'being': Being warm and comforted in a soothing bath; being nourished by a meal later; being refreshed by a good night's sleep.

No planning for tomorrow until tomorrow.

Maybe I'll write a few postcards later.

But for now, it's time to soak and switch off my mind.

Angel Inn Dining Room

10 p.m. Monday, 15ᵗʰ June '98

That was a tonic Dad. Just what I needed.

I lolled in the bath for almost an hour. All tensions have melted away from muscles and mind.

And since Mr Visa is helping my cash flow, tonight I've decided on another indulgence for dinner. The Special Seafood Platter has scallops, prawns, cod and sardines. Yum!

I love sardines – real sardines, not the tinned ones. They remind me of sunshine in Portugal.

The dining room here reminds me of winter, cosy fires and hearty soup. It's kept a lot of the old coach house atmosphere. I'd say the heavy oak beams have some stories to tell of times gone by.

A sign on the wall says: 'The Telegraph Coach left from this inn each day at 5 a.m. and 5.45 p.m. Southampton 2 ½ hrs. London 11 hrs.'

I guess the 5.45 p.m. was the red-eye to London. But that was long before motorways. What would those coach travellers think of the travel times today?

Southampton ½ hr, London 2 ½ hrs! Such speed!

But little time to appreciate the journey or the views.

I've managed to avoid the motorways so far, Dad. One motorway is pretty much the same as another – fast and bland. It's in the slower lane that the living is done. So I've chosen a slower pace for this trip. Yet perhaps the modern sense of time is ingrained in me. Is that why I've been packing in so much sightseeing? So much to do, so little time? Change that thinking! From now on, I'll be doing less cross-that-off-the-list sightseeing and taking more time for observation, reflection and appreciation.

Isn't that what holidays are for?

My appreciation of the background muzak is starting to wane. Nineteen-fifties rockabilly tunes seemed cheerful when I first came in, but now that the other diners have left, the sound seems ill-matched to the history seeping out of the timbers. So I think I'll retire to the powder-blue room to write some postcards before I sleep. But will I sleep alone?

The inn advertises 'many resident ghosts, to keep you company'! Perhaps the Angel Inn will also provide me with an angel to guide me while I sleep.

Goodnight, Dad.

The White Horse
Salisbury

Tuesday, 16th June '98

I woke this morning with a Peter Gabriel tune on my mind; Solsbury Hill. But this is Salisbury. No matter, decision made; destination Salisbury Hill. It was early when I woke to sunshine streaming in the window. The forecast on the radio promised 'only occasional light showers'. Make hay while the sun shines! So a ramble around pretty Lymington seemed to be a good way to start the day.

By the time I got down to the quayside, the boat people were just coming awake. Aboard *Petrol Blue*, the girls were removing the covers from the mainsail. *Strongbow* had a baby on board and the parents were absorbed in breakfast drill. On the deck of *Cosantes*, the skipper enjoyed a shave. Six sharp lads on the *Pirouette* were the first away – motoring out to sail away the day. That's the life, Dad!

I found a signpost for the Solent Way, and followed the path past the Yacht Haven. A haven it is indeed. Some of the yachts just screamed money. Walking back by leafy lanes and red-brick houses, it struck me that this is a very well-to-do sort of town. The High Street was bustling by the time I got back, and most of the shops were open. So I swung by the tourist office for information on Salisbury, before returning to the Angel Inn to collect my thoughts and belongings.

The sun suggested a coastal drive to Bournemouth, before turning inland to follow the Avon north to Salisbury. But a lot of other people seem to have had similar thoughts about Bournemouth. The nearer I got, the more the traffic thickened. And traffic jams were not in my game plan for today. So I took a diversion towards Hengistbury Head Nature Reserve. That was the perfect antidote to traffic trauma.

The Nature Reserve trail took me past the marshlands of the Avon estuary and through woodlands with fantastically shaped trees. Then it skirted a run of candy-coloured beach houses. When the path forked it was decision time again. An uphill climb to the top of the headland? Or take the 'low road' following the bleached sand to veer back towards the car park? I fancied the notion of feeling the sand between my toes. But the beach had been basking in Mediterranean-style sun for the morning and my soles rebelled against the heat of the sand. By the time my sandals got me back to the car park, I was sweltering.

I thought that the top of the headland might provide a bit of a breeze to cool me down. The climb wasn't too taxing. It was certainly worth the effort for the breeze and the view. Poole Bay stretched out to my right and Christchurch Bay to my left. I could even see the Isle of Wight in the distance. My legs were tingling from the walk and the climb, so I sat on the grass to rest them and listen to the bees buzzing. I sat there for ages, relishing the view and the breeze from the height of the headland. It gave me a whole new perspective, Dad.

I think that I need to start looking at my life from that perspective too. Start seeing the bigger picture, if you know what I mean. I've been so focused on what's been happening in work, but there's so much more to life than just the job.

My mind went into free flow, and I fished my journal out of my bag to capture some of my thoughts before the breeze carried them away. But I couldn't find my pen. Then I saw it – in my mind's eye – sitting on the bedside table in the Angel Inn. It was a strange feeling, Dad. I suddenly felt handicapped without my pen. Strange paradox indeed. I feel so happy to have escaped from the paperwork of the office for a while. Yet I feel lost without a pen – as if I had lost my means of expression.

When I got back to the car park, I discovered that I was a lawbreaker! I must have been so distracted by the earlier traffic trauma that the Park-and-Pay sign escaped my attention. To my cost, I didn't escape the attention of the inspector! My 'first offence' would set me back thirty quid – Ouch!!! – but discounted to a tenner if I paid within ten days. I opted for the discount rate, and made a beeline for the nearest Post Office.

Fine paid, postcards mailed and well stocked with pens, I headed north for Salisbury. Passing through Fordingbridge, I spotted a pretty pub beside the bridge. It had tables outside, so I stopped for a coffee and sat in the shade of the trees, watching the river Avon flow by. Perhaps I should have had something to eat there too. The river should have calmed me, but instead I felt anxiety rising. I had phoned a few B&Bs from the brochure, but they were all full. It was getting late in the afternoon, and I was starting to fret about finding accommodation. So I decided to press on.

Salisbury is a much bigger town than I had imagined. Worries crept in again about getting lost in the traffic system. Jitters at every junction. Which way?

I followed the signs for Central Parking, to leave the car and get my bearings on foot. The cathedral spire gave me a good landmark and I started to walk toward the town centre. Then I found myself on Castle Street, opposite the White Horse Inn.

My first port of call and they had a single room vacant, and they took Visa. Bingo!

No need for my earlier anxiety.

I'm starting to notice a pattern, Dad. Despite my best resolve not to worry, the anxieties and insecurities still creep in – especially when my energy is low when I'm tired or hungry. Energy seems to be the key to keeping my fears at bay and keeping a positive outlook. But I think that I still have a lot to learn about balancing the energy books!

After I had washed off the dust of the day, a dish of hearty lasagna soon boosted my energy. The pub downstairs is warm and friendly, and quite possibly the only Official Football-Free Zone in town. An added bonus!

While I was paying for my meal at the bar, I noticed a 'World Cup Penalty Box' on the counter. Curiosity got the better of me, and I enquired how it was filling up.

But I made the mistake of using those dreaded two words – World Cup – and I got stung for 50p. Oh well, it's going to a good cause – the local hospice.

But it's a good job they didn't have a swear box on the counter too!

Writing doesn't come easy this evening, Dad. Perhaps my unnecessary anxiety has run my energy so low that a dish of lasagna is not enough to top it up. Maybe a good night's sleep will help to balance the energy books. I think that I may stay two nights here and avoid accommodation anxiety tomorrow. There's so much to see in this area that I could even stay for a few days. But I'll be happy enough just to see the cathedral and Stonehenge before I move on again. To where? I don't know yet. That's a decision for tomorrow. Meanwhile it's time to retire for some shut-eye.

Goodnight, Dad.

Banks of the Avon
Salisbury

Wednesday, 17th June '98

You'd love this spot, Dad. I found it earlier this morning, following signposts for the Riverwalk. It was a lovely walk here from the White Horse. The path led me past a dinky little bridge. Underneath it swans and cygnets were having a breakfast of soggy toast courtesy of a generous grandmother. The little boy and girl were assisting with smiling delight on their faces. It reminded me of Granny Quinn and feeding the ducks in St Stephen's Green. Simple pleasures.

After the bridge, there was a shady stretch of walkway smelling of damp hawthorn. The river runs deep and quietly here. It was so peaceful walking to the sounds of whispering leaves and birds twittering. A lone angler sneezing was the only human sound. The cathedral is only a few hundred yards away, but you wouldn't know it. You can't see the spire for the curtain of willows along the riverbank.

The path turns where two rivers converge – the Avon running slow, the other running fast. Just at the turn, there's a majestic weeping willow. It's a Siamese twin tree.

A very long time ago, it had only one trunk. But now there are two, leaning away from the centre, each crying their leaves into a different river.

The willow splits in two just at the point where the two rivers meet. It forms a perfect frame to watch the unified river carry on towards the sea.

And some thoughtful person has built a bench here, for

walkers to sit and marvel at this oddity of nature. It's a magical place, Dad.

I walked back towards the centre of Salisbury earlier this morning to visit the cathedral. Another feat of engineering. But its elegance is partly cloaked by scaffolding at the moment. Inside, organ music filled a vast cavern with almost tangible sound. It took a few minutes for my senses to adjust to the scale of space and sound. Then I found a leaflet to guide me through the cathedral.

First on the list was a mechanical marvel – an olde medieval clock with no face, yet it chimes on the hour even still. I guess time doesn't need a face. Then a stained-glass window caught my attention. It was a commemoration to all those who served in World War II, at all stations. The caption on the glass banner extolled: 'Freedom from fear, freedom from want.'

It struck a chord with me somewhere deep inside. Or perhaps it was just a reminder to me that I have been slipping a bit in my resolve to free myself from fears and letting the jitters creep in again.

I could have spent a lot more time lingering and absorbing the energy of the cathedral. But the leaflet said that the Magna Carta was on view in the Chapter House. So I decided it was time for a history lesson. I lit a candle for you before I moved on.

The entrance to the Chapter House was through the cloisters. And the peace and beauty there held me enthralled…as if I had stepped back in to the thirteenth century. The church was pretty well-to-do in those days, judging by all the gold and silver among the ecclesiastical exhibits. But peace wasn't the norm then. Even so, there must have been some forward-thinking guys around. The text of the Magna Carta was hard to decipher in 'ye olde English', but the translation certainly had echoes of the American Constitution – Freedom and Independence.

'These truths we hold to be self-evident …'

From George Washington, my mind skipped forward to *Shirley Valentine*: '…Why do we get all these hopes and dreams if we don't ever use them?'

Afterwards, I sat in the cloisters for a while to reflect. In the quiet I tried to hear what the cathedral had been shouting at me. But it was too calm there. The place stilled my mind. So I came back here to the bench by the magical willow. Watching the rivers flow helps my thoughts to flow.

There seems to have been a freedom theme to my sightseeing this morning.

And somewhere in there is a message for me, Dad. But what is it?

Freedom is calling me. But like the twin-trunk willow, there are two freedoms: freedom <u>from</u> and freedom <u>to</u>…

I know what I want freedom from… Freedom from the paper piling up on the desk, from the endless deadlines, from the frustration. Freedom from my own mental constraints and fears.

But to what end? What of the other sort of freedom?

Freedom to… What? There are lots of things I want to do.

I'd like to write more – for myself – to travel more, to learn more about sailing, to learn to speak French. I'd like more time to read and think. I'd like to ski, to visit Australia. I'd like to learn more about technology and human energy and how to balance it all.

Yet all of my thoughts are of doing… So busy doing. What of being?

Freedom to be. Be what or who? Maybe just me.

My thoughts are flowing too freely now. I can't keep up with them.

There are so many choices. If I had the freedom to… Where would I start, Dad?

Maybe I should start by climbing a hill again, to see the wider perspective. And let the question float on the air until an answer comes to me.

I know just the hill too!

Old Sarum, the original Salisbury, is next on my visiting list – en route to Stonehenge. Time to move on.

Old Sarum

2 p.m. Wednesday, 17ᵗʰ June '98

It's a bit early in the day for seeing the city lights but there certainly is a spectacular view from up here – south over Salisbury and northwest over Salisbury Plain.

I can't help but wonder what majesties lived here, enjoying these breathtaking views. Though I'm sure they had their own cares and concerns too – of invaders coming over the horizon. Where are their worries now?

Where are your worries now, Dad? Where will my worries be years from now?

Where do worries go? Is there a deep, dank well somewhere where worries gather in the dark to party together… or fester?

Or do they float around the air until they find some solution that lets them glide away bright and carefree?

I throw my questions to the wind and trust they will come back to tell me when they find an answer.

Like the song says, the wind is blowing and time did stand still, temporarily.

But, the wind has brought some miserable drizzle.

So it's time to drive on to find Stonehenge.

Stonehenge Coffee Shop

4.30 p.m. Wednesday 17th *June '98*

On the road here, I passed some army tanks with soldiers in full battle dress and a civilian tailback behind them. It seemed incongruous in this rolling, windswept landscape. But as I drove up to the car park, the tourist throng around this ancient enigma seemed even more out of place.

The car park was full and there was a long queue for tickets. Americans by the busload – young and old. Some tragic fashion victims among the younger set!

I bought a polystyrene coffee and fed apple cake to some wily little birds while I waited for the queue to abate. At the next picnic table, some elder Americans were in get-to-know-you mode with their new neighbours.

'Yes, we know people in North Carolina, but I can't remember if they live near Charlottesville.'

I enjoyed eavesdropping on their friendly chatter with former strangers – so Irish-like.

It was refreshing to hear such openness, especially after the last few days of the famous English reserve. Or perhaps that has just been a reflection of my own reserve.

My daydreaming was interrupted by the realisation that the queue had gone. Quick dash to view history – look but don't touch – like a child in a china shop.

My attempts to capture these ancient stones on camera were confounded by a technical challenge – how to keep people out of the picture? Especially the woman in the dayglow raincoat. The brooding rainclouds were an appropriate backdrop to the stone circle but not so her raincoat.

It reminded me of my last visit to Newgrange. It's changed a lot since your last visit, Dad. They've built a new interpretive centre on the south side of the Boyne River. From there a minibus brings visitors up to see the ancient mound. They still bring you inside through the narrow passageway and they still turn off the lights to simulate the solstice sun creeping along the ground and lighting up the central chamber. You can still feel the energy there too, and a sense of ancient wisdom… of secrets locked in time. Time without a face.

Unfortunately, my last visit coincided with that of a group of young Americans – agricultural students from the Midlands. On the minibus, some of them asked the driver to stop so that they could take photos of some cows! Are cows so rare in Amerikay? But the same depth of appreciation didn't quite extend to the 5,000-year-old legacy of Stone Age man. The tour guide did a very good job of building an atmosphere of awe at the ancient mystery. Then she turned out the lights. In the air of hush and expectation, a lone voice twanged, 'Gee! Look, my buttons glow in the dark!' Silence shattered!

I guess it's a sign of the times, Dad, when luminous buttons are more noteworthy than the amazing achievements of ancient man. No wonder we have lost so much of his ancient wisdom too, being so absorbed in modern trivia.

Dawn or dusk are definitely the times to visit Stonehenge when tourists are thin on the ground. I can't feel the energy of this place with so much noise and distraction around. I'm tired of tourists now. Or maybe I'm just tired. It's time to head back to Salisbury for a quiet evening studying brochures and making decisions for tomorrow.

Winchester

12.00 p.m. Thursday, 18ᵗʰ June '98

It's amazing what a bit of planning can do for your peace of mind. No accommodation anxiety today, Dad. I made an early call to book a room in Southampton before I left Salisbury this morning. Then I decided on a scenic drive through Stockport and Winchester. I fancied that I might stop in Stockport to while away some time over a cup of coffee overlooking the river Test. But in Stockport, the Test manifests as several duck ponds flowing under the main street. Not what I had imagined. So I pressed on to Winchester.

It's not what I imagined either – more of a city than a town. Back in traffic again, I headed for Central Parking and then took a stroll around. The High Street stretches uphill, lined with Tudor facades. They look authentic, as if they should enfold some welcoming hostelries. But looks can be deceptive. On closer inspection, Boots, Next, Debenhams and other chain stores peep out from underneath the ancient eaves. It gives the term mock-Tudor a whole new meaning.

I went for a ramble around the college streets and past the house where Jane Austen spent her last weeks. Perhaps it's the college influence, but I sense a sort of rarified atmosphere of gentility.

Call me a philistine, Dad, but I gave the cathedral a miss. Two cathedrals in two days would only confuse my impressions of both.

My impression of Winchester is… hush. 'No talking in the corridors, please!'

The hush seems to extend to the street entertainers too. On my way back to the car, I came across a gold-clad mime artist entertaining a crowd of shoppers. In smiling silence, he teased a miniature cyclist with a sugar treat. The little boy eventually won out by making a lunge for the sweet. The crowd smiled. Even the competing reggae buskers seemed to enjoy the amusement. It struck me how few smiles I have seen since I arrived last Saturday. Is this part of the famous English reserve, or just the gravity of the current economic climate? There's certainly no Celtic Tiger bounding around here, Dad. Perhaps things will be livelier in Southampton. Time to get on the road again…

Ibis Hotel
Southampton

6.30 p.m. Thursday, 18th June '98

Well, if I thought that the city would be livelier, I thought wrong. After I dropped off my bags and the car at the hotel, I set out to explore the shopping precinct and soak up some of the city atmosphere. Atmosphere? What atmosphere?

On the High Street there were plenty of lunchtime shoppers about – shopping in silence. I spotted a few smiles, but there were few sounds of chatter and no laughter. What was I expecting? The prattle and buzz of Dublin shoppers, perhaps. After passing an entrance to the Bar Gate Shopping Centre, I doubled back to explore it. There was an even greater hush there – quiet as a church. A stark contrast to the noise of shopping at The Square in Tallaght!

The side door of the shopping centre led me on to East Street. An interesting mix of shops there, but little interest on the faces of the shoppers. People walked as if their spirits had been drained. Do you remember *Invasion of the Body Snatchers*, Dad? Or *The Stepford Wives*? Maybe I just picked the wrong day to visit – the day the Stepford shoppers came to town.

I lost interest in shopping and decided to walk the old city walls down to the Maritime Museum. From the top of Arundel Tower, a vista unfolded of McAlpine's Fusiliers building a mini city. The West Quay Development site stretched out over acres.

Cranes, cranes and more cranes, and hi-vis jackets scurrying around like a luminous ant colony. The cranes reminded me of the Dublin skyline since the Celtic Tiger came to stay. Construction equals confidence. So maybe the economy here is on the road to recovery only the shoppers haven't noticed yet. Maybe we're all just like scurrying ants in any city. We all scurry around, so busy that we can't see that there is life outside of our own little microcosm. Heads down, spirits drained. But how come some have more spirit than others? What happened to the spirit of Southampton?

I think I found part of the answer in the Maritime Museum, Dad.

The *Titanic* was a big blow. Southampton provided her crew. Almost every family here lost someone in that tragedy. Loss without warning; without time to say goodbye.

Then there was the wartime bombing – a city shell-shocked, again.

But the final blow crept in during the 1950s. Technology killed the passenger liner trade slowly. Airplanes won the day.

The city doesn't seem to have adapted well to the change. It lost its glamorous identity and its spirit by the look of things today.

How can a city live without spirit? How can people live without spirit?

There was an air of melancholy in the museum for times gone by.

I feel it hanging over me still. But times move on… And it's time for me to move on. To soak my swollen ankles and then find some place to eat.

TGI Fridays
Southampton

8.30 p.m. 18ᵗʰ June '98

I take back anything I ever said about the Yanks – they sure know how to generate energy! I'd heard of TGI Fridays before, though I don't think that there are any in Ireland yet. It reminds me of my waitressing days in the Swiss Chalet Bar-B-Q – though that was a Canadian franchise. A hostess welcomed me at the door. The staff are young and enthusiastic. The music is upbeat, but a little bit too loud. My Thai chicken salad was delicious. And my fortune cookie promised: 'You will make a profitable investment.'

Glad to hear it! But, I wonder… Is the investment in money, time or energy? That got me thinking, Dad. How have I been investing my time and energy lately? So much of it has been going into work. And what is my return on that investment? Not enough to balance the books out of the red and into the black. I really do need to take another look at how I'm investing my time and energy and maybe do something completely different; something more rewarding to me.

Claire, my waitress, has been dancing attendance since she introduced herself to me. No rush. No hassle. Just attention.

'Is everything all right? Can I get you anything else?'

She's well trained in customer service. It makes a pleasant change. In fact, she could give lessons to staff in some of the pubs I've visited.

Some don't even offer you a beer mat! In one pub, I asked for a beer mat so the condensation wouldn't drip onto my clothes when I lifted the glass. Do you know what the barman said, Dad?

'It's OK. I'll wipe the table when you're finished.'

I was stunned speechless. The saddest thing about it was he seemed to think that he was being helpful! Customer service is obviously an alien concept for him. You'd think that the pub existed for the convenience of the publican, not the customer. (Oops, sorry for dripping on your table, Mr Barman.)

Granny would be horrified! Her pub was always a 'public

bar' for the use of the 'the public'. So much so that we used to joke about her catch phrase; 'What'll the public say?'

What would she think of all the sticky tables in pubs here? I can just imagine her face!

Claire makes sure her tables are clean. There's a little paper pyramid on each of them advertising:

WANTED – VIP DADS
Bring Dad to TGI Fridays for a meal
On Father's Day – 21st June.
And we'll make him feel Very Important.

If only I could! I'm sorry, Dad. Sorry for all the missed opportunities. Sorry for the Father's Days when I didn't take the time to make you feel important. Sorry that I won't have that chance again. I miss you, Dad. But you know that, don't you?

I'm feeling that melancholy again... Despite the birthday celebration at the table in the corner. They're bursting balloons now. I think that's my cue to leave.

Ocean Village
Southampton

2 p.m. Friday, 19th June '98

I found another side to Southampton today, Dad – an old spirit in a new place. The shops and restaurants of Ocean Village are quite new, as is the marina. There's a spirit of adventure here. I could sense it as I walked around the marina looking at the boats. There are some magnificent boats moored here. From sleek, lazy cruisers without the challenge of sails to the ultimate challenge of sails – Global Challenge yachts, aerodynamically designed for speed to race big brand logos around the world.

At one of the restaurants, I found a waterside table so I could watch the boats over a sandwich. The spirit of adventure came to join me. I didn't catch her name. She was an old lady looking for seats for four. She said her family were out to celebrate her daughter's forty-ninth birthday. I was happy to share the table. Her teenage grandson squirmed with embarrassment as he was despatched to find his mother. I enjoyed the old lady's friendly chatter. She told me of her boat moored on the Hamble at the Mercury Boatyard and of sailing at Cowes. I told her of my tentative sailing progress and my capsizing lessons in the Toppers.

Sailing is in her blood, and that of her whole family. Her daughter fell in love with boats at the tender age of four. And her son earns his living by travelling the world, delivering boats overseas. Her pride in him is palpable. She told me of her voyage to Gibraltar, as crew, with him: the terrors of Biscay, the thrill of arrival, and the anticlimax of the flight home.

Her tanned arms looked thin and deceptively feeble. But she is not. She's well past retirement age, but still not ready to retire from the sea. Her vitality was a tonic. And our brief conversation was an antidote to any fear I may have had of the sea.

I was sorry when her grandson came back to say they'd found another table. I'm sorry now that I didn't ask her name, or that of her boat.

I might see it later, as I'm swinging back by the Hamble today.

The Spinnaker Pub
Swanwick

10 p.m. Friday, 19ᵗʰ June '98

It felt great to get out of the city today and back near the river. I checked into the Spinnaker early this afternoon. I'd stayed here last Saturday night and the barman remembered me. He asked about my travels and I enjoyed chatting with a familiar, friendly face. The novelty of newness is starting to wear thin at this stage of the holiday, Dad. I'm happy to revisit more familiar surroundings.

The barman gave me some tips on local walking routes. So I spent the afternoon walking leafy lanes and riverbank paths. By teatime I was ravenous. My route took me by the Jolly Sailor pub. It's a beautiful spot, Dad, with a beer garden overlooking the boats and the river. It was glorious in the sunshine. And the seafood pie was delicious. The wasp buzzing around the meagre remains seemed to think so too.

I spent a few hours there, out in the air, watching the world go by with the smell of the tide coming in and writing a letter to my friend. The weekend boat people were starting to return for some unwinding over a pint, before setting down to boat business. Perhaps my friend will return this evening too, perhaps not. I'll call to the boatyard in the morning to leave the letter or say hello – whichever.

At the table next to mine, a young guy presented a 'Jolly Sailor Tankard' to one of the older men – a gift with a wish for a Happy Father's Day.

I started to feel chilly. The sun had gone down below the

treeline. And melancholy settled on me again. So I walked back here, to the warmth of the lounge in the Spinnaker.

I feel that I've come full circle on this trip, Dad… almost. Perhaps I'll complete the circle tomorrow and return to Netley and tell my holiday stories to the landlady who said that she envied my freedom.

The pub is busy tonight with Friday evening revellers. I wonder what they make of the solitary scribbler at the table in the corner. Or do they wonder at all? I'm in no humour for revelling tonight. I feel the Guinness going to my head and my skin is hot after the day in the sun. One more for a nightcap and I'll sleep like a log.

The Rising Sun
Warsash

12.30 p.m. Saturday, 20ᵗʰ June '98

A jolly little man served me breakfast this morning. When I adjourned to the bar counter for a cigarette, he remarked on my accent and we chatted for a while. He told me of his days in the army and of some of the 'Paddys' he'd served with – and of his sons serving in the North. I told him of my travels and my family connections 'up North'. We talked of politics and religion, despite the taboos. Perhaps this is where peace starts, Dad – with talking and hearing another's perspective.

After breakfast, I called back to the boatyard. But still no sign of my friend. So I just left the letter for him and carried on with Plan B. I still have some sightseeing I've kept in reserve. It's my last full day with this nifty Polo so driving is the name of the game today.

The Cormorant
Porchester

4.30 p.m. Saturday, 20th June '98

Well, I've covered some ground today, Dad. Warsash was charming. Lee-on-the-Solent was lonely. Stokes Bay was sunny. Gosport was grey. And Porchester Castle was… spooky. It really shook me.

The Romans settled on the site for its security and its command of sea and land for miles around. But the castle keep was built much later. The notice said it was once used as a prison housing over 3,000 men. I couldn't help but wonder in what squalor and despair, so far from France?

I felt pain in the air. So I climbed to the top for some sunshine.

The view was breathtaking. I could make out Port Solent and Gosport, and Portsmouth further away (a whole week away).

But when I looked down, I thought how far it was to fall. And what depths of despair would drive a man to take that dive?

Black thoughts indeed.

A shiver ran down my spine and I felt the need to leave immediately.

I was too shaken by my thoughts to drive very far. Then I spotted the Cormorant pub, which serves food all day – a rarity. I feel a bit better now, after tucking into a tuna sandwich and tea. And the sun in the beer garden has warmed the shivers out of my bones. But I feel a coldness again when I think of the castle.

I sense it holds a dark energy, perhaps from its past as a prison.

But the air of despair spreads further than the castle keep.

I've felt that weight in some of the towns and cities that I've visited too – from people trapped in prisons of their own making. Just like me.

But my prison is a comfortable one. And I'm happy to return to it now to plan my escape.

Bewley's Café
Eastleigh Airport
Southampton

11.30 a.m. Sunday, 21ˢᵗ June '98

Sipping Bewley's coffee, I feel like I'm home already, Dad.

I said goodbye to my nifty Polo, and left the keys back to Mr Avis.

It's strange to think back… Was it only a week ago when I was so nervous about driving her? Well I certainly conquered that fear, and a few others.

It's been a week of ups and downs. Although I learned a lot about myself this week, Dad. It's been wonderful to have had so much time to myself to think.

I enjoyed the challenge of travelling solo.

So I wasn't exactly conquering Everest, but, hey, one step at a time!

I know now that I can do that too… if I want.

It's strange to think that I'll be back at work tomorrow. Back to busy-tizzy days, again. I'm sure the desk will be swamped tomorrow with a full week of paper.

It'll probably take me all day to clear it! But… Change that thinking!

Before I came away, the boss gave me his approval to do the Mindstore training course. So I have that to look forward to on Tuesday and Wednesday.

I have the feeling that it's going to be another eventful week with little time for letter-writing.

Today is the summer solstice. It seems an appropriate day to be heading home to a new beginning. Karyn's heading off tomorrow for a new beginning too on her round the world trip to Australia. I must call over to her tonight to wish her luck on her travels, and share what I've learned from mine.

They're calling my flight now, Dad. So, gotta go!

Happy Solstice!

Love,

Clo

Chapter 6

CONNECTIONS

The Waterside
Ringsend Road
Dublin 4

Saturday, 27th June '98

Dear Dad,

I can hardly believe that it's a full week since I left Hampshire. If feels like so much longer. But that's probably because there has been so much happening this week. It took me the best part of the day on Monday just to deal with all the mail from last week. Although I did have a little time left over to do some planning for a couple of meetings I'd arranged for later in the week. Then I parked the office at the back of my mind and took off for two days of training on the Mindstore course.

The course was fantastic! It's almost two months since I started using the relaxation techniques from the book and that has made such a difference. I know that it works, Dad. I don't get so stressed out anymore – even in situations where I'd fly off the handle before. I wanted to learn more. Why was I getting so stressed out in the first place at things that other people just seem to take in their stride? As it turned out, I learned much much more than I had expected.

There must have been over 200 people in the function room when I arrived at the hotel. It took me a while to find a seat. The room was buzzing with conversation. I thought to myself: 'If Jack Black is going to hold everyone's attention for two days, he'd better be good!' He was. It must have been the most entertaining course I've ever been to – and it was fun.

Perhaps it had something to do with his Glasgow accent, but at times he struck me as being a polished version of Billy Connolly. He has a similar gift of telling a story, with that strong sense of the ridiculous in looking at some of the things that we all just take for granted. Like the way we spend our working day – rushing, rushing, busy, busy – wasting energy at every step along the way. But he had a serious message none the less: Stress Kills! (Don't I know it!) Apparently, that's what motivated him to develop the course. So many people he knew were dying from stress-related illnesses – unnecessary, untimely deaths like yours.

He started off talking about stresses – the avoidable, the unavoidable, the ones we put on ourselves and how we deal with them – or not, as the case may be. Then he went on to explain about how relaxation is the only natural antidote to the stress reaction. Not the put-your-feet-up-in-front-of-the-telly type of relaxation; more like that deep, deep relaxation when you're lying in the sun and almost doze off. We put it into practice too. As he talked us through a deep relaxation, I could feel all tension melting out of my muscles. My neck muscles were so relaxed that they started this occasional jerking to stop my head from falling over. But not everyone experienced that distraction judging by some of the snores around the room.

After the break, he explained how the brain works at different levels of relaxation; about the different types of brain waves (beta, alpha, theta and delta); the two hemispheres – the left brain and the right brain.

That was a revelation to me.

Oh, I knew that the left side of the brain dealt with logic and reason and analytical things while the right brain was the more creative, imaginative and intuitive side and that for most people, one side is usually stronger than the other.

But I always thought that the strength of one side of the brain over the other was in some way hereditary. I thought that our gifts of analytical or creative abilities were passed on in the family genes.

Our Fiona was always good at arts and crafts, drawing and dress design, so I thought that she had inherited the creative genes. While I was always better at maths and science and geography, so I must have inherited the logical academic genes. But that's not true, Dad! I have a creative right brain too. It's just that I haven't used it as much as my logical left brain so it's gone a bit flabby – like my right arm muscles were, after those few weeks in plaster.

There were a few times, though, that I really made an effort to be more creative.

One winter I took up patchwork. I enjoyed making a design out of the different patterns of fabric. But then the sewing got to be a bit of a chore and a bit of a bore.

The quilt covers the top of the bed now, but it'll be a long time before it reaches the floor.

Last summer, I had another little artistic urge and painted a jasmine tree on the bathroom wall. The one on the balcony was so pretty in bloom and I missed having a bathroom window for light to grow plants indoors. The wall looked so bare with just pale yellow. I didn't know what paints to use, but then I remembered the poster paints from school days. It was fun weaving the trunk and the branches with brown, yellow and green. The leaves and white flowers were good amusement too, but very fiddly and time-consuming. I ran out of steam halfway through. So now, one side is spring and the other is winter and I like it that way.

Friends keep asking me when I'm going to finish it. I've come up with an excuse: It's a metaphor for life… a work in progress! Feeble excuse for my laziness, I know.

But I don't have to finish it. I'm just going to leave it that way.

Oops, there I go, Dad. Off on a tangent again!

What started me on that detour? Oh, yes… Back to the course. It seems that there's a bonus to this deep relaxation, on top of helping to cope with stress. Apparently, when you're in that state of deep relaxation, it helps to kick-start the right half of the brain and to develop imagination, creativity and intuition.

I had a strange experience while he talked about imagination, Dad.

It happened after lunch on the first day. I was feeling good when we all settled back into our seats, looking forward to the next stage of the presentation. Jack Black started off talking about imagination and dreams and the way children use their imagination without any preconceived limits or constraints; the way we all used to imagine – and dream – of fantastic futures. But, somewhere along the line, we stopped doing that.

Then he asked a question: 'When did *you* stop dreaming?'

The question hit me like a punch in the heart. I felt a lump in my throat and tears welling in my eyes when I realised that it was such a very long time ago. Do you remember when I was a kid, Dad? I was always a bit of a tomboy – climbing trees, building tents and treehouses, going exploring, and building my fantasy land in the treehouse of my imagination. I couldn't answer his question as to <u>when</u> I stopped dreaming. It was so long ago. But I think that it was a process – a slow insidious process, where the fears start to creep in along with the word *can't*. I felt a real sadness and sense of loss when that dawned on me. Then I felt exhilarated at knowing it. Because now I can take action to get my imagination back and start to dream again.

It's funny the way 'can't' works. If I say it to myself often enough – 'I can't, I can't, I can't, I can't, I can't, I can't' – then I start to believe it. And, 'I can't' becomes true. But the opposite works too. 'I can, I can, I can, I can, I can, I can.' I can feel my shoulders pulling back and my head lifting higher and I believe that I can and I will… if I choose.

Granny Quinn used to say: 'Couldn't is wouldn't, and can't is won't!'

It took me a long time to understand what she meant by that. But I think that she was saying: 'You're not helpless. You're wilful.' And, 'If you're going to be a wilful child at least put your wilfulness to positive use!'

I learned a lot from the course about the way the subconscious mind works and how I've been holding myself back with my self-limiting beliefs. All those 'I can't's from over the years. They all add up to the luggage of life; weighing down my reality, my

101

present and my future. I've been taking the knocks of life on board, taking them to heart; knocking my own self-esteem and holding myself back to my ever-shrinking comfort zone. But I can change all that if I just change my thinking.

Jack Black says that 'thoughts are things', and 'the quality of our thoughts determines the quality of our lives'. Just like the song says: 'What we believe is true!' I know that's true. When I was a child, I could 'think myself sick' if I wanted an afternoon off school. I never needed blotting paper in my shoes. All I had to do was spend a few classes thinking: 'I am pale and weak and shivery.'

The more I thought it, the more I believed it, the more I became it. A doctor might have called it psychosomatic. But the headmistress wasn't taking any chances. It worked every time! Although I didn't use it too often in case she copped on. I always had a miraculous recovery about five minutes after I left her office just as I bounced out through the school gate. It never took me long to think myself back to being well again.

Is that what happened to you, Dad? Did you 'think yourself ill'? I don't mean on purpose. But did you just stop thinking, 'I'm fit and well and healthy', when you were under all that stress?

Speaking of stress… We did a couple of self-evaluation questionnaires on the first day of the course. Twenty questions apiece. From the first one, I found that my stress level isn't really as bad as I thought. Or maybe that is just because I've started to take it in hand. But the second questionnaire was another revelation: 'Behaviour Contributing to High Levels of Stress'. I'm starting to see how much stress is my own fault – taking on too much work, setting my own ridiculous deadlines, getting so impatient with myself and rushing, rushing, rushing. But perhaps fault is the wrong word. Blame achieves nothing. Responsibility – that's a better word. It's my responsibility. So it's up to me to take responsibility for it: my stress levels, my health, my future, my life.

The second day of the course was all about the future. Defining goals for the future, adopting the right attitude and seeing the outcome. Do you know, Dad, I'd never actually written down my goals before. In fact, I felt that I was making them up as I went along. I guess I've been plodding along a fairly predictable path without question. I haven't really had a good look toward the horizon to see where I'm going, or where I want to go.

It was a useful exercise, even just writing down the goals that sprang to mind. But we had such little time on the day. I want to find some time over the next couple of weeks to sit down and really think about my goals and do that whole exercise again. Especially after learning about the importance of the right attitude: Desire, Belief, Expectation. Without those, it's not a list of goals. It's just a wish list. It won't really happen. So what do I really want for the future?

We did some practice of seeing the outcome of goals.

Imagine the future. What does it look like? See it, feel it, smell it, taste it. Imagine it has already happened and play that movie over in your mind every day.

I had a bit of a challenge with that as my imagination has gone so rusty. Maybe it just needs more exercise and practice.

Then, at the afternoon break, I got chatting to a woman called Barbara. She had done the course before and found the techniques so useful that she came back for a 'refresher'. When I told her that my rusty imagination was having a challenge with visualisation, she recommended a book called *Creative Visualization* by Shakti Gawain. There's another one for my shopping list!

I met some wonderful people over those two days, with some amazing stories to tell. Like Paulette. I was introduced to her by Anne O'Neill, who organised the course. We shared the same table at lunch on the first day. At first I thought that Paulette was about thirty. But after our conversation, I reckon that she has to be a lot older than that. She certainly doesn't look it. There was an aura about her, a sort of serenity. And yet she was full of vitality.

We started a predictable conversation: 'How did you come to be on the course?'

I told her of my job, the increasing stress and frustration at work, and my realisation that I need to learn to balance my energy better than I have been doing.

She could relate to that. It seems that she's been there too.

Paulette told me that she used to train corporate executives on one of those outdoor activity training programmes. High intensity stuff, both physically and mentally. But after a few years of that she literally burned herself out – at twenty-seven! She injured her back and was laid up for nine months. That must have been some frustration – to be so physically active and then so totally laid up.

Through the physiotherapy for her back she became interested in yoga, and learned about a lot of complementary healing therapies that work with body energy. She mentioned chi kung, or qi gong. I'd never heard of that one before.

It seems that it's an ancient Oriental system for cultivating personal energy and managing that energy for better health and vitality. It sounded very much like tai chi.

Paulette is certainly a walking advertisement for whatever type of exercise she practices. I asked her to tell me more about it. She told me a little about the different body energy systems.

I'd heard about the meridians before; who hasn't heard about them from acupuncture? But the Indian theory of the chakra system was new to me. I knew that yoga helped to stimulate the endocrine glands, but I didn't realise that they were connected to energy centres too.

This body-energy stuff is fascinating, Dad. I want to learn more. How come I never learned about this in biology at school? We really are such complex creatures. The mind and the body are so… connected. But when did we become so disconnected?

On the subject of body energy, my own is a bit low just now, as is the stock of food in my fridge. So it's time that I took a break from writing to scrape a sandwich together and then hit the supermarket. The library is on the way back, so, I may drop in there too, to see if I can find an answer to my disconnection question…

The Waterside

Sunday, 28ᵗʰ July '98

Libraries are dangerous places, Dad. They're almost as bad as bookshops for me. I lost a few hours in there yesterday, but I found a mine of information. And I think that I found an answer to my question.

It seems that it goes back to the seventeenth century when some guy called Descartes reasoned that mind and matter must be two separate things.

A philosopher – not a physician – decided that the mind and the body were separate. A mind and a body machine!

He was the same guy that wrote: 'I think, therefore I am.' I heard you use that quote quite a few times. So you must have heard of him, Dad.

But, I wonder… How did he reason that thought down his arm, through his pen, onto paper if he reasoned that his mind and body were two separate things.

In the library, I came across a lot of books on body-mind connections and the power of the subconscious mind. And I found a book on the chakra system. So I borrowed that, along with another good book on yoga. Which brings me back to Paulette.

She told me that she works with the Life Foundation in Wales. I'd never heard of it before. She said it was set up about twenty years ago by a group of students from various different fields of study – science, philosophy, sports, medicine, etc – from Bangor University. They run a School of Therapeutics near Snowdonia in Wales, where they teach dru yoga, tai chi, chi kung and various other body-mind-heart techniques. By coincidence, their annual conference is on at the end of next month in Bangor, Wales and they'll be running workshops on everything from nutrition to shiatsu. Sounds interesting. Like a one-stop shop for learning more about body-mind-heart connections. I gave Paulette my address and she said that she'd send me more information on the range of workshops and accommodation in Bangor.

Looks like July is shaping up to be a busy month. I've had two invitations from friends to visit them on their holidays in the country. Aine and her husband, Andrew, are renting a house in Ballyvaughan, County Clare for two weeks next month. And Matty and Martien are bringing the kids on holidays to a country cottage near Westport. The only trouble is, they're all going away at the same time. It's so long since I've spent time with them, I'd like to visit them both. And why not? I've still got a few days leave in reserve. So I may take a long weekend and do a grand tour of the West.

Work is going to be pretty busy again (still!) for the next couple of weeks; catching up again (still!) after my time out of the office. So I'll be glad to get out of the city for a long weekend, some good country air and a rest. Work! Aargh! Back to reality!

Time to iron for the morning and then dream of walking in the wilds of the West.

Goodnight, Dad.

The Waterside

Saturday, 4th July '98

Well, true to her word, Paulette sent me the information brochure on the conference in Wales. It's running for four days, from Thursday 23rd to Sunday 26th July. I'd love to go for the whole four days. But I can't really afford to take another two days off work, especially with two weeks holidays coming up in August.

Although, if I get the fast ferry over on Friday evening, I could get into Bangor just before midnight. And if I catch the ferry back on Sunday afternoon, that should allow me to take in at least three workshops without taking any time off work.

I don't know anyone else going over. But Paulette said that they are expecting about 800 people from all over the world, so I certainly won't be on my own. And everyone is staying in the university residence, so there should be no problem meeting people.

Decision made, I sent the booking form off yesterday to confirm two nights' accommodation and three workshops: Shiatsu on Saturday morning, 'The Success Formula' in the afternoon (that one sounds a bit like the Mindstore course) and 'The Secret of Vitality' on Sunday morning (there seems to be a bit of yoga in that one too).

This has been a reading week, Dad. I'm really enjoying the freedom of the summer break from the business strategy course. No prescribed reading. Wonderful! Now I have time to read whatever takes my fancy.

I've been making inroads into those library books that I borrowed last Saturday. And I'm getting a deeper understanding of yoga. It's not just about stretch-and-tone and breathe-and-relax. You can use the breathing and postures to manage your energy too – to calm down or re-energise. I've been practicing a few of the exercises from the book and I can really feel the difference. But some of them are a bit too complex for me. I lose track of when to inhale or exhale. It's so much easier when someone talks you through it. Perhaps I should consider going to a class again.

But I've put the library books on hold over the last couple of days.

I've found a new book.

On Thursday evening, I was over in the Blackrock Shopping Centre – this late-night shopping really does help to take the pressure off time at the weekends. Anyway, I almost passed the bookshop. Almost… but not quite.

I remembered that book that Barbara had recommended, *Creative Visualization*. So I went in to see if they had a copy. But it was sold out.

Scanning the shelves, I found another by the same author called *Living in the Light*. The cover blurb said it was about developing intuition and learning to use creative abilities. I dipped into a few pages… And then I couldn't leave it behind.

I've almost finished it now.

The author, Shakti Gawain, writes about the left brain and the right brain too.

But she talks in terms of male and female energies within us all – like yin and yang. The female energy is the more intuitive, creative side; while the male energy is more action-oriented. It seems that we all have both – just like we all have a left brain and a right brain.

But we need both energies working in balance to really live a creative life. It's a different way of being: listening to intuition, trusting it and acting on it. I like the sound of it. Though I imagine that it could be a bit scary. Especially if my intuition tells me to do something risky and outside of my comfort zone.

My intuition has been telling me that I need a change of job and I've been looking at some alternatives logically, with my left brain. What are my options for doing the same job with a different organisation? I have a sense that if I changed jobs that way life wouldn't change very much at all. Within a few months, I'd probably be back to same stress, different setting. So perhaps I should look at the dilemma differently and ask my intuition. Here goes! Time to relax, connect to my intuition and ask it a few questions…

Strange stuff this intuition, Dad.

I asked myself: 'If I had absolutely no constraints in the world, what would I <u>like</u> to do?'

One word popped up in my mind: Write.

That's odd! As you well know, Dad, I hate report writing with a vengeance.

Yet I love writing letters. I can lose all track of time when I sit down to write to you or to a friend.

OK! So if that's what my intuition is telling me, let's work through the options: What do I write? A book? About what…? No idea!

Travel. That's always a good way to see the world differently and maybe come up with some ideas for writing en route.

Maybe I could write travel articles… Now there's an idea!

But how do I fund the travel?

I could save up for a year and then take off for six months or a year.

Yes, I like the sound of this!

And since I've been made permanent in work, I could apply for a career break.

That would give me a safety net – a job to come back to if things didn't work out.

So what's stopping me?

Financial commitments: the mortgage on the apartment.

So why not rent it out?

Good idea! The rent would cover the mortgage and give me the freedom to go walkabout and still have a home to come back to.

What if they say no to the career break?

Well, I like this idea to travel and write, so I think that I'll do it anyway. But there's still no harm in asking for a career break.

What else could hold me back?

My own fears! Mind over matter… I'm working on that.

But back to the present. I lost track of time there… again. And I've to meet our Fiona in town in an hour. I haven't seen her in weeks. I'm looking forward to lunch and a natter.

It'll probably be busy in town today. There's a lot of Americans around this weekend for some big American Football game to celebrate Independence Day. Maybe it's just the day that's in it, Dad, but I'm feeling a great sense of independence myself today too.

The Waterside

Sunday, 5th July '98

I called over to see Mum this morning. She's just back from holidays with her friend, Frances. They had a great time with Pina in Italy. Mum sounds in awe of Pina's vitality. At seventy-five, she bakes her own bread and paints, and she's just started studying for a degree in music. What a lady! She sounds so full of life. As the saying goes, you're never too old! I'd love to meet her sometime. It sure sounds like she has been an inspiration to Mum.

Fiona seemed quite inspired yesterday too. She's starting work on a new movie next week, and she's all talk about the details of period costumes. She's always so full of confidence when she starts a new job. But it seems to be a feast or a famine in that business. It's long hours and mega-stress when she's working on a contract. Then it's total rest for a few weeks before the insecurity sets in, wondering when and where the next contract will come from. It's very different to the way I'm used to working: regular hours, regular pressures with surges of stress.

I guess I should think about that. If I'm going to change from the day job to travel and write, there's still no escaping from some stress. It'll just be in a different pattern. I can see how lack of time structure on activity could bring about its own stress and insecurity. So I'd better work on keeping my confidence up. Positive thinking!

What got me on to that train of thought? Oh, yes… It was something that happened last night, Dad. An insight into my own confidence and self-esteem. But first, I should explain how it came about. I was practicing one of the Mindstore techniques – a mental visualisation.

Eyes closed, I thought myself into a deeply relaxed state. I imagined myself by a river, lying on the warm grass with sunlight dappling through the pale leaves of a lime tree overhead. I rested there awhile to let my mind clear of thoughts. Then I crossed over the river in my mind, via some imaginary stepping-stones, and I stood on the right bank of the river looking out across the landscape (the creation of my right brain). It's a beautiful view. Though I can't actually see it, I sense it is there.

I stood on the lush green grass and felt a balmy breeze coming from the beach on my right carrying the smell of the sea. On my left, a field of red poppies danced in the wind. Behind them, a gentle hill rose clad in purple heather. Straight ahead of me, in the distance, a blue, blue sky silhouetted mountains to the right in many shades of green that were rolling down to the azure sea. And, in the midst of this imaginary landscape, I saw an imaginary house with a red roof – that represents me. It's sheltered on the left by a grove of silver birch trees that rustle in the breeze. From where I'm standing, I can see big windows on the right side of the house that look out over the sea.

The grass is soft underfoot as I walk to the front steps, and the wooden boards give a welcoming creak as I walk up to the door. When I open the door, an explosion of golden light greets me. The walls either side are of glass bricks that let the sunlight flood through.

The entrance hallway holds a symbol of my potential – a crystal bouncing the sunlight off into little rainbows that dance around the walls.

I don't know what it means, Dad, but it lifts my heart every time I see it.

Through the entrance hallway, I come to my conditioning shower – a cascade of warm, bubbly spring water that washes away all negative thoughts from my mind. I turn off the shower and let sunshine flood over me. It leaves me feeling warm, dry, positive and glowing.

Then, if I need an energy boost, I step into my energising

beam.

Mine is a bit like *Star Trek*'s Transporter Room.

Beam me up energy, Scottie! I imagine energy tingling up from my toes to the top of my head and I feel a new lease of life.

No, I haven't been smoking any 'funny cigarettes', Dad! I'm just letting my imagination run free. And believe me, it works. After I think myself through this imaginary journey, I feel so positive and full of vitality that nothing or nobody can drag me down.

But that's just the start.

Next comes the central corridor and there are many more rooms off that. In the central corridor (a symbol of my self-esteem), I put recognition of my achievements to remind myself of past successes – all part of boosting positive thinking. The first time I created my central corridor, I guess my logic said: 'Corridor equals straight walls… like a hospital or a school.'

I framed all the achievements I could think of, and hung them aligned on the walls. But last night, I went in to visit and found things have changed.

Instead of a hospital corridor, I walked into Aladdin's Cave! It was a huge, high-roofed cavern with treasure chests strewn on the floor and spotlights beaming up through them. I couldn't see all that was in the treasure chests but I was filled with a feeling of power and delight.

Later, my logical side compelled me to interpret what my imagination had shown me of my self-worth.

In the hospital corridor, I had framed the things that other people value in limited narrow confines.

Have I been doing that all my life, Dad?

Seeing my value through the limited lenses of other peoples' eyes?

Well, this Aladdin's Cave has given me a new perspective of my own worth.

It has shown me talents and gifts that I hadn't recognised before – treasures inside me that I didn't know were there.

Yes, the mind does work in mysterious ways. How long have I been holding myself back to the confines of a hospital corridor? How long have I been sabotaging myself subconsciously? No matter. That's past. My mind has shown me my Aladdin's Cave – not a picture that I can see, but one that I can feel. I feel a greater worth and value… for the present. But I also know now how to maintain that feeling so that it lasts for the future.

While I'm on the subject of the Mindstore course, I almost forgot to tell you… I met a guy there who also writes to his dead father. I have no idea how we got into the conversation. But when I told him that I write to you, he seemed somehow relieved and told me that he still writes to his dad who died six years ago. They didn't really talk a lot when he was alive – sounded like some sort of father-son friction. But he finds comfort in talking to him now on paper, just like I do talking to you. But I still miss talking with you.

Goodnight, Dad.

Monk's Pub
Ballyvaughan
Co.Clare

Saturday, 11th July '98

Sorry I didn't find time to write during the week, Dad. Work has turned mad busy again. It's a funny thing, though. I'm actually enjoying the job again now that I've got it back in perspective as a means of financing my ends not as an end in itself.

But, gee, it's great to be on the open road again. I left the city early this morning and arrived in Kinvara before noon. It seemed a nice place to break the journey. So I stopped for a cuppa and phoned Aine's mobile to tell her I was only a half-hour away from Ballyvaughan. But the best-laid plans are made to be changed. She and Andrew were still on the M50, just leaving Dublin and the traffic was manic. They didn't expect to get down before four o'clock. So that gave me a few hours to kill.

First on the list was to stretch the legs. I took a stroll down the pier. The smell of turf smoke and low-tide seaweed confirmed I was far from the city. Although I thought that I could just make out Galway City across the bay.

There were a few boats in the harbour, precariously propped by the mud, stranded by the tide. Some of the old wooden boats had interesting names – *MacDuach*, *Siochan* and *Asurnai*.

But there was one misnomer for sure – a big, bedraggled rust-bucket called *Fairy Queen*.

It no more resembled a fairy! But maybe it once did in the eyes of its owner.

I rambled back to the village and found a gift shop open. So

I went in to browse, and found some tourist guides.

What to do for an afternoon in North County Clare?

The Aillwee Caves!

The day was overcast but hot and humid, so I thought that a tour underground might help cool my skin. It certainly did.

The tour guide said that bears used to hibernate in the caves and that the bear bones were dated much later than their supposed extinction. The last bastion of the Irish brown bear! But the bears wouldn't have had fire or light to appreciate the inner beauty of the caves. The colours and shapes of the rock forms were magical and accentuated by man-made light. There was a wonderful waterfall too – a sparking stream of liquid tinsel pouring out of the dark.

At the furthest depth of the cave, the guide told a story of the intrepid potholers who discovered the cave by candlelight.

Imagine the courage of those two men, exploring the darkness.

Imagine if one candle went out.

Imagine if both candles went out.

Blackest darkness deprives the senses.

I've never seen such darkness before – even if I close my eyes there are still some pinpricks of light. But this blackness absorbs everything and disorients.

Which way is up? Which way is out?

I was glad when they turned on the lights again and directed us towards the tunnel for the way out. Walking that tunnel was strange. Maybe it was the uphill slope, but I felt sort of unbalanced; as if I was walking on sea legs.

I was happy to emerge to the warmth and the daylight.

There was still an hour to go before meeting Aine and Andrew in Monk's Pub. So I found my way to the house they are renting, parked the car and walked toward Ballyvaughan Pier. A soft drizzle had descended by the time I got to the pier, so I ducked into the pub for shelter. I was wrapped in warmth as soon as I walked in the door. A turf fire was smoldering in the grate – in July! There were no seats free but by the fire. So I've settled into a big cosy armchair to swelter and wait. Though the Guinness helps to cool me down.

But I've been so intent on writing that I've only just noticed the details of the décor. A series of amazing pictures line the eaves. Scenes of transformation; elements of nature turning into crafts of man. An eagle and a swordfish merge from air and water to form a speeding spinnaker in full sail. A shower of starfish descends from the heavens to blossom into a multitude of billowing white sails. A pterodactyl turns into a butterfly, a magic wind in its wings then shapes them into an Oriental junk. Waves curl into wings, and a windsurfer leaps. Swans' wings soar to become schooner sails. A fish sprouts wings and evolves in stages into a technical drawing of a deep-keeled yacht.

The artist has a wonderful insight into function and form. His creations bring the genius of Leonardo da Vinci to mind. Creative transformation by human imagination. He has a precious gift to see the world so differently and with such an innovative eye.

And with my eye, through the square window, I spy... Aine and Andrew coming towards the door. Got to sign off now. Until later...

Leenane
Co. Galway

6 p.m. Sunday, 12ᵗʰ July '98

I've covered a fair bit of ground this weekend. From Dublin to Clare to Galway. A few more miles and I'll be in County Mayo to rest overnight before I head back to the city again. But I'm enjoying the driving, Dad. Despite the potholes, it's a joy to drive through Connemara in this wonderful green wilderness. It's good for the soul.

I had a very enjoyable evening with Aine and Andrew last night. Andrew is big into computers and science. And, somehow, the pub conversation wound its way round to energy, science and physics. Quantum physics, no less! I'm still fascinated by energy. Although, at some level, I've been carrying a mental block against physics. I think it goes back to when I scored that glorious F in my Leaving Certificate Exam.

But Andrew made it all sound so interesting, talking about atoms dancing at different wavelengths. Seems that we're all made of atoms of energy. From the rocks in the cave, to humans and all forms of life. It's all made of energy, just buzzing at different vibrations. Each atom of energy buzzing beside the next. And, somehow, they're all connected by energy in a dance that permeates life.

I didn't quite grasp all the details. But Andrew recommended a book that thankfully explains it in layman's language: *The Dancing Wu Li Masters*. Another one for my list!

Aunt Kay was buzzing with energy too, when I call by at lunchtime. It's a long drive from Ballyvaughan to Westport, so

I decided to stop off in Oughterard to say hello and scrounge a cuppa. Kay is so like Mum in some ways, and in other ways… they're not at all like sisters. A bit like Fiona and myself. It's funny the way a family gene pool mingles and jumbles.

Kay asked how life was treating me. So I told her of my stress and frustration, and my decision that it's time for a change. I told her of my asking my intuition, and my embryonic plans to travel and write.

'You should talk to your Uncle John then.'

As soon as she said it, I knew she was right. He's written two books at this stage. As it's all new to me, I'm sure that I can learn a lot from his experience. Perhaps I should start talking to other writers too, and learn more before I leap.

I've had so many thoughts popping up on the drive – of things I need to learn, things I need to do and questions I need to ask before I make that leap of faith. Faith in my intuition and myself. So, I've stopped off here in Leenane to jot my thoughts onto paper and capture my ideas for later. I've noticed something, Dad. The more I talk to people about my ideas for change, the more ideas they give me for how to make it happen.

I'm looking forward to seeing Matty and Martien this evening and bouncing my ideas off them too. They've been such good friends to me for so long. How long is it now? Yikes, almost twenty years. Time do fly! They still call over on Christmas Day to visit Mum. And Matty still passes the comment that it's somehow different with you not there. They'll be worried if I'm too late. So, time to move on…

The Waterside
Ringsend Road

Saturday, 18ᵗʰ July '98

Yet another week goes by without time to write. Even my reading has gone by the wayside this week. Work has been rush, rush; busy, busy... One step forward, and two steps back. But I've still found time to keep practicing the deep relaxation and that helps keep me on track.

I'm glad that I took last Monday off. It was such a pleasure spending time with Matty and Martien. I'm only sorry that I couldn't stay longer. The house they rented was so calm and peaceful – a modern cottage out in the middle of nowhere. On Sunday, we sat in for a cosy night of chat. The sun was shining on Monday, so we started the day with a climb up the hill behind the house. It was a fairly steep climb, but well worth it for the breathtaking view – south to the mountains of Connemara and north over Clew Bay. After that we took a drive in through Westport, and on west to Murrisk for a walk on the beach. There was just time for a quick lunch before I had to get back on the road. But I felt so much better for the climbing and walking and talking, and all the fresh air. It really set me up for the week.

Over the last few weeks, I've been a bit remiss about walking. Sometimes it's so hard to find time amidst the pressures of city life. But no time like the present. If I've time to be writing, I've time to be walking. So I'm off now to walk the South Wall and refresh my perspective on life.

University Residence
Bangor, Wales

1.30 a.m. Friday, 24th July '98

Greetings from Wales! Although I haven't seen much of it yet
– just lights from the train in the darkness. The ferry crossing
passed quickly. It was a bit of a rush after work, to get to Dun
Laoghaire in time for the ferry. When I got on board, it was
such a relief to relax into the journey. Destination Bangor. And
from there… I didn't know just what to expect.

I had phoned earlier this week to say that I'd be arriving late.
In a soft Welsh lilt, the girl on the other end of the phone gave
me directions to get from the train station to the University
Residence. She said that she'd leave an envelope for me at the
porter's desk with the key for my room.

It was almost midnight when the train arrived at Bangor
Station. Only three others got off. They all seemed to know
where they were going. I took a few moments to get my bearings,
then found my way to the taxi rank. The girl on the phone said
that it was only ten minutes' walk from the station, but I'd best
get a taxi if it was after dark. I was glad that I did. As the taxi
man drove up a steep, tree-lined road, I felt it would have been a
sinister walk in the shadows of the trees. Delivered to the door,
I paid the small fare and noticed a sigh of relief escape on my
breath in the night air.

Inside the front doors, a large entrance hallway opened up
and I detected a faint smell of disinfectant – like in a hospital
or school. The cold speckled wall tiles and the stairwell banister
reminded me of hospitals too. A 'Porter' sign hung above the

window of an office. I peered in, but there was no one around. No sounds but the echo of my footsteps on the marble floor. Then I saw the table with a few dozen white envelopes laid out. Names and room numbers. But none had my name. And no one around to ask. So… what to do next?

My first thought was that if this was six months ago I'd be starting to panic. But not now. It was a bit disconcerting, though. I thought that perhaps the security man might be doing his rounds. So I moved over towards some seats and sat down to wait.

Twenty minutes later, I heard the echo of some voices bouncing off the walls.

Two women came through the doors from a corridor. I asked for their help.

They said they were going down to The Haven, the place where the central registration was based. It was well after midnight, but they said that there may still be someone from administration there and they'd ask about my key.

I stayed on alone to wait for the security man.

After another twenty minutes, my two saviours returned with my key. I felt a wave of comfort and relief with my key in hand and directions to my room. After they left, the walk down the corridor seemed endless. The key turned in the lock – another relief. I was fit to collapse when I finally flopped on the bed. But now I can't sleep.

Perhaps it's over-exhaustion from travelling, or delayed nervous tension about finding the key. Maybe it's just down to arriving in unfamiliar surroundings in the dark. But enough of this fretting! I'm not going to let anxiety deprive me of sleep.

I know how to get past this… Just think myself into deep relaxation, imagine a soothing shower washing away all my worries, and then invent a soft cosy room with a deep featherbed where I'll sleep like a baby. It's time I engaged my mind-body connection and put my imagination to positive use.

Goodnight, Dad.

And… help me sleep tight.

Love,

Clodagh

Chapter 7

HEARTFELT

The Waterside
Ringsend Road
Dublin 4

Wednesday, 29ᵗʰ July '98

Dear Dad,

Well, despite my Friday night jitters, I had a wonderful time in Wales. But it was so eventful that I had no spare time to write. As I had no idea what to expect from the weekend, I went with a totally open mind. I didn't know anything about the Life Foundation apart from what Paulette had told me – that they run courses, seminars and workshops on various body-mind-heart techniques that help to maintain health, well-being and peace (something I could well do with, living in this crazy modern world!)

But I discovered that there is more to it than that. They're a non-profit organisation, and the funds they raise through the courses are redirected to help promote world peace. They organise walks into war zones and bring techniques for emotional healing to people suffering trauma in places like Bosnia and Chechnya. Trauma I can't even imagine from the comfort of my home. It sure puts my stress in perspective. I met some wonderful people there; people with a warmth, an openness and such vitality. They radiate life.

On Saturday morning, I went down to The Haven to check on the venue for my first workshop on shiatsu. But as things turned out, that one was fully booked.

My name was listed under my next choice, a workshop called 'The Power of the Heart'.

It took place in a hall that reminded me of school assemblies, with polished wooden floors and big, bright, airy windows. Annie and Shannen presented the workshop. Annie was five foot nothing and full of bubble. She must have been in early- or mid-forties, but at a distance, I'd have put her around mid-twenties. Shannen had an ethereal air about her. Her hair fell in strawberry blond waves to the middle of her back and she carried herself with the elegance and grace of an angel. I recognised her voice. It was her soft Welsh lilt that I'd spoken to on the phone.

They spoke about the flow of energy in the body and the importance and power of the heart. And of how the energy gets blocked by judgement and criticism and lack of compassion – a sort of hardening of the heart. But they weren't just talking about the physical organ; it was more about the energy of the heart and the flow through the heart chakra. They claim that the heart is ten times more powerful than the mind. So, Dad, if the mind is so powerful, then the power of the heart must be… Wow!

But it wasn't all theory. They talked us through a sequence of exercises of movement and gestures to release energy blockages and open up the heart chakra. And honestly, Dad, I could really feel it!

Towards the end of the sequence, we all stood with our palms facing towards us at chest height, about a foot from our bodies. I felt something like a ball of heat in my hands from the energy in front of my heart. I think that the workshop opened some other hearts too as everyone seemed to be smiling and happy as we left the hall.

At lunch in the cafeteria, I found myself sitting opposite an amazing lady. Her skin was weathered and tanned, and her face carried the lines of many stories. She was all dressed in black, apart from a few wisps of rebellious grey hair.

'Oh, you're from Ireland,' she said to a place somewhere just above my head.

That took her onto the subject of travel. It sounded like she had been all over the world.

'Yes, but I still have so many places to visit. I want to go to Lake Titicaca next. But I haven't been able to find somebody to come with me yet.' (Lake Where?)

'Lake Titicaca. It's in Peru! Don't you know it?'

Guess I must have missed that geography lesson, Dad. But I can see her climbing the Andes no bother – age no impediment. And her stories fuelled my imagination and gave me some ideas for my own travels further afield.

I enjoyed the conversation so much that I was almost late for the next workshop: 'The Success Formula'. Of course, everyone was curious about 'the formula', but the workshop started off with talk about success. What is success? What type of success? Success in work, in sports, in finance; success as a mother, a father, a son or a daughter; success as a friend, as a person.

Anita, the presenter, said: 'Success means different things to different people.' And ain't that the truth!

I thought of your struggle with the business… All those years, striving to make it a success. But the success (or failure) of your business didn't matter to me, Dad. In my eyes, you were always a success as a father. The business may have failed, but you were never a failure… You were always a success. Couldn't you see that?

But back to the workshop. Anita spoke of the importance of balance and energy if you really want to achieve your goals. You need energy to take action and you need energy in thought. A list of goals is just a wish list if there's no energy behind it. And a wish has no energy if it's not backed by a driving desire.

'You are what your driving desire is…

As your desire is, so is your will…

As your will is, so is your deed…

As your deed is, so is your destiny.'

Some of the ideas reminded me a bit of the Mindstore course. Like: Our thoughts create our reality. We can only live in the present moment. Our deeds determine our future. Believe in the power of your potential and the power of your imagination. Trust your intuition. And learn to flow with life. Don't waste energy fighting to control life's flow.

But this workshop put more emphasis on energy; the energy of the heart, as well as the mind. When you plant the seeds of success, it must be with a deep heartfelt desire if you want them to grow.

That prompted me to think back, Dad, to my own goals.

Oh, I have a wish list all right. But what is my deep, heartfelt desire?

I guess deep down it's the same as everyone else's: to love and be loved.

But how does that relate to my goals, and what do I want to do with my life?

When I ask my heart and my intuition, they still tell me to write and to learn and to share what I learn.

I learned a lot from the people I met in Wales; people who were so open-hearted and sharing. At dinner on Saturday night, there was such a buzz of conversation as strangers got to know each other, sharing things that they had learned from the various workshops during the day. So even though I only went to two workshops, I learned about some of the others that I would have liked to attend. Like the one on nutrition and herbal remedies; another on balancing the chakra energy system; and another on crystals for balancing energy in the home. But I still want to learn more. People shared book recommendations too. So my reading list is now as long as my arm.

I called in to The Haven after dinner to check the venue for my Sunday morning workshop. And I lost myself for almost an hour browsing among the bookstalls. But I decided to postpone any buying until Sunday, as I didn't want to be carrying books with me to watch the show in the main hall.

Nobody knew what to expect from the show, it was just billed as 'An evening of entertainment'.

It started with a play based on *The Wizard of Oz*, my old childhood favourite.

The curtain went up on the scarecrow, centre stage amid a pile of rubble and bricks. He was searching for a brain so he could know how to lay out the bricks to build a path: The Yellow

Brick Road.

From the audience, the lion and tin man came to help him.

The lion hoped for courage, and the tin man wished for a heart.

Courage, Heart and Intellect.

And then Dorothy came on stage looking for her home.

I've been a bit of a tin man, Dad. With my intellect on centre stage, I've been letting my head rule my heart. I need more than just courage to overcome my fears. I need the full balance. Maybe that's why I found myself at The Power of the Heart workshop. I still can't fully see my new path. It's a bit like that pile of rubble and bricks. I can see some of the pieces, but I can't quite see how they fit together. But no worries… I trust a picture will emerge with time.

After the play, there was dancing. A beautiful Indian woman from Leeds glided across the stage with elegance, skill and a beauty of movement in a traditional dance. She had the audience mesmerised.

Then Annie and her sister, Jane, sang a Welsh song that they had sung to their father when he was dying of cancer. They said the words were about opening up to life in the moment and remembering through the dust that settles over time. They sang it in Welsh with really sweet voices. It was a magical song. I'm sure it was a great comfort to their father as he came to the end of his time.

Time! Where does it go to? I completely lost track. I had only been planning on writing for an hour and now it's past 1 a.m. And I've an 8 a.m. meeting tomorrow. So it's time for some shut-eye. I'll try to write some more tomorrow and tell you the rest of my story from Wales.

Goodnight, Dad.

The Waterside

Saturday, 1st August '98

These last two days have passed in a blur. My mind is juggling so many thoughts: projects at work, summer project for the strategy course, holiday plans for next month (this month! Yikes!) and longer term plans.

I called over to visit Mum last Thursday. It was on the tip of my tongue to tell her of my plans for big change. But I held back for the moment. She'll only start worrying as I don't have the answers yet, for the expected questions of: How? How are you going to support yourself? How are you going to travel? How will you finance it? How are you going to get a job when you come back? I don't need to ask myself those questions. The answers are coming to me anyway in flashes of insight. I get an insight, with energy behind the thought and another brick is laid on the path. Somehow, a picture is forming – while I keep up the deep relaxation and visualisation – of a different lifestyle next year.

Mum was concerned enough with my holiday plans turning uncertain. I was supposed to be going to a wedding in Seattle mid-August. But there's been so much changing and rearranging that I've decided to let that plan go by the wayside. I cancelled the long-haul flight, so I'm left with a return flight to London and two weeks of freedom on my hands. I told Mum that I might pick up another flight in London and go visit Maureen in

Greece. That seemed to put her mind at ease.

And then, up pops another coincidence! Last night I had a call from Maureen. She's back in Dublin to look after her mother. I didn't get all the details – some sort of emergency operation – though she said her mother is recovering well. I'll know more tomorrow when I call over to see her.

But I got a bit sidetracked, Dad. I wanted to finish telling you the story of last Sunday in Wales. After breakfast, there was another presentation in the main hall before the last of the workshops. It was a graduation ceremony. Annie presented diplomas to the finishing students of the Dru Yoga Therapy course.

'What's dru yoga?' I hear you ask.

It seems that it is like the exercises we did in the Heart Workshop – a mixture of yoga and chi kung. It's energising and fun. The three-year diploma course trains people to teach it.

There were about twenty people on the stage to receive their diplomas: men and women, old and young. The class had elected the eldest to make a speech at the end – a jolly graduating grandmother called Vera. She told a heart-warming story.

One day she was practicing her yoga in the living room at home. Her young grandson walked in and asked: 'What are you doing, Granny?'

'I'm doing my homework,' she told him.

He paused for a six-year-old thought, and then asked: 'So what are you going to be when you grow up?'

Vera laughed with such a hearty chuckle, I could tell that, whatever she's going to be, it wouldn't be a serious and grumpy old granny.

She was chuffed with her success in receiving her diploma. Justifiably so. She had overcome many challenges in doing the course; including high blood pressure and a bad back. It had obviously worked for her. She looked a picture of health and so full of vitality.

Then Vera shared some of her learning. She said that she never knew before that there were so many different ways to breathe, and talked a bit about pranayama – the practice of yoga of breathing. She said that she would like to share one of the breathing exercises that she had learned. The audience followed her instructions:

'Take a deep breath in… hold the breath for a few seconds. Then breathe out slowly and evenly while saying "Ha". Take another deep breath in… hold it… and… out slowly, saying "Ha". Keep breathing that way, slowly and evenly. Now breathe a little bit faster, still saying "Ha" on the out breath. Next… breathe a little bit faster… and faster again… still faster… even faster. Breathe faster… faster, faster, faster…'

Soon we all got the message. 'Ha, Ha, Ha, Ha, Ha, Ha, Ha…'

Everyone was laughing with her. What a wonderful way to learn!

Then Vera introduced the Children's Choir. They sang with such heart and hope of finding their path that leads to a brighter world. It was a powerful song. I was overcome with emotion. Tears welled in my eyes; not tears of sadness, but tears of joy. Do you know what, Dad? I can't remember the last time that I shed tears of joy. Listening to the song of the children, I believe in their bright future. If only all children had that view of the world; what a fantastic world it would be.

The last workshop I went to was run by Joshna from England, and Regina from France. It was called 'The Secret of Vitality'. But there's no great big secret – it was all very much common sense.

They ran through the Keys to Vitality:

– Eating – You are what you eat.

– Breathing – Trillions of cells in the body, and all of them need air.

– Exercise – Aerobic exercise enhances breathing,

like walking, cycling or swimming.

– Positive Thinking – Your thoughts determine your present and your future.

– A Strong Healthy Body. And

– An Open Heart.

The workshop focused on the last two. They guided us through another sequence of movement and gestures and some strong yoga postures. We had to pair up with a partner for some of the stretches.

I was matched up with Edward from London. He certainly had a strong healthy body. I asked if he worked out in a gym. But, no, he said that he just practices yoga a few times a week. I could tell; he wasn't just muscular, he was fit and supple as well.

Some of the postures were quite strenuous, and I was pleasantly surprised that I could manage them all. Though the 'Lake Titicaca Lady' beside me seemed to be struggling with one of the stretches. She appeared to have a stiffness in her right leg. I spoke with her afterwards. It turns out that she has a gammy knee, like Mum. It's been like that for a couple of years; since she broke her leg while tap dancing… at seventy-four years of age!

But it won't stop her from climbing the Andes. Vitality! She's certainly got it!

After lunch, I called back to the treasure trove of bookstalls in The Haven. I bought a lovely little book called *The Dance with Joy and Pain*. It's all about managing emotions. And it has some marvellous insights on life as well as details of some of the energy block release sequences. I won't remember all that we did in the workshops so the book will be a good little refresher for me. I bought a book by Louise Hay as well. But I haven't had time to read any of it just yet.

As I was about to leave The Haven, I bumped into Paulette. She invited me up to visit Snowdon Lodge for the afternoon. That's the training centre up in the mountains near Bethesda. But I had a ferry to catch. And to tell the truth, Dad, I was feeling a bit overwhelmed. I'd met such wonderful people over the weekend, but I needed to spend some time on my own to let the experience really sink in. Although I was sad to be leaving, I knew that I'd be back to visit again.

In fact, Dad, I've been thinking about doing the dru yoga teacher training course. The diploma course is four weekends a year over three years. So it's quite a commitment. And I don't know where I'll be next year if I'm taking time out to do some travelling. But I'll keep the course in mind – on the back-burner. First, I should finish the courses I've already started.

The business strategy course lectures are starting up again at the end of August. I'll need to start putting some work into my summer project if I want to get it finished by then.

Aine is back from her holidays, so we're going to finish the sailing course this weekend. It seems so long ago since we did the first two lessons. I hope that I haven't forgotten everything that I learned back then. Well, I'll find out in about an hour when I'm back on the water again. Better sign off now, and get myself organised. Until later…

The Waterside

Sunday, 2ⁿᵈ August '98

Guess what, Dad? This sailing lark is a bit like riding a bike. Once you've got to grips with the basics, it all comes back to you. Although I had to concentrate hard for the first half-hour or so, I soon found myself whizzing across the water. No capsizing this time! Aine has pretty much mastered it too. We're doing our last three hours of the course tomorrow afternoon – a great way to spend the bank holiday.

On our way back from the Surfdock, I was just thinking that I must find a way to get more sailing practice in. Then… another coincidence.

I bumped into Gerry Allen. He used to live downstairs from my last flat in Sandymount. It's hard to believe that it's three years since I lived there.

Anyway, it turns out that he runs the boatyard, and he asked what brought me down there. When I told him of our sailing exploits, he said that he has a dinghy that we can use anytime. Excellent! What a generous gesture.

But now we've got the use of a boat to practice in, the challenge will be finding the time.

I've block-booked next weekend to finish my business strategy project. It's been hanging over me all summer, somewhere at the back of my mind. But now it's time to just knuckle down. I'm going to stick with it, even if it takes the whole weekend! I want to get shot of it before I go on holidays the weekend after. So I probably won't have time to write much until then.

On the subject of holidays, I called out to see Maureen last night. She's still staying over at her mother's house. Her mum seems to be recovering well after the operation. Although it sounds like it has been a stressful time for the whole family.

I can well imagine.

Anyway, Maureen expects to be back in Greece the day before I leave for London. She said that I'm welcome to come over to visit. I just hope that I can get a flight now. But she said that there's usually no problem on standby from London.

This afternoon, I went for a walk on the South Wall and did a lot of thinking. I'd spent the morning reading – that book by Louise Hay. She has an amazing story to tell. She said that she had been diagnosed with cancer. The doctors wanted to operate, but she bargained for time. The doctors gave her three months. Then she read everything she could find on the subject of cancer… and she learned. And she learned. She said that she changed her lifestyle and her thinking and she went through what she called 'a thorough mental and physical cleansing'. Six months later, the doctors could find no trace of the cancer. It's amazing, Dad… She cured herself of cancer!

But what causes the cancer cells to grow in the first place? Some say that they've always been there, but our immune system keeps them in check as long as the immune system is strong. Other researchers say that some types of cancers can be caused by radiation and by environmental pollution. Yet others say the majority of cancers are a result of poor lifestyle – environment, diet, lack of exercise or psychological distress. It's been called 'the disease of civilisation'… Some civilisation!

But so many books confirm a mind-body connection; that physical disease can be the result of mental and emotional distress and stress. Denise Shapiro maintains that cancer 'appears to be the result of many years of conflict, guilt, hurt, grief, confusion or tension surrounding deeply personal issues. It is connected to feelings of helplessness, inadequacy and self-rejection… It is as if the deeply embedded resentments or conflicts eventually begin to eat away at the body itself.'

That was the origin of your cancer, Dad, wasn't it? I know that it's true.

On my walk earlier, I was thinking: When did you stop dreaming, Dad? When did you lose heart? When did your dream become a chore, a pressure, a stress?

If that's what you thought it, then that's what you made it!

OK. So the business failed, but not you. You were never a failure. You were the best father and I love you dearly. But couldn't you have just let it go?

We could all see your pain, you know. And your grief over the loss of your brainchild. Mum said that she saw you cry over it… just the once. She said you were sitting alone down the end of the garden. She saw the back of your shoulders quiver as you let go of each heartfelt sob. Was that once enough for you to let all those feelings go? Why did you have to put on the brave face? Didn't you know the price of pushing your feelings down to eat in on you?

'Big boys don't cry!'

What rot! Whoever came up with that stupid notion? How else are men supposed to release painful emotion? Tears are healing – they're a natural part of grieving.

I watched you grow tired over the years. You tied up so much of your energy in thoughts of blame. It kept cropping up in conversation: 'The bloody taxman'; 'The banks!'; 'They're all the same!' What does blame solve? Nothing! But you held onto the thoughts of blame, and the thoughts stoked up the emotions. The bitterness, the resentment… they ate in on you, sapping your energy.

You didn't have the energy then, to fight the January cold as well as the cancer. So your immune system went for the cold and the cancer ran riot. Although we didn't know that then. You were concerned about the cough, which persisted for two months. So much so, you even overcame your resistance to visiting the doctor. Would it have made any difference if you had visited earlier? Probably not. Even by St Paddy's Day they still thought that it was pneumonia. I remember that's what they said when you went into hospital for the tests.

And I remember two days later. It was late when I went in to visit you. The ward was dark and quiet. You seemed to be feeling pretty low and said that you'd been fasting.

'See Christy over there. He came in for tests too… two weeks ago! And he's still there. I don't think I'll ever get out of here!'

'Nonsense,' I said. 'You're just saying that cos you're tired.'

My mind then woke up. 'Fasting! Why is he fasting?'

You said that you would have to take barium meal for the test in the morning. Barium meal? That's hardly respiratory!

That was my first inkling.

The following day, Mum said the oncologist had been in to see you.

'What's an oncologist, Mum?'

'A cancer specialist.'

'Cancer!' It was the first time I had heard the word mentioned… A terrifying word. Yet, there are treatments if they catch it in time. But they didn't. From the results of the tests they gave you a few months. And then it took off like wildfire. The months turned into three weeks.

But what if you'd known earlier? Not weeks or months earlier, but years. What if you'd known the impact of the stress and the blame before it took its toll? Would you have changed your thinking? What were you trying to prove, Dad? You didn't have to prove anything to us. We loved you for just being you. Maybe we just didn't say it enough. Maybe it's a family trait, this bottling up of emotions. I know I do it too.

I'm not trying to blame you – or me – for holding back feelings.

I read somewhere that emotionally, 'we're all victims of victims'. And ain't that the truth. I know so little of your early life and the childhood that shaped you.

But I know that your dad died of cancer too. Perhaps it's a family pattern. But patterns can change.

And change starts here…with me.

I've let go of my anger and I hold no resentment.

I forgive you, Dad… for not always being the way I wanted you to be.

I forgive you and I set you free.

The grief will still come in waves, I know.

But, I'm learning, Dad, to just let it flow.

I'm taking responsibility for my life, my thoughts and my feelings.

I'm the only one responsible for my own health and well-being.

It's not that I fear death; we all have to go sometime. It's just that preventable death – avoidable illness – it's all so unnecessary.

There's so much I want to do with my life, Dad. The to-do list keeps getting longer and I'm still not entirely sure what is my heartfelt desire. I really don't know where to begin. So I'll begin with the present moment… and let the past go. That's the only way I can build my path to my bright future. I may eventually see where the path is going. But, for now, I can only lay the bricks one by one; moment by moment.

Goodnight, Dad… and sleep in deep peace.

Love,

Clodagh

Chapter 8

MISSED CONNECTIONS

Aylesbury Guest House
Maidstone
Kent

6.30 p.m. Friday, 14ᵗʰ August '98

Dear Dad,

Greetings from Kent!

What am I doing in Kent? That's a very good question... I'm not quite sure myself. It seems that I am having another wing-it holiday – another holiday on flexi-plan. I feel like I have been travelling for the best part of the day.

First there was the flight from Dublin, which got me into Heathrow late morning. Maureen had told me that one of the airlines flies direct from London to Santorini, and that it's a much handier route for travelling on to Ios than going through Athens. But she didn't say which airline. When I got to Heathrow, I enquired at a few of the booking desks. Standby flights to Greece this weekend seem to be non-existent. A helpful man at the BA desk said that he could get me onto a scheduled flight to Athens for £800! Way, way over my budget! Thanks, but no thanks!

After an hour of airline enquiries, it became apparent that I wouldn't be flying to Athens at a reasonable price until at least Monday or Tuesday and I still hadn't found out which airline did the direct flights to Santorini. So I decided to wait and phone Maureen later when she got in to work.

That still left me with a dilemma… Where do I spend the weekend? London? No thanks! I've had enough of the hustle and bustle of cities. Then I remembered the last conversation I'd had with Martin, my friend in Hampshire. He said that he had been working a lot near Maidstone in Kent. It's called the Garden of England and only an hour from London. Sounded good to me!

I tried to call him from the airport to find out if he was still working there. But the network lady, in a refined pre-recorded voice, said: 'Sorry, it has not been possible to connect your call. Please try later.'

Decision time.

I'd have a couple of days to kill before I could get to Greece. London didn't appeal. Why not go to visit the Garden of England anyway? Why not indeed!

Decision made.

The British Rail lady said that I'd have to change at Victoria. Victoria! Flashbacks to working in Burger King in Victoria en route to my first summer holiday in Denmark fifteen years ago now… Oh my, how time do fly! I remembered that there was a tourist office near the station where I might pick up some brochures on Kent. And since I had to change there anyway, I thought that I might step across the road from the station for a nostalgia lunch break. But not in Burger King. The restaurant where Fiona and her friend, Jean, used to work had a much better and more varied menu.

It's still there, though it's called the Shakespeare now. I can't remember what it was called back then. Young Australians seem to have taken over – there's not one Irish accent to be heard… except for mine.

I was glad that I'd taken a break on the journey to park my rucksack for an hour and get my bearing on Kent from the brochures. But the heat in the city was exhausting, and I was happy to see the landscape change from city to country through the windows of the train. It was a pleasant train journey, which delivered me to Maidstone West Station by 2.30 p.m.

From the map, I discovered that the tourist office was on the other side of the town. Planes, trains and automobiles all in the one day? No, I decided to forgo a taxi. It didn't seem far to walk, so I worked out a route that would give me a feel for the town centre. But, laden with luggage, I was in no mood for window shopping. First priority was to find a bed for the night.

The lady at the tourist office was very helpful. She made a few calls, which saved me trudging around town. And she found a room for me at this guest house within walking distance of the town centre. I only booked for one night, in case I'm in luck with a flight cancellation tomorrow.

The River Medway flows behind the tourist office. I sat for a while there on a wooden bench watching the swans on the water and the pigeons on the wall, basking in the sun. I felt relaxed and contented… Until niggling thoughts started to creep in:

What if I can't get a connection to Martin's mobile?

What if he's not working in Kent anymore?

Guess I'll be spending the weekend on my own.

So what! I'm sure there's plenty to do in Maidstone to pass a couple of days.

What if I can't get a phone connection to Maureen?

She won't know whether I'm coming over or not.

What if I can't get a flight out next week?

Oh, shut up, Chatterbox. Go away!

I refocused my thoughts on my new way of being – on trusting my intuition. The river reminded me of my resolve to 'go with the flow'.

Following the tourist office directions, I crossed over the river and found myself climbing Rocky Road to the guest house in the heat of the afternoon sun. I was out of breath when I got there – hot and tired and wondering if I was meant to be elsewhere. But I feel much better now after a cool shower and a rest. So I'm heading back into town to find someplace to eat. I'll make a few phone calls later and see what transpires.

O'Neills Pub
Maidstone

1.10 p.m. Saturday, 15ᵗʰ August '98

I've had such a morning of frustration, Dad. Although I got a connection to Maureen last night, it seems that I phoned at a bad time. In the background, the restaurant sounded manic and Maureen sounded hassled.

'Can I call you back?'

'No, I'm calling from a phone box. I just rang for the name of the charter firm you mentioned that do direct flights to Santorini.'

145

'I think that it's called something like Phileas Fogg,' she said.

'OK, I'll check directory enquiries and call you back tomorrow.'

If I was hoping for a chat, I picked the wrong time to call. But it was easier to get a connection to Greece than to a mobile in England. I still haven't managed to get through to Martin.

After several calls this morning, I finally got the number for Phileas Fogg Travel Agency. A pleasant voice answered my call and introduced herself as Mandy. She said that the direct Santorini flight only goes on Tuesdays and it's booked out this week. But she could get me out to Heraklion on Tuesday and back to Heathrow for my flight home on the 28th. I could then get the ferry from Heraklion to Ios. Mandy had to check out some details and wanted to call me back. But there was queue forming outside the phone box. So I told her that I'd phone back in half an hour. It's at times like this that I can see the merit of having a mobile. Anyway, Dad, it's time to call Mandy back now...

Darn and tarnation! Mandy said the Heraklion flight is now full as well. Life seems to be conspiring against me going to Greece this summer. But I'll make one more attempt after I finish my sandwich. There's a travel agent across the road.

Small consolation, but I managed to get a connection to Martin's mobile while I was at the phone. Turns out that he's en route to Wales to visit family for the weekend. When I mentioned that I had tried to call earlier, he explained that the networks can sometimes be a bit dodgy, especially when he's driving through the mountains. Then he asked how long I was planning to stay in Kent. I had just started to tell him of my challenge in getting a connecting flight when the line started to break up. End of conversation. Darn networks! Oh, well… Maybe I'll have better luck at the travel agent across the road.

Banks of the River Medway
Maidstone

3.30 p.m. Saturday

Confounded again, Dad! The travel agent was called Going Places. All they could tell me was where I wasn't going… and that's Greece. Oh, I could get out there anytime next week. But the difficulty is in getting back for the 28th. It seems that it's the last week of the school holidays so the flights back are all full of families returning for school. I half-joked to the girl at the travel agency, 'It's tempting to go and maybe not come back! But I don't think that my boss would be impressed. I'm not quite ready to chuck the job just yet!'

'Maybe it's an omen,' she quipped back.

Maybe it is. But to go to Greece… or not to go? The travel agent gave me another phone number to try – a Greece & Crete travel specialist. My last resort.

In search of a phone card, I rambled in to the Royal Star Shopping Arcade. There I found myself outside a shop called Destinies.

With a name like that, I just had to go in. Inside, I found crystals and wind chimes and books galore.

At this stage, Dad, I had just about given up hope of getting to Greece. So I stood in front of the bookshelves, closed my eyes briefly, and asked my intuition to give me a sign of which way to go. I opened my eyes and the word *Signposts* jumped out at me from the spine of a book. I thought, 'Well, there's a sign, if ever I saw one!'

The book was written by Denise Linn and is another book about listening to intuition! So I opened it at random with a mental query of where I should go next. It opened at a page that explained the symbolic significance of rainbows and rivers. With a clear blue sky, rainbows are highly improbable today. So I decided to come back here to sit by the river and let my thoughts flow free of frustration.

I've let go of the notion of going to Greece now, Dad. But I can't stay in the Aylesbury tonight. The landlord mentioned this morning that they are fully booked for this evening. I'll have to collect my luggage from there soon. On the way here I stopped at a phone box with my local accommodation guide. After a few calls, I finally found a vacancy… At a B&B called Wits End!

It seems so appropriate, Dad, to my frame of mind today.

But I've changed my thinking now. Sitting by the river again, a thought sprang to mind: 'Don't push the river, it flows by itself.'

A boat called *The Jester* glided by. Is life playing the jester with me and my plans for Greece? If so, perhaps it's time I stopped fighting the game, go with the flow and enjoy it more. I'll stay in Maidstone for the weekend… But what then?

I've no car. I'm laden with a rucksack and plenty of beach clothes. The weather forecast is good. But I don't fancy sweltering inland. A sea breeze would be welcome.

So what are my options?

A ferry to France? Dover and Folkstone are both nearby.

No, I've had enough of travel arrangements already!

What about a beach? Brighton! There's a beach there and I've heard that it's an interesting town.

Yes, there's energy in that idea.

So, after the weekend, next stop is Brighton. I'll be passing the train station on the way back to collect my rucksack so I'll call in to check on the schedule and fares.

Speaking of luggage, it's time I moved on to settle in to Wits End.

Wits End Guest House
Maidstone

5.40 p.m. Saturday

Synchronicity seems to be at work again, Dad.

After I had collected my rucksack, I was trudging up the Tunbridge Wells Road in the heat, yet again, thinking: 'This walk is further than I thought. I wish that I'd called a taxi.'

Next thing, a BMW driving toward me slowed down and pulled in at the kerb beside me. I had a map in my pocket so I leaned toward the window, ready to help with directions. The driver leaned across the passenger seat and opened the door.

Appearing well-dressed and sounding well-spoken, he said, 'I don't normally do this, but I saw you carrying the rucksack and I thought that you might need a lift.'

I was a bit taken aback. I'd say my expression must have told him so.

He seemed a bit embarrassed as he explained, 'It's just that I saw you earlier in Destinies and you were reading a book by Denise Linn. I've read a few of her books too. And then when

I saw you again just now... well... I thought it was a bit of a coincidence. I'd actually passed by on my way home. But then I thought that you were going the same direction. So for some reason, I turned the car around to see if you wanted a lift.'

Now, don't get mad, Dad. Though I'm sure Mum would flip if I told her after all the years of 'Never accept lifts from strangers.' I've been programmed to fear not to trust. Yet I felt no fear of this man. In fact, he seemed more apprehensive than I was. My intuition tuned in to assess the situation as soon as he started talking. When he mentioned the shop and the book and the coincidence, my intuition said, 'It's OK.'

So I told him, 'Well I don't normally do this myself... In fact, I was brought up not to accept lifts from strange men – not that I'm saying you're strange, or anything. But, as you mentioned the coincidence and Denise Linn... Well, I'd really appreciate a lift. I'm going to a guest house called Wits End. Do you know it?'

He seemed relieved that I didn't shout at him or accuse him of anything odd. I threw my rucksack into the back seat, and by the time I sat into the passenger seat he had visibly relaxed. I was relieved not to have to walk with the weight anymore, and to have the rucksack, and myself, delivered to the door.

We had a good conversation on the short drive. I gave him the potted version of how I had come to be in Kent travelling alone. He told me his name was Alan. He runs his own business and seemed interested in my job working with small businesses, and in my fascination with mind-body energy. We talked of books, and he told me that he had met Denise Linn at one of her workshops several years ago. He asked of my motivation...

No, the word he used was 'agenda'. I said that I'd no agenda but learning and told him of some of my experiences following up on coincidences and trusting my intuition, but that I didn't quite know where it was all leading me.

Outside the guest house we chatted for another five or ten minutes. I was enjoying the conversation, but I felt that I should go. Alan said that he'd like to continue the talking and asked if I would like to meet him for a drink tomorrow evening. Well… Why not? I'm looking forward to meeting him again tomorrow. With all the coincidences, I sense that we have some things to learn from each other.

But, for this evening, I feel the need to walk, unencumbered by rucksack. I still have a few hours left before the sun goes down.

The Fountain Pub
Tunbridge Wells Road
Maidstone

9 p.m. Saturday, 15ᵗʰ August '98

The landlady gave me directions for a good walk out of town. I think that I took one or two wrong turns, but I wasn't too concerned. I still found my way to the river and back to a bus stop on the main road.

Her route brought me up along the main road first, then down a lane, across some playing fields, past an old rectory and along some country roads. It may have been at one of those signpostless junctions that I took the wrong turn. But I met a young cyclist and asked him for directions to get to the river.

He pointed back the way he had come, along a dirt lane between the hedges.

'Turn left at the end and it's downhill from there.'

My nose was struck by a strong smell of apples. Then I realised that the lane cut through an orchard – a huge orchard. The trees seemed to stretch out for miles. Above it, the sky had turned into those beautiful pink and blue pastel hues. In the distance, two giant balloons hovered. One was in vivid rainbow colours. The other was red with white script spelling Virgin Atlantic. I used them as a landmark. Or, should I say skymark? In any case, I found my way to the river by the time they'd floated away.

When I arrived at the footbridge, I could see no sign of my objective – the Victor pub. But an elderly couple were crossing the bridge coming toward me. So I asked them for directions. 'You've come a bridge too far,' the old man joked, and then he redirected me downstream along a riverbank path.

Crickets chirped merrily in the grass as I started along the path. I passed a sign proclaiming 'Private Fishing'. It certainly was private. The banks were concealed by the reeds and shoulder-high greenery. I only caught occasional glimpses of the fishermen… silent in their nests.

The path narrowed, and narrowed again. Then gigantic nettles encroached from either side. I dithered about whether to turn back to avoid getting stung. A blackbird appeared on the ground about two feet in front of me and hopped along the trail. I decided to follow him. Using two elderberry stems to coax back the nettles, I found myself in a sort of tai chi dance through the nettle patch. It was slow-going, but I got through without a sting. Then the path opened up again for a more comfortable walk.

I must have walked for well over an hour by the time I got to the Victor. My legs were tingling as I sat down at a table in the beer garden to savour a rest and refreshment in the balmy evening. The baked potato I'd ordered seemed to be taking forever. So I moved inside to remind the barmaid that I was still alive… and starving! But when the food finally arrived, it was well worth the wait.

Then the peace of the pub was shattered by an invasion of noisy likely lads. Their voices started to grate. I wasn't alone in my irritation. The landlord told them to quieten down. But their beat on the jukebox urged me to move on.

It was a straight walk back up the hill to the main road. Darkness had fallen as I reached the top of the hill. There were few streetlights on the last stretch and I was starting to feel a bit nervous walking under the shadow of the trees.

Then, as I reached the corner, a neon sign jumped out at me from the front of the Fountain Pub: 'Take Courage'!

Courage? I will, when I need it. But the walk uphill was thirsty work… so, I thought, 'Make mine a Guinness!'

It's quiet in here for a Saturday night. So the barman had time to chat. He's young and friendly, but a bit self-critical. After commenting on my accent, he passed remark on the pulling of a pint.

'I hope I'm doing it right. You're supposed to draw a shamrock on it, aren't you? I heard that from a mate who works in O'Neills.'

I reassured him, 'What's in the glass is more important than what's on the surface. And anyway, the shamrocks are just for the tourists. I prefer a smiley face myself.'

I picked up a matchstick and drew a smiley on the pint.

The barman grinned, as I showed him my pint smiling back at me.

It's a comfortable pub and I feel at ease here. Though my limbs are pleasantly weary, I know they appreciated the walk. I'll give them more exercise tomorrow exploring the Medway, but further down river.

One pint was enough. Now it's time for my next big adventure… Finding a bus back to my bed at Wits End.

Wits End Guest House
Maidstone

10.30 a.m. Sunday, 16ᵗʰ August '98

I woke to another sunny morning, but my sunny humour didn't last long. When I turned on the radio for the weather forecast, I was shaken by the news of the devastation of a bomb blast in Omagh – twenty-eight dead! So much for the peace process, Dad. The psychos up North are off again. How could they do that to fellow people? People – fathers and brothers, mothers and sisters, grandparents… and children! People out for a Saturday shopping! What butchers do such things in the name of religion or faith? Faith in what? Man's inhumanity to man? Faith in what God demands they kill children? No God could condone such wanton destruction of lives and the freedom to live. What fools follow religion blindly into fear and hate and stupidity? Do they expect their reward in heaven? From who?

I'm sure they'll get their reward… If not in this life, then in the next.

As the saying goes, 'You reap what you sow.'

But, Dad, I can feel my blood boil at their self-deluding stupidity.

Freedom! Don't make me laugh!

They don't have the courage to claim their own personal freedom from the puppetmasters of hate.

Oh, Dad, when will they learn? Freedom is in the heart and the soul, it's not a line on a map.

Yesterday I walked off my frustration. Today I must walk off my anger.

Benchley Gardens
Maidstone

3.30 p.m. Sunday, 16ᵗʰ August '98

My map brought me back to the river and the Medway Walk. On my way there, I stopped at a phone box to call Maureen to tell her that my plans for visiting Greece had been scuppered. She sounded disappointed. I think that she was looking forward to company and news from home and conversation in Dublinese. But she'll be back home in November. So I'll catch up with her then.

At the start of the riverbank path, I walked fast. But then the pace of the river slowed me down. Once I got past the concrete bank, the trees and the reeds had a calming effect. I tuned in to the names of the boats. Each had a story to tell…

Captain Webb – Sea Mist – Tara – Fantasy Too – Carefree – Gentle Lady – Happy Days – Blue Dawn – Forty Knots – Blue

Knight – Sea Swift – The Joker – Diamond Wings – Ocean Breeze – White Hot – Monaco Prince – Pollyanna – Little Gem – Temple Moon – Smell the Roses – The Dolphin – Fortuna – Sundaze Lady

As the path emerged from the shade of the trees, I saw a row of Dutch sailing barges moored by the bank. They no longer carry cargo and some had been made into homes. Shiny brass portholes and pretty lace curtains showed the care of the owners. A couple were having a late breakfast on deck.

Imagine living on a river, Dad. Such peace!

Going about your everyday business floating above the water's constant flow.

After the barges, I came to a Beefeater pub, the Malta Inn. I sat for a while at a table outside, watching the river traffic flow by – boats, joggers, cyclists, dog-walkers – all travelling at their own relaxed pace. Then a thought struck me… Malta! On the phone, Maureen had mentioned Malta as another holiday option. I considered it briefly. But the thought of more airport bustle put me right off. I'm enjoying the pace of my random rambling now. Though I still feel a need to be near the sea. So I'll stick with my plan for Brighton after a couple more nights here.

Moving on from the Malta Inn, I strolled along the same path back to town. The museum was next on my flexible list. I only got as far as the front door of the museum. Wafts of music drew my attention and curiosity steered me around the corner into Benchley Gardens. I followed the *Mary Poppins* tunes to the bandstand. The museum will still be there tomorrow, but the brass band and the sunshine may not.

I've done enough walking today, Dad. It's so pleasant just sitting here on the warm grass, watching a wide range of humanity enjoying the same sun and the same music. Foot-tapping geriatrics in deck chairs. Families gathered around picnic baskets. Toddlers in rhythmless, uninhibited dance. Teenagers trying so desperately to look bored. And the band plays on…

Wits End Guest House
Maidstone

11.30 p.m. Sunday, 16th August '98

I've just spent a thoroughly enjoyable evening with Alan. He phoned just before six to ask if I'd eaten. I hadn't. So he suggested dinner, as well as that drink, and called to collect me shortly after. We drove to the Malta Inn. The car park was chock-a-block. It would have been a long wait for a table. So we drove further out of town to a lovely little country pub called the Tickled Trout. They do have such curious names for pubs here.

Over a drink in the beer garden, we settled in to conversation. It sounds like he has had a lot of challenges in his life – three children, two failed marriages and one failed business. But he seems to maintain a very positive outlook and has learned from the past. Though I get the sense that he's at another crossroads in life – like me. He's recently started up a new business. That led back to the subject of my work with small businesses and my path evolving over the past few months from frustration and fear to positive thinking and yoga and energy-balancing.

When I mentioned energy, he asked if I had read *The Rainbow Journey*. Never heard of it. It was the book that he'd bought in Destinies yesterday and was still in the car, unread. He went back to the car to get it. Scanning the cover, I discovered that it's all about balancing personal energy with a separate chapter on each individual chakra. It seemed to be much more detailed than others I had read.

Alan said that I could borrow it as he won't have much reading time until his holidays next week. I didn't know if I could get it back to him in the post before his holidays. As I had Shakti Gawain's latest book in my bag, I offered to lend him that, as substitute holiday reading instead.

Over dinner, I told him of how my holiday plans had changed and my new plan to follow my intuition towards Brighton. Alan gave me the phone number of a friend of his who lives in Brighton.

'You should get on well with him. He talks a lot too.'

That reminded me of Shakti Gawain's notion of 'people as mirrors' that reflect back attributes of ourselves. We are drawn to people who mirror and reflect back some aspect of ourselves, whether that be a strength or weakness or something we have to learn.

And oftentimes we are drawn to opposites; to people who express energies which are less developed in our own personality. In some way, they can help us to develop those energies and become more balanced in our own self.

Reflecting on that, I see that myself and Alan are both searching for some sort of direction. But he listens with patience while I prattle away. Perhaps I should talk less and listen more. He's a good listener. Maybe that's it; maybe it's patience that I need to learn.

He's back to work tomorrow, and I'm off to Brighton on

Tuesday, so I won't see him again on this holiday. But, apart from returning books through the mail, I'm sure that we'll be in contact again. It's funny how paths cross, Dad. And you do meet the most interesting people when you're open to learning on this rocky road of life.

Cafe Rouge
Maidstone

2.30 p.m. Monday, 17ᵗʰ August '98

The banks are open again this morning. So I walked into town to change my drachmas back to sterling. I lost out on the transaction. No matter. I gained in the learning process.

Maidstone seemed different with all the shops open in the hustle and bustle of commercial life. After I'd stocked up on postcards, I quickly tired of the shopping precinct. Chain stores are so much the same. The tourist guide said that Union Street was the place for specialty shops and some hope of individuality. When I got there, I took a break for a coffee. Following a sign for The Heart of Kent Hospice in Staines Court, I found a haven of peace from the pedestrian traffic and a worthy cause. Inside, the shop was a mishmash of interesting bric-a-brac priced in pence, not pounds. And the courtyard tables outside provided welcome respite from the noise of the main shopping street. Peace and quiet to scribble some postcards to friends back home.

My amble up Union Street provided a wonder of window shopping – a feast for the eyes. Model trains, old toys missing bits. A thirty-year-old stereo without a stylus. Antique battered furniture. Gaudy baubly jewellery. Budget tattered books. More knick-knacks and bric-a-brac.

A shop called Red Feather caught my eye – or more precisely, what drew my eye was a pair of overwrought candlesticks in the window, surrounded by tacky gilt-edged delph. In contrast, a small Grecian urn peeped out from behind them.

A reminder of the holiday that wasn't to be. It was stereotypical holiday souvenir – terracotta and black provided the background for the face of an ancient sage with curly marble white hair. His name was written in white too: Hermes. God of what? I remember that Aphrodite was love and Mercury, the messenger – but Hermes? Which god was he? No worries. I'm sure the answer will come to me.

Heading back through the shopping precinct, I spotted a phone box and thought that I should make some arrangement for accommodation in Brighton. From the brochure, Marina West on Oriental Place looked interesting. The voice on the phone was cheerful and friendly. So I booked a room for Tuesday and Wednesday and, provisionally, Thursday. They're pretty full up after that with a stag party block-booking for Friday and Saturday. But at least it gives me a base to check out the town and decide it I want to stay longer or move on elsewhere.

Soul Café
Maidstone

7 p.m. Monday, 17th August '98

I had a funny experience on my way home from window shopping this afternoon, Dad. Walking up the Tunbridge Wells

Road, I noticed some activity outside the Maidstone Spiritualist Church. I must have passed by several times over the last few days, but I hadn't noticed it before. A sign advertised the annual Open Day. My curiosity woke and my instinct steered me to explore. But, for some reason, I walked on.

As I rested back at Wits End, I wondered at my earlier hesitation. From somewhere inside me a voice asked: 'What were you afraid of?'

The people at the door had seemed very open and friendly – no horns on their heads or anything like that. What had I expected? Some psycho cult? Then I started to see how much the church of my birth has programmed me to fear: to fear difference; to fear their opinion and viewpoint; to fear expressions of individuality.

I knew nothing about them, their views or their outlook. So why should I fear them? I regret today that my fear held me back from learning more about others. As I walked back to town later, the doors of the church were closed for the night.

The Soul Café is welcoming this evening. I stopped for a coffee here earlier and previewed the menu on reconnaissance for dinner. My Hungarian waiter from lunchtime is spruced up in his evening apron. This place has a really nice ambience, with low lights and candles on the tables and mellow music to soothe the soul. It's not very busy, being a Monday night, I suppose. I feel at ease here.

I ordered the Ravioli Conchetta. It seemed the lowest calorie option. Although I've been burning off a lot of energy with all my walking, I'm still keeping an eye on the food intake. I don't want days of guest-house breakfasts to start taking their toll!

This looks like my meal coming now. Time to take a break for eating and maybe a little reading...

Soul Café

10.30 p.m. Monday

It's zany, Dad. Talk about things arriving in the right place at the right time! The meal hit the spot and so did the book. Well, I've only read the first third of it. But it seems to be the right book in the right place at the right time.

I'd only scanned the cover and the index when Alan first showed it to me. I've only read the introduction, the background and the first couple of chapters, and the author has really taught me a lot.

She started her career as a pharmacist, and then trained in medicine, progressing on to surgery. And then she retrained in clinical psychiatry. She's also had a gift since early childhood of spiritual healing. I know what you're thinking, Dad, with your logical left brain – woo, woo, spooky, spooky, prove it, prove it. But, it's not at all spooky. As she explains it, it's very much common sense.

When it comes to healing there's so much more to it than 'the gall bladder in bed number 10'. Though that may be the illness the doctor is dealing with, what about the rest of the person in bed number 10? What's happening in their mind, in their heart and their soul? Who's treating the whole person? Who's treating the whole of the patient in bed number 10?

After her years of experience, Dr Davies shared what she had learned of the importance of healing and balance at all levels of being: body, mind, heart and soul. But the book was more of a guide to self-healing through understanding and clearing energy blockages. It gave me a better insight into some of the things I had experienced in Wales, and other things about me that I have still yet to learn.

She spoke about energy or life force – what the Chinese call *chi*, or in India, *prana*. That life energy that pervades every living thing is as vital to living as eating food or breathing air. Without that vital energy, there is no life. She gave a beautiful description of the human energy field, or aura, and how it is animated by the swirling discs of energy in the chakras.

I've heard that some people can see the aura. And some can sense it – or feel it – as I felt heat from my heart chakra at the workshop in Wales. It must be a beautiful sight, Dad, to see someone's aura. But, if the aura is really the energy of the soul, maybe it's best that we can't see it. It would be an awful intrusion – like seeing into another person's thoughts… An invasion of privacy.

But you don't have to see things to know that they are there. Like wind, or electricity, you can feel them. Sometimes you can feel the vibes when you walk into a room – you can sense if someone is happy or sad, agitated or peaceful. People emit energy that others pick up.

I picked up on your weariness a long time before you became ill.

I sensed your determination when you got the results of the tests.

You had such focus – to dot all the i's and cross all the t's for the taxman, the insurance man and the rest. You did it, Dad!

In such a short time, you did it all with your mind working overtime in the hospital bed. And then... I sensed you let go.

I was glad to be there at the end. I'll always love Liam for standing up to give me his seat by your bed. It was such a privilege to be holding your hand as you left. I know how much Liam loved you – as a brother, in business and in the trials of life. And I know how much it meant for him to give that seat up.

It was painful to listen to your chest heaving, wondering if each gasp was the last. And then... I knew that it was. I knew, in that instant, that you had stopped your struggle for air. Holding your hand, I didn't need to feel for a pulse. I knew it was gone.

Your life force, your essence, had left. But where is it now, Dad?

Where is your soul, your energy, your essence of being?

Energy has to go somewhere; it can't just cease to exist!

There I go again with the logic!

What does it matter just where your soul is? I feel it's at peace.

But, speaking of logic... This book, *The Rainbow Journey*, reminds me of another book. One you gave me for Christmas many years ago.

Do you remember, *Tell Me Why?*

It was a marvellous book, Dad. It answered so many questions of my twelve-year-old curiosity. Like, how is a rainbow made?

It explained all about light refraction, the different wavelengths of light, the colour spectrum, and about prisms and raindrop reflections.

The author of this rainbow book also talks about the search for logical proof. Of the flow of human energy and the answers she's found through her research. After the scientific bit, she made an interesting point: 'Rainbows didn't wait to exist until man understood why.'

Yes, there's so much we don't know, Dad. Like: Where does the soul go when it has no need of the body anymore? Is it out there somewhere in a different form? Somewhere in space and time? Maybe your light shines through again occasionally, for a fleeting moment, like a rainbow... A beautiful smile of light in transient time.

Tomorrow is another day of transience for me too. I'm planning on catching the mid-morning train to Brighton. So, it's time to settle my bill at the Soul Café and haul myself back to Wits End to repack my rucksack for the next stage of the journey.

Maidstone East Train Station

11 a.m. Tuesday, 18ᵗʰ August '98

Sitting at the railway station, got a ticket for my destination... Hmm, Brighton bound. I do like train stations, Dad. They're such great places for people-watching. Not much opportunity for that now, though, as there are only two others on the platform. But I've got twenty minutes to kill before my train arrives. So I've time to tell you about my lesson this morning on crystals.

I was trundling down the hill towards the station about an hour ago with thoughts of walking on further to sit by the river and read in the sun for a half-hour or so. When I came to passing the Christian Spiritualist Church again, I saw a new sign out on the pavement: 'Fayre Today'. As I glanced over the wall and across the grass, billowing white muslin caught my eye. A sort of canopy had been erected in front of the door and underneath it was a table with a couple of chairs. A woman was laying out brochures and leaflets on the cloth-covered table.

My curiosity got the better of me today. I turned in through the gate and walked up the path. A smiling, fair-haired lady with a perfect perm and wearing twin-set and pearls greeted me. She threw a curious glance at my rucksack. I explained that I was on my way to the station, but I had been sidetracked by the sign outside on the path. She seemed a bit perplexed. So was I, to be honest, Dad. I wasn't quite sure why I was there. My eye latched onto the leaflets on the table. The nearest one advertised times for spiritual healing. So I asked her to tell me more about that.

'My husband would be better able to answer your questions. He's a spiritual healer. I'm expecting him here at about 10.30 if you'd like to talk with him. You could have a look around the fayre inside while you're waiting.'

'Why not?' I thought, as I had time to spare before catching the train.

I parked my rucksack at the door and wandered inside. Through a short corridor, I walked into a carpet-tiled hall with more cloth-covered tables along each side. I veered to the right. Displayed on the first couple of tables was a sparkling array of crystals and gemstones. Not what I had expected. But then… What did I expect?

On the table, little baskets and bowls held stones and gems in every colour of the rainbow. Vivid yellow and orange starbursts cut out of cardboard advertised 'Bargain Rates' and prices in felt-tip pen. Amber, amethyst, aventurine, hematite, carnelian, quartz, tiger's eye, malachite, citrine, turquoise, fluorite and rose quartz, among others. Some of the names I'd never heard of before. And others, which I knew, strictly speaking, weren't crystals.

From somewhere way back in my mind came a flash of a long-ago geography lesson. I could see Miss Murphy in front of the blackboard talking about igneous and sedimentary rocks and the evolution of rocks from the earth's core of molten magma. 'The oozing liquid rock then cools and can crystallise through heat and pressure, forming igneous rocks.'

These rocks then work their way to the surface to be eroded eventually by water and wind and their broken-up bits are then redeposited as sedimentary rocks. Then the plates of the earth's surface shift to swallow up the sedimentary rocks, enfolding them back to the core where they melt down. After which the whole process starts all over again. But she stressed that really it is an ongoing process, though it takes zillions of years. When Miss Murphy started to talk about mineral composition and the symmetry of atomic structure in crystals, my mind started to wander.

The lady behind the table of crystals reminded me of Miss Murphy a bit. Pretty wasn't a word you'd use to describe her, though she did have a very friendly disposition. Her long, lank hair had a few strands of silver, matching some of the threads in her cheesecloth Indian skirt. The black T-shirt she wore hadn't seen an iron in a while. All in all, she was very unteacher-like in appearance. But then, teachers do sometimes appear in unusual guises. Mentally, I christened her 'the Crystal Lady'.

She saw my interest in the table display – loose stones, cut stones, pendants, rings, necklaces, bracelets, crystal balls and key rings. My eyes were still taking in the array when she started pointing out the best bargains.

'Those citrine necklaces are very good value... only five pounds.' She wasn't pushy and seemed sincere.

'What's citrine?' I asked her.

'It's a type of quartz,' she explained. 'It's good for the kidneys, the liver, the gall bladder and all the digestive organs. It's also good for raising self-esteem, giving hope and warmth and energy. And it also attracts abundance.'

I was fascinated by her knowledge of the properties of these stones and quizzed her on others. She knew so much about them and told me more about the latent energy that they hold, and their uses in healing. It wasn't heavy sales talk. She seemed to have a natural understanding and love of the crystals and gemstones. Prompted by my questions, she gave me a copy of a chart on the uses of the various gems and minerals.

I wanted to buy something. But the style of the citrine necklace wasn't quite me, so I dipped into some of the baskets to see what else I could find. A silver dolphin drew my attention. It clasped a clear crystal with colour striations of green, blue and mauve.

'What's that crystal?' I asked.

'It's fluorite.'

'I thought that's what they put into toothpaste,' I joked.

But crystals are no joking matter to her.

'No, that's fluoride. This is fluorite. It's where the word fluorescence comes from. It sort of glows for a while after it's been exposed to ultraviolet or sunlight. '

She said that it was also called Blue John, and it's a powerful healer.

'It helps to calm the over-excitable by bringing greater concentration in meditation, and helps to connect to the higher self.'

Intuition again! It seemed to be just what I was looking for at some level… and the silver dolphin was pretty too. I bought the fluorite pendant and thanked her for her help.

Then I moved on to the table at the end of the hall. A range of books was spread out, face up across the tabletop. It looked as if someone was clearing out their bookshelves and lying them flat, to cover more space. There was an interesting mix of books. From titles on yoga and chakras to the life of Mother Teresa and *Dear God, This is Anna*. Someone was sharing their spiritual library.

Again, I started to wonder what I was doing there and my chatterbox started off: 'If anyone from work knew what I was doing they'd call for the men in white coats.'

Oh, shut up, Chatterbox. Go away; I'm learning.

I picked up a book called *The Art of Spiritual Healing* and scanned the Table of Contents: Introduction, The Danger of Fear, The Healer Within, Mental Dis-ease, The Alpha/Theta State, the Chakras, Prana…

Then I opened a page at random – page 6. The word 'Hermes' jumped out at me! Coincidence again! I found an answer to my question of Hermes on the little Greek urn. Was he a god… or was he not? Whichever, it seems that in ancient times he gave man a set of teachings that have influenced philosophy and religion ever since.

My curiosity was activated again. I read a few pages to pick up the gist of Hermetic Philosophy. It seems there are seven basic principles:

- The ALL is mind: The Universe is mental.
- As above, so below; as below, so above.
- Nothing rests; everything moves; everything vibrates.
- Everything is dual; everything has poles; everything has its pair of opposites; like and unlike are the same; opposites are identical in nature but different in degree.
- Everything flows out and in; everything has its tides, all things rise and fall; the pendulum swing manifests in everything; the measure of the swing to the right is the measure of the swing to the left; rhythm compensates.
- Every cause has its effect; every effect has its cause; everything happens according to the law; chance is but a name for law not recognised; there are many planes of causation but nothing escapes the law.
- Gender is in everything; everything has its masculine and feminine principles; gender manifests on all planes.

Funny thing, Dad, as I read, the ideas seemed familiar and yet somehow sort of cryptic. It's like a cross between quantum physics, Eastern religions and Shakti Gawain. I decided to buy the book to read at my leisure and to understand more.

Yet again, I asked myself, 'What am I doing here?'

I'd had my lesson on crystals and found this book to learn more about Hermes. So did I need to hang about any longer just to ask some questions of the husband of the lady in the twin-set and pearls?

Then an idea came to me. 'Why not apply the first principle of Hermes?'

If 'ALL is mind' or thought, then I thought, 'If I am to meet a spiritual healer, they will come to me and answer my questions.'

Almost immediately, the Crystal Lady appeared at my elbow to show me more pendants and some of her favourite stones. She held out one pendant with an opaque jet-black stone. It shimmered in a clasp of silver.

'This one is obsidian. Isn't it lovely? They also call it Black Velvet.'

I could see why. It really was a beautiful stone.

I showed her the book that I was about to buy and told her of my curiosity and interest in books on human energy and healing.

'Oh, the healing... It just comes to you. You don't want to mind them books with all that fancy talk.'

It turned out that she's a natural healer. She spoke so matter-of-factly and answered my questions.

She asked me some questions in return about Ireland. By coincidence, she's been invited over to visit some friends there next month. Then another coincidence... When we got back to the subject of healing, I discovered that she specialises in cancer healing. I told her that you had died of cancer.

'Oh, cancer,' she said, with the voice of experience. 'It all starts from emotional stress.'

Just as I was about to launch into some more questions, the lady in twin-set and pearls came to join us. She said that her husband had been delayed, but would arrive soon. My reminder of time and my train! Meanwhile, the Crystal Lady was called back to her table of gems. I would have liked to talk with her some more. But there were several people around the table demanding her attention and time was moving on.

I thanked the twinset-and-pearl lady as I paid for the book, and explained that my questions had been answered already, in one form or another.

Maybe that wasn't entirely accurate. How could I know that my questions were answered when I hadn't even known what they were?

Suffice to say, my curiosity was satisfied.

I collected my rucksack and headed for the train station.

So here I am, Dad, and the train is running late. I hope it's not too late. I don't want to miss my connection. But, no matter. It gives me some time to chew on the food for thought I've found in the last hour – and the last few months. I've had so many new concepts coming to me; so many new ideas drawing my energy.

Yet they're not new really. They're just new to me. Somehow they all seem connected. But how? I need time to digest these ideas; to filter the nourishment from the chaff, so that I can absorb what's relevant. There's so much learning available in this Grand University of Life, yet I need time for discerning what is pertinent to me.

Oh, here comes my train now. Gotta go…

Love,

Clo

Chapter 9

JIGSAW PIECES

Druid's Head Pub
Brighton Place
Brighton

Tuesday, 18th August '98

Dear Dad,

Greetings from Brighton!

I've only been here a few hours, yet the place seems somehow familiar. With a map from the train station tourist information, I had no trouble finding my bearings – straight down Queen's Road, turn right at the Clock onto Western Road, then find a turn to the left to reconnect to Oriental Place. It looked straightforward on the map. But the walk along Western Road seemed never-ending under the weight of the rucksack.

At the junction with Montpelier Place, some outdoor tables and chairs looked inviting. Café Esprit seemed like a good spot to take a break and recheck the map. A sulky teenager served me a coffee as if a smile would kill her. I brought it to a table outside before the milk turned sour.

Watching the world go by, I was struck by the variety of people and dress styles ambling along. Why did this place seem so familiar?

Gazing downhill to the sea, it hit me – San Francisco. Of course!

The hills, the streets stretching down to the water, the relaxed pace, the expressions of individuality in the clothes people wore, the sunshine warming my skin – it all brought me back to another holiday three years ago. Perhaps that's why Brighton seemed so familiar. Or maybe the sense of recognition was just from forgotten photos, or stories that I'd heard from Mum. I recalled that she had been over here a few times to visit Auntie Ellie. If I'd known that I was going to end up here, I would have asked Mum where Ellie is buried. It would be nice to have brought her some flowers. But maybe the thought is enough.

When I found Oriental Place, at first glance it seemed very quaint – very olde worlde resorty. But, on closer inspection, peeling paint and rusting wrought-iron balconies give it an air of dilapidation. The sea air must take its toll.

A bubbly guy called Barry welcomed me to Marina West Guest House. I recognised his Welsh accent from my phone call from Maidstone. He walked with a bounce in his step as he led me along the hall to the reception room, which was like somebody's living room with a big brown leather sofa – very 1960s. An ancient episode of *Coronation Street* was playing on the TV. Copies of the *Sun* and the *Pink Paper* were strewn on a footstool in front of a matching brown leather armchair. A neon rainbow sat on the windowsill inside the venetian blinds. There was more lively colour in the mahogany display cabinet – red and white ribbons, rosettes and trophies filled the glass case. I guessed there was a proud dog-owner in the house.

As I checked in, Barry said that I'd been upgraded to a room with a shower. Boy, was I glad! After sweltering for the day under the rucksack, I made immediate use of it. Refreshed and revived by the shower and a deep relaxation, I happily left my luggage and set off to explore.

Turning right at the pavement to head for the seafront, I saw a curious thing, Dad – little pieces of jigsaw on the ground. First I saw one, then two, then three… then more. There was a trail of them scattered along the street. I guess somebody must have dropped then while moving house. I hope it wasn't a 5,000-piece jigsaw. Imagine only discovering that you're missing some pieces when you're 4,000 pieces through the puzzle! I have a funny feeling, Dad, that somehow Brighton holds more pieces of the jigsaw for me.

I treated myself to an ice cream at Ye Olde Brighton Rock Shoppe and then rambled along the upper esplanade for an overview of the beach and an updraft of sea breeze. The smell of the sea felt like a homecoming.

There were throngs of people on the beach and the promenade. It was a riot of colour and activity, too much for my travel-weary senses to absorb. In the sunlight, the West Pier looked sad and neglected and the Palace Pier looked absolutely manic!

At the Old Ship Hotel, I turned away from the seafront, in search of The Laines and the tourist office. I found the tourist office first and stocked up with postcards and guide brochures. By the time I'd found my way to The Laines my energy was flagging. Passing through Brighton Place, a sign caught my eye: 'Welcome to the Druid's Head – where past meets present!'

I felt the call of refreshment of a liquid variety.

There were no seats left outside for me and my pint of Fosters. So I'm ensconced by the window, looking out on the former 'House of Correction'.

On the wall beside me, there's an old pencil sketch of Stonehenge struck by lightning! Very druidic! It reminds me of my visit to Stonehenge on the trip to Hampshire. Was that only last June? So much has happened since and that trip seems like a lifetime ago.

I've been tuned in to the conversation at the next table, listening to a voice that oozes with studious boredom.

'Yeah, I just got back yesterday. I've been sleeping on the beaches in Greece,' a dishevelled twenty-something man told two girls. They've been talking of holidays, mayhem in the Star Apartments, the pick-up lines of water-ski instructors, and throwing up in the bar. What fun… not!

After earwigging on their conversation, Dad, somehow I'm very glad that I'm not in Greece just now!

Things usually turn out for the best in the end. But not always as we expect them to.

A clock outside has just chimed five, so I guess that's the end of my shopping today, but there's always tomorrow. After the pint of refreshment, refuelling is next on my agenda. I think that I'll ramble back along the seafront and find someplace to eat and watch the sun go down later.

Alfrescos Restaurant
West Pier Beach
Brighton

10 p.m. Tuesday, 18ᵗʰ August '98

Well, the West Pier may look run down by day, Dad, but by night, when the lights come on, it has a magical air. It looks so pretty in its evening dress with reflections of its electric sequins shimmering in ripples over the night water. The sunset was spectacular too. I walked the promenade towards Hove while the sky turned shades of cerise and dusky red. By the time it faded to pastels, I'd reached Hove and started to walk back again towards the fairy lights of the piers.

There's a Mediterranean feel to the air here tonight. With so many people out walking for the sunset, it's the best show in town. I feel very safe and part of it all. My table here gives me a good vantage point to watch the walkers and the water. As I tucked into my pasta earlier on, I thought, 'I could almost be in Italy.'

Perhaps it was the balmy sea breeze that set me on that flight of fancy. More likely, it was the smell of the pasta and the Italian waiter singing along to 'Strangers in the Night'.

But now 'Old Man River' plays out… 'He just keeps rolling along.'

And it's time for me to roll home to Marina West. It's been an eventful day, Dad. I've earned an early night. But I do like the feel of Brighton. There's so much to do here. I think that I may stay on longer than just two days.

Royal Pavilion Gardens
Brighton

1 p.m. Wednesday, 19ᵗʰ August '98

I had a jolly start to the day, Dad. Barry was chirpy and cheerful as ever while he served breakfast. A smiley face impressed on the toast brought a smile to my face too. I confirmed my booking for Thursday night. But they have a full house on Friday, so I'll have to look elsewhere if I want to stay for the weekend. I can do that tomorrow. Today I have designated a shopping day.

After an hour of reading, I rambled up to Western Road and then back down Preston Street. Then I found myself on the seafront again. Stopping for postcards at the Brighton Rock Shop, I managed to cross a few pressies off my list. What else could I bring back from a holiday in Brighton but Brighton Rock? The shop had an amazing selection of names in the rock. I got 'Mother' and 'Fiona'. There was no sign of the name 'Brendan', so I got 'Brother' instead. And for Niall? 'Liverpool', in red-and-white stripe, of course!

I drifted through a few gift shops and department stores on my way up toward The Laines. But the sun was shining and I felt the need to spend some time outdoors. When I stepped out of Henningtons shoe department, I caught sight of the domes of the Pavilion peeping through the skyline.

I wandered around the Pavilion gardens with no inclination to go inside.

Whatever treasures the interior may hold, the exterior is feast enough for my eyes today. At the back of the building, a stone seat provided a resting place while I had my lunch of fruit and water. And now a stepped pillar gives me a perfect writing desk while I contemplate the Pavilion and the lily pond.

As I rest my mind, long forgotten words from Coleridge and my schooldays float back to the surface.

In Xanadu did Kubla Khan
A stately pleasure dome decree.
Where Alph the sacred river ran
Through caverns measureless to man
Down to a sunless sea.

The Pavilion basks in the sunshine, faded pink and ivory against a clear blue sky. Spires and onion domes. Minarets without muezzins. Lattice lace and regal feathers. Crowns and coronets. Wide balconies and lofty canopies.

It's a pretty palace, Dad, fit for a queen – the Queen of Sheba – or an Arabian Prince.

But there's more beauty in the lily pond. I wonder, is the lily a cousin of the lotus? One bright white lily is in full bloom. Its heart of yellow shines out from snow-white petals. Others are in various stages of opening, struggling to reach their full potential in a battle against the algae rising from the murky depths. Flies are feasting on the surface of the pond. And now they're starting to feed on my arms. So it's time to move on, to explore the North Laines for the afternoon.

The Green Dragon
Sydney Street
Brighton

3.30 p.m. Wednesday, 19ᵗʰ August '98

After the peace of the Pavilion garden, the market stalls and colourful shops were slightly disorienting. But it didn't take me long to adjust to browsing again, especially when the acid-yellow façade of Brighton Books drew my attention. I started scanning the shelves of the local history section – books about smugglers and princes, bathers and divers and dippers. I always thought that 'dippers' were Dublin pickpockets. But the word has a different meaning in Brighton, Dad. Here the dippers were a sort of lifeguard in ye olden days. Well, you learn something new every day!

None of the books on local history really jumped out at me. So I moved over to the philosophy section to see if I could find out any more about old Hermes. The few books I picked up were all exceedingly heavy and none of them caught my energy. So I ambled along past the cash desk to the back of the shop and found myself in front of some free-standing shelves. The top shelf bore a title: 'Fairy Tales and Myths'.

I wondered, 'What am I doing here?' But I let intuition guide me.

Tall books, small books, thick books and thin books crowded the shelves. At the far end of one shelf, a momentary glitter of gilt caught my eye. It came from a small thin book with a grubby beige spine. The lettering on its spine was age-faded and indistinct. I had to pick it up to read the words: *In the*

Great God's Hair. It was the same height as my hand; a perfect fit. Contrasting the beige, the rest of its cover was a deep slate blue. It felt warm and furry, almost like fuzzy felt.

Inside the front cover, a faded ink inscription read simply: 'F. to G. 1909'.

The thread binding creaked as I flicked through the rough-edged pages, releasing a faint whiff of must. Pencil highlights and question marks in the margins added character. I wondered who was F. to give this book to G. – this little Indian fable, dedicated to husbands and wives?

It was only four pounds for this little book of eighty-nine years. I felt that I had found a treasure, Dad, and I couldn't leave it behind. I'm looking forward to reading the story and getting a sense of the previous owner from the markings they left behind.

I sauntered in and out of a few more shops, but the heat of the day was making me weary of walking. When I turned into Sydney Street, I seemed to have hit the Australian enclave. Ozzie signs abound. I thought of Karyn on her Antipodean adventure. I really must start a letter to her tomorrow.

A chalkboard outside the Green Dragon advertised a beer garden. I thought a rest in the sun with a beer and a sandwich sounded like heaven. When I walked in the door, it took my eyes a few moments to adjust to the lack of bright light. Three Ozzie lads at the bar gave me directions out back to the beer garden.

But the 'garden' was concrete paving enclosed by four whitewashed walls. No breeze. My notion of heaven wasn't a sweltering sauna. So I've moved back to the cool indoors.

It's quiet here in the bar, so I hope that my sandwich won't take too long to arrive. Apart from the barman and the three Ozzies, there's only one other guy at a table in the corner. I've found a prime seat for writing and reading, with the sunlight streaming in the window behind me.

This looks like my tuna sandwich coming over now. So it's time to rest my pen, Dad, and fish out my newly acquired treasure from its little paper bag cover.

West Pier Beach
Brighton

6.30 p.m. Wednesday, 19ᵗʰ August '98

The sun-warmed stones on the beach are surprisingly comfortable for sitting and writing, and the roll of the sea is so relaxing. It's mesmerising just watching the late sun reflect on the water while I reflect on the day. Coincidence struck again today, Dad, in a big way.

This afternoon, as I settled down to eat and read my new-found old book, I heard a voice from the corner table say, 'Did you just buy that in a second-hand bookshop?'

I told him I had, and gave him directions to Brighton Books. But I was curious. How could he tell from a distance? I asked if he could tell me about the book, and brought it over to his table. He seemed very knowledgeable about books. After examining it, he said there was another from that era that I should try to get hold of: *The Roadmender* by Michael Fairless.

'She was a local woman, but she used a man's name as a nom de plume.'

'Why?'

'Women weren't supposed to think in Victorian days, let alone write,' he explained. 'She wrote it nearby in Shermanbury in Sussex. It was one of the last books that she wrote before she died.' He spoke almost as if he knew her.

I gave him a pen and paper and he wrote the name down for me.

On impulse, I invited him to join me as I returned to my table to finish my sandwich. He picked up his glass and moved over, introducing himself as Roger. He told me that he works in the electronics industry. Why is it that people always introduce themselves by their name and their job?

Anyway, by coincidence, Roger had been to visit Ireland recently to do a job in some electronics plant near Dublin (Intel, I guess). I told him of my roundabout road to Brighton – via plans for Greece and maybe Malta! The last beach he was on was at Santa Cruz near Silicon Valley a few years ago. It sounded like the job takes up a large part of his life, and I passed that remark. But he said that he also plays guitar and sings with a rock band and did some travelling with them too.

I was dumbstruck when he mentioned his future plans – to chuck the job for a year and travel to Tangier to write! Coincidence indeed! I explained it to him by telling of my own notion to take time out, to write and perhaps travel. Tangiers sounded very exotic to me. But he's been there before. In fact, he's done a lot of travelling and writing en route.

So I asked for his advice from his experience. He gave it freely.

Writing style and discipline, time consumption, travel article construction, publishing networks, lead times and how to generate income 'on the road'. So many questions answered, almost before I'd asked them! Coincidences still fascinate me, Dad, even if they don't surprise me so much anymore.

It was valuable advice that he gave me.

'Don't let the writing interfere with the travel experience. Just go with the flow!'

Now where have I heard that before!

As we discussed the merits of pen over PC, I came to realise something. If I'm going to take this notion seriously, then I may have to invest in a laptop computer.

Aargh! There's no getting away from technology in this modern age!

That led us on to the subject of technology, its commercial impact, and its social impact. Roger has some concerns about the consequences of technology for the human condition, as I do too. I shared my observations with him of the increasing stress levels in business – an inevitable consequence of the accelerating pace of technological change.

Who was it that wrote, 'Sometimes I don't know what I think until I say it'?

I can't remember… but that's me all over.

Through the conversation, I started to realise that I'm not alone in my frustration with work and the way 'the organisation' is adapting to change. It's all about people really. It's people that make up any organisation. It's people that have to learn to adapt, to embrace or reject the things we've created. The ostrich approach won't work anymore in this day and age. We've all got to face up to change.

The sun is low in the sky now and the sea air is turning chilly.

To my left, toward the West Pier, I see little black dots gathering in the air above the run-down pier buildings. Are they starlings? Or swallows? They're starlings, I think… swarming in a sort of formation.

Oh, Dad, you should see this! They're dancing en masse!

The cloud of birds swirls clockwise. Then it twirls anticlockwise. It hovers for a few seconds and then dives in a corkscrew spiral down to the roof. A few minutes' rest… and the dance starts again.

It's amazing to watch. They dance in such close formation, in dense concentration, and then the bird-cloud dissipates for another rest. What communication do they use for such synchronisation? Perhaps they send out signals, or thoughts, or some form of energy.

Well, if birds can do that, I guess people can too. They say that everything is connected – atom by atom – in the universal energy field.

It certainly seems to be working for me. I put out thoughts of changing my lifestyle – of writing and travelling – and guidance comes to me.

But other things are drawing me too. Like all the books that have come to me over the past few months; books on energy and complementary therapies and healing on various levels. So many books – and so many that I haven't yet had time to read. Somehow they're all connected too… like another piece of the jigsaw.

Yet the full picture is still a puzzle to me.

Do you remember when I was a child, Dad? I always had an answer to that age-old question: 'What do you want to be when you grow up?'

I never had any hesitation. For years the answer was always the same: 'A nurse.'

But then, when I hit my teens, financial reality started to dawn… or maybe it was just greed. I thought, 'Hey, doctors make more money! Maybe I should study medicine instead.'

It's ironic, really, that it was my failing physics that knocked me out of that points race. Or maybe my subconscious was making me wait for the syllabus to catch up to include quantum theory and the energy of beings.

I'm glad that I didn't make the grades for medicine. When I see the hours that doctors now work treating pieces of patients, I think that I would be terribly frustrated – limited by time and resources to dealing with limbs and gall bladders and other parts, instead of whole people.

Isn't it funny, Dad, how we only reflect on our past when we come to a crossroads in life? With hindsight, I see now that my zig-zag path has led me to learn about people – through waitressing, cleaning hotel rooms, supervising the warehouse and the factory floor. And my path has also taught me of business – from restaurants to factories, from marketing to finance; big businesses and small. But where is my path leading me now? I seem to be setting my own syllabus of learning to put my experience to alternative use. Though that's not exactly correct. Synchronicity seems to be setting the syllabus for me. Where will it lead me next?

Thinking of the books that I've been drawn to, I seem to be coming full circle. Not back to my childhood image of nursing, but to some alternative sort of healing somehow related to technology and business and stress. I'm beginning to see the frame of the jigsaw, though there's still a gaping big hole in the middle. Perhaps more time spent writing and travelling – away from the stress of the desk – will help me to see the picture more clearly. I trust my intuition to lead me to more pieces of the jigsaw, and, in time, I'll see the big picture.

But enough of this mental rambling! The sun has gone down and the sea breeze is cold now. The warmth has gone out of the stones too. My intuition is talking to me again. It says, if I don't get a move on, I'll be back to nursing tomorrow – nursing a nasty old cold. So it's time to head home to the warmth of Marina West.

Goodnight, Dad, and… thanks for listening.

Marina West
Oriental Place
Brighton

5 p.m. Thursday, 20ᵗʰ August '98

I woke before six this morning, disturbed by the noise of teenage clubbers returning home from a night on the beach. Although I was wide awake, I was far too cosy to get out of bed. So I curled up to start reading my new little treasure, *In the Great God's Hair*, feeling a sort of reverence for the age of the book. As the story unfolded, that reverence deepened as I discovered some of the gems of wisdom within.

Though some of the language and notions were a bit old-fashioned for one brought up in the post-feminist age, it held much wisdom all the same.

It told a tale of 'Hindoo' gods sitting on top of a mountain playing at dice, and telling stories of their various games playing with the lives of mere mortals. Chance and change were the name of the game – interfering with the outcome of the future and the impact of the past.

'And do not therefore be too apt to estimate the future of our lives by the past: for while life itself endures, there is the possibility of change…

'Moreover, there are instants and atoms of time containing in themselves causes and consequences that run both ways into the two eternities of the past and the future, being as it were the fruit of one and the seed of the other: and many times it happens that the twinkling of an eye determines the destiny of a soul.'

Do the gods play with our lives, Dad? Or is it as Hermes said? That 'Chance is but a name for law not recognised… Every cause has its effect and every effect has its cause.'

By chance, today I found more pieces of the jigsaw… pieces about healing. By chance, I wandered in to Public House Books just around the corner in search of Roger's recommendation, *The Roadmender*. The shop assistant was very helpful, but said that they didn't stock it and I should try an antiquarian bookseller. By chance, I wandered to the back of the shop and discovered a wide array of books on healing – everything from aromatherapy to Zen meditation. I earmarked a few to buy before I leave Brighton.

By chance, it started to rain as I walked back towards The Laines to find Brighton Books again. I ducked into the nearest doorway for shelter, and found myself in a healing shop. It wasn't a New Agey sort of shop. It was staffed by qualified practitioners in aromatherapy, homeopathy, therapeutic massage and reflexology. Mellow music was playing, and I detected the smell of lavender oil from a burner. Then the relaxing ambiance was shattered by an angry voice.

An irate man started sounding off at the man behind the counter, who was evidently a homeopathic practitioner. The potential customer complained that he was in constant pain from his left leg, somewhere just below the knee. The doctor had not been able to cure it. He was aggressively demanding a guarantee that a homeopathic remedy would heal it before he forked out more money. The practitioner was wise. He calmly offered advice, but no guarantees.

It struck me how impatient we've become in our aspirin culture – expecting instant relief, but no time to consider where the pain may be coming from, or how we might help to heal it ourselves.

The rain eased off. I left the shop, somewhat upset by the man's anger and aggression.

At the tourist office, I continued my search for accommodation for Friday night. The lady behind the desk said that sometimes it could be difficult to find weekend accommodation at this time of year. She recommended that I try some places nearer to Hove. I made a few calls to no avail.

Then I decided to kill two birds with one stone.

I'd picked up a little brochure called 'Hidden Brighton on Foot' so I spent the afternoon walking some routes from that and knocking on doors of any guest houses that I passed. The walk was thoroughly enjoyable, but the search for accommodation left me downhearted.

I was weary when I got back to Marina West, thinking that I'd have to pack and move on tomorrow. But there's still so much I want to see in and around Brighton. I really wanted to stay on for the weekend.

Then Barry and Ken came to my rescue. They were watching TV in the lounge as I returned. I told them of my trekking the back streets and my fruitless search for a bed for tomorrow night. They have a room for me here on Saturday and Sunday. It's just Friday that poses the problem. But Ken kindly offered to make up a bed on the big sofa in the lounge if I was really stuck.

That has put my mind at ease. Though I'll still try the tourist office in Hove in the morning. Now I can enjoy my fish dinner at Melrose, and finish writing my postcards in peace.

Brighton Marina

Friday, 21ˢᵗ August '98

After breakfast, I strolled down to Hove. The lady in the tourist office had the patience of a saint. She spent twenty minutes on the phone on my behalf. But the only single rooms in town tonight are executive suites at £90!! Forget it! Barry and Ken's big leather sofa was starting to look like a godsend. So I decided to take them up on the offer.

On my way back from Hove, I stopped for a coffee at the Meeting Place Café. Walking towards it, I passed a big statue of an angel, but missed a marvellous photo opportunity. Streaks of angel-wing clouds soared up in the sky behind it. At the right angle, they could have been an extension of the statue's wings.

Why, oh why did I not have my camera to hand? Anyway, Dad, since I'll have no fixed abode until later, I've designated today as a roving camera day.

A walk along the seafront exercised my photo-spotting eye. I enjoyed playing with light and angles – composing pictures of piers and people, deck chairs and a carousel. Then I ventured to explore the Palace Pier.

The first stretch of the pier is dedicated to dietary indulgence: donuts, burgers, shellfish, fish & chips, Belgian waffles, bratwurst and, of course, Brighton Rock.

Then there is food for the curious: 'Palmscan'– your future by computer!

Graphology, the secrets of your signature revealed. An Indian fortune teller. And 'Gypsy Jim, will read your palm – for only a fiver!' He claims to be the only Australian gypsy in town! His vintage caravan seemed authentic. It wouldn't look out of place behind a horse on the Kerry roads.

Next, I came to the temple – a modern-day temple dedicated to 'Amusements' and noise pollution. One-armed bandits looked tame compared to the more dangerous techno games – 'War Games', 'Scud Attack', 'House of Horror' and 'Death'. The noise assault jarred my senses. Mental torture. A grown man screamed in primal delight, as he 'killed' a hologram invader with his laser.

Not my idea of 'amusement', Dad! I find no entertainment in such expression of aggression.

I walked on to the end of the pier to find thrills of a gentler era: go-karts, waltzers, helter-skelter, and I watched the children's faces lit with laughter on the bouncy castle.

Still, the noise invaded my ears. Then the wind brought the smell of the sea to my nose. So I ducked between the bouncy castle and the waltzers to stand at the railings for a while looking out across the waves and breathing in the salty air. I started to feel my connection to nature again. In the distance, I saw masts peeping above the breakwater of Brighton Marina. I felt the call of their comforting clinking. So I ran the gauntlet of the noise assault again, back to the start of the pier, and turned eastward for the long walk to the marina. My feet took on a life of their own and kept me moving past the boats, across the lock and on to the end to the breakwater and back.

As I walked the breakwater, the sun was shining, warming my face. A wild wind, refreshing. Waves crashing. Wings of sea spray, uplifting. My thoughts went wandering as free as the ocean, until my legs demanded rest.

I'm sitting on the wall near the start of the breakwater watching the seagulls and the surfers bobbing on the waves.

What endless patience surfers must have, Dad, waiting for The Wave?

They paddle out to sit astride the board, watching and waiting, waiting and watching – a meditation in itself. They're ready when the big one comes; propelling themselves into the oncoming rush.

Walking on water, twisting, turning, spinning in displays of agility, balance and flexibility. The thrill, the buzz, is their reward for the effort and the waiting.

I feel a sense of expectation today, Dad. Expectation of what, though? I'm not quite sure. It's almost like I'm waiting… Waiting for some sort of wave to lift me and propel me forward.

To what or where? I don't know. But, like the surfers, I'm waiting with anticipation ready to dance on water when the wave crest unfurls.

Marina West
Oriental Place

2.30 a.m. Saturday, 22ⁿᵈ August '98

After a long day of walking, I was thankful for my bed on the big leather sofa. Though it creaks when I move, it's comfortable and cosy. I slept well for a couple of hours. Then I woke with a start. A door slammed, drunken loud whispers and laughter came through the wall from the hall – late night revellers returning and scrambling up the stairs.

All's quiet now. But I've lost my grip on sleep. The neon rainbow light hums on the window ledge, casting a soft glow into the room like a child's nightlight, banishing the scary monsters of the dark. I fear no monsters out there. But there's a monster in my mind tonight, Dad. It growls with too many thoughts. The monster of mental indigestion is force-feeding me half-thoughts. I've no time to grasp one before the next one roars up. My body is at rest, but my mind is racing in a frantic game of chasing my thoughts. I must quiet my mind. Perhaps if I focus on the rainbow, it will cast out this monster and give my mind peace to sleep.

Marina West
Brighton

5 p.m. Saturday, 22ⁿᵈ August '98

Last night's full house was evident this morning in the breakfast room. There were people at every single table when I walked in. Barry asked if I'd mind sharing a table with the Italian gent from number 8 and said that I shall inherit his room this afternoon.

The man from Milan said that he'd come over to escort his daughter. She's attending a summer school here. My expression must have changed when he told me her age. Twenty-two! And still in need of an escort?

'We Italians are quite fearful,' he explained.

I could understand his concern when he told me that he had lived in London for a year in the late sixties. Brighton is still swinging, Dad, but to a nineties' beat. I hope the man from Milan can conquer his fears for his daughter. She'll never grow up until he learns to trust her to live her own life.

Mr Milan had been here for ten days and told me of some of his excursions. A few days walking the Downs, up around Devil's Dyke, and several day trips – to London, Dover, Canterbury, Chichester, Arundel, the Isle of Wight, Portsmouth and Southampton.

'How far is it to Southampton from here?'

'Only one hour by train,' he explained.

I thought of my last trip there on my Tour de Hampshire in June. I've no great urge to revisit the city, but a thought crossed my mind… I might call over to Bursledon to visit Martin, if he's around, since it's only an hour away.

After breakfast, I tried to phone him, to no avail – the phone just rang out.

But at least the networks seem to be working again.

Then it was decision time again. What to do today?

Barry said that there was a market on Saturday mornings up near the train station. So I rambled up through the back streets, making my way toward the station. I found the market. But I must have been too early as there were very few stalls. I didn't stay long. Veering back down through The Laines, I headed for Brighton Books to look for *The Roadmender*. Bingo! They had it in stock.

In fact, they had several copies of different editions. The bookseller showed me a selection, apologising for not having the original from 1902. That didn't matter. I'm a reader, not a collector. I was drawn to a pocket-sized edition from the 1940s, while the man behind the counter pointed out the merits of each of the others. While making my choice, a picture flashed in my mind – the picture on the wall above Public House Books. A white-haired man held an open book in his hands, with rays of white light radiating from its pages. The caption underneath carried the words: 'The book shall be a ball of light in the hands.'

I bought the little pocket-sized hardback. It felt right. But whichever edition, I sense that the words hold some wisdom for me.

I browsed through some more shops on my way back to base. At the corner of Ship Street, an art shop drew my eye. The range of paintings in the window were crafted with beautiful nuances of colour. They were all scenes of Brighton Beach and the piers, at dawn and twilight in glorious shades of sunrise or sunset. I went in to see if I could find a print as a souvenir.

The prints were too big and would only get squashed in my rucksack. So I chose a large, glossy postcard of one of the paintings by Philip Dunn instead. It's a sunset silhouette of the West Pier with seagulls in the foreground casting shadows on the sand ripples of low tide. In the shallows, a man is digging for bait, mirrored by his shadow on the wet sand. It's a beautiful picture called 'It's never too late'.

But it'll need the right frame and the right wall and the right light.

After I chose it, the next rack of gift cards caught my eye. Mainly because of the contrast of a very different style. The sketches of landscapes in shades of gentle greens seemed insipid at first next to the vivid reds and indigos of Philip Dunn's sky and sandscapes. Yet these landscapes seemed vaguely familiar. The first one I picked up was of Devil's Dyke, where I haven't yet been. The next was closer to my home – Dingle Peninsular, so of course it would look familiar. I've been there several times before. But the third was of a place that I'd been only once – Brandon Creek. I recognised it before I turned the card to find the name.

It's a wild and magical place, Dad. I remember it well. Martin brought me to see it last March when we went down to visit his parents in Kerry. It's so remote there, you'd search hard to find a postcard of it, even in Kerry. Yet I find such a card here in Brighton of all places! Another coincidence? I was thinking of him only this morning!

On my way back to base, I tried to phone him again – still no answer. While walking, my mind wandered to the coincidence and to chance. Are the god's playing games again, Dad?

By chance, I first met Martin at a party in Kerry last New Year's Eve. A party I wasn't supposed to be at. By coincidence, he was coming back to visit Ireland in March for his father's sixtieth birthday. Several phone calls and letters later, he visited Dublin en route. We spent a week together in such ease of company. It felt like I'd known him forever. By chance, we haven't met since.

By chance, I'm only an hour away by train, and it's my birthday tomorrow. It would be nice to spend the day with a friend. But perhaps he's not there. Maybe he's working away again. Unlikely on a Sunday. Oh, I'll try the phone again... later.

Alfresco
West Pier Beach

7.50 p.m. Saturday

Well the gods seem to be playing games with the phone networks, Dad. I almost got a connection on my way here. I heard half a 'Hello' then crackle, crackle and the line went dead.

Walking up to Alfresco, I heard 'Old Man River' playing again and again and I was reminded to 'go with the flow'.

So I found a table with a good view of the sun going down and I can move to the opposite chair to watch the fairy lights of the West Pier when the sun has gone. I'm settled here for the evening.

In only five days, this has become one of my favourite haunts. Mellow music, good food, excellent views and a comfortable ambience to read or write, as is my pleasure. Tonight, I'm not much inclined to write. I'm eager to delve into my new treasure

– *The Roadmender.* I'll fill you in tomorrow…

The Druid's Head
Brighton Place

Sunday, 23rd August '98

Another year older, another year wiser… Isn't that what they say? I like being thirty-five, Dad. It feels so much better than when I was twenty-five. 1988, yeugh! That was a horrible year. But this is a good one and I feel a great sense of hope for the year to come. Life's such a grand adventure, whatever it holds. But there were times today when I did feel very alone.

I started the day with a ramble up to the market behind the station. It was a big one today with row upon row of stalls. But somewhere among them, I lost my enthusiasm. So I decided to catch a bus up to the downs to take in the view from Devil's Dyke. The weather turned watery en route. Drizzle descended to greet the bus as it laboured its way uphill. Not quite the right weather for an open-top bus ride. But I wasn't the only lunatic sitting upstairs, enjoying the spritzer on my face. Four others seemed to share my elation, and they had wide smiles on their faces too.

By the time the bus reached the top, the drizzle had turned to a heavy mist. The wonderful view that I'd heard so much about was obliterated. My view was limited to a few hundred yards. It was too wet for walking. So I adjourned to the warmth of the restaurant to read my book. It absorbed me for a couple of hours until it was time to catch the last bus back down to the seafront.

Leaving the restaurant, I stepped out into a cloud and a wild wind blowing in from the north-west. It seemed that the weather was heading downhill too. So I opted for the lower deck on the return journey. But I got soaked again on the walk back from the bus stop.

I met Ken in the hallway when I got back to Marina West. He thought I was mad going up to Devil's Dyke in such weather. Maybe I am. But no madder for venturing out again later in search of a pen. What is it with pens, Dad? I usually have four or five. But when one runs out, they all run out!

The rain had turned back to drizzle as I walked the length of the seafront looking for a shop. They all seem to close early on a Sunday. When I got as far as the Palace Pier, I stopped to ask the security man for directions to a convenience store where I might buy a pen. He didn't know of any shops nearby that would be open after eight. But he kindly volunteered a gift of his own pen. Little did he know that it was a birthday present. I thanked him for his help and told him how much I appreciated the gift.

Then I remembered that there was a band playing tonight in the Druid's Head pub. So I decided to stop for a pint to dry off a bit before braving the elements again.

The band is late starting. There aren't too many people out in such miserable weather.

My spirits seem to have taken a dip this evening, Dad, and I'm feeling sort of flat. Maybe it's because I'm spending my birthday alone. Or perhaps it's just the abysmal weather. Although I have a sense that this feeling started creeping in earlier, while I was reading *The Roadmender*. I wonder why.

It was a lovely story, filled with the joy and simple pleasures of a man who works close to nature breaking stones and mending country roads. He enjoys his work. And sees the fruits of his labour in the road he creates to serve the footsteps of his fellow men. Yet, even in that bygone age, he saw the impact of technology encroaching: 'The swift stride of civilisation is leaving behind individual effort, and turning man into the Daemon of a machine.'

I know what he means. Sometimes, in work, I feel like a paper-processing machine. I'm dealing with entrepreneurs on a daily basis, and I have great admiration for them. They create businesses and employment. And they see the fruits of their labour as their businesses grow. But what do I create, apart from a mountain of paper?

Maybe that's where my urge for change comes from. The urge to create something of value, something of service to others. Perhaps one day I'll create a business, but I've a lot to learn before then. So, meanwhile, I'll stick with my original plan – to take time out, to learn and write.

On the subject of writing, I'm reminded of Rogers's advice not to let writing get in the way of experiencing life. Perhaps I have been writing too much on this journey, maybe my pens running out together were telling me that!

My train of thought was interrupted there, Dad. A man started playing the fruit machine across from my table. It makes a dreadful noise. As I looked over, the name of the game lit up. 'Aladdin's Cave'. A timely reminder – my symbol of self-esteem.

I have been neglecting that lately; no wonder I'm feeling so flat. So I think that I shall take a break from writing for a few days and put more time into boosting my energy with yoga and the Mindstore techniques. I have a few more excursions in mind, but I think that I shall spend more time drifting, and see where my energy takes me.

Charlie's Café
St Ann's Well Gardens
Brighton

3 p.m. Wednesday, 26th August '98

Bless me, Father, for it's been a few days since I have written – although I must confess that I have thoroughly enjoyed myself, just drifting. And, guess what, Dad? I'm still in Brighton. By this stage, I think that the lads at Marina West must reckon that I'm a bit eccentric. Each morning at breakfast, they ask of my plans for the day.

Each day my response is the same: 'I haven't decided yet. Any suggestions?'

On Monday, Ken recommended a day trip to France. So I caught a bus over to Newhaven. Mais, quel dommage… I just missed the ferry. I didn't fancy hanging around for two hours for the next one. So, after consulting the map, I walked down to Fort Nelson for a slice of history.

There were some vivid exhibits in the museum there of life in wartime Britain, showing what people endured during the Blitz. Talk about strength in adversity! I wonder what happened to that fighting spirit? The newspapers today are so full of misery and woe. Now that 'fighting spirit' seems to only find expression on football terraces.

But perhaps that's unfair. People fight adversity in various ways… Like the guy on the corner of Western Road who sells the *Big Issue*. I bought a copy of the new edition from him yesterday. Then he furthered my education, handing me a magazine with the headline and lead article, 'How to make money by travelling and writing' – more useful information for me.

This morning, Ken said that he was taking the dog to see the vet and he'd be passing the Natural History Museum on the way if I wanted a lift. I accepted with thanks for the thought.

It's a fascinating place, Dad. And it's there because of one man's passion for nature and birds. Apparently, Edward Thomas Booth's love of birds led him to learn taxidermy and it seems that he originated the practice of displaying the birds in their natural settings. They look so much more lifelike than those caged in the zoo.

He was such an avid collector, that his collection outgrew his house. So, in 1874, he built a museum in his garden! When he died without heirs, his collection was left to the people of Brighton. What a legacy!

Two brown bears guard the entrance hall, standing upright behind the glass. Believe me, Dad, those guys are tall! They gave me a bit of a start as I walked in the door.

Inside, the walls are lined with awesome displays of birds in their natural habitat – eagles, hawks, swifts, starlings, eiders and more. The little auk was so cute, like a furry teddy bear with wings instead of paws.

One whole display case was dedicated to nests of birds, wasps and bees. An edible nest of a swift. The skeleton of a dodo (very rare!). Butterfly beauties. Sea mats and sponges. Insects and other creepy-crawlies. Beautiful bugs and furry spiders. Lobsters, crabs and shellfish. Black butterflies with emerald green eyes on their wings.

I turned a corner to face a me-sized turtle shell hanging on the wall, and skeletons galore. The rest of that hall was dedicated to mammals that had forsaken land and adapted to the sea – whales and dolphins. Turning another corner, I came to more birds and fish – swordfish and sailfish. Another turn left, and I was surrounded by minerals, crystals and fossils.

The place was amazing; a veritable history of evolution.

As I was leaving, I couldn't help wondering… Where does it go next?

Did evolution stop when man stood upright?

No, he kept on evolving, for good or for bad.

So, why should evolution stop now?

And where does it go from here?

Oh dear, Dad… There I go again! Mental rambling and asking the big questions! Perhaps I should ask myself a smaller one:

'Where do *I* go from here?'

For now, I think that I'll just drift back toward the seafront and decide from there.

The Lion & Lobster
Bedford Row
Brighton

6 p.m. Wednesday, 26th August '98

Well, as they say at home in Dublin, 'Ye can go nowhere!' This pub is only around the corner from my temporary home, but I hadn't noticed it before today. As soon as I walked in, there was something vaguely familiar about the place. I spotted a Harp lager tap behind the bar. It seemed an unusual brand for Brighton. Then, on the wall near the TV, an aerial photo of a city in sunshine caught my eye – Dublin from above the bay.

'Is this an Irish pub, then?' I asked.

The barmaid confirmed my suspicion. Although I needn't have asked if I'd looked further at the posters on the walls: Irish pubs, Irish postcards, Irish loos and Irish castles.

There's a framed photo collage too, with signs from the Gaeltacht: *Taisteal Go Mall, Géill Slí* and Ui Flathertaigh's pub in Dingle.

From Dublin to Dingle, Irish signs abound.

Dingle! Now there's a coincidence. I've just had a flashback, Dad, to a thought that popped up in the shower this morning. It was one of those early morning insights of such clarity that it was almost like hearing a voice in my head. I remember it clearly, even now.

'Well you could always sell the apartment and buy a house in Dingle!'

It wasn't a vague 'house in the country', or 'move out of town', it was specifically Dingle. How strange!

Yet, thinking of it now... Why not? What's to stop me? Only myself.

The idea has merits.

I could get a good price for the apartment. Its value has increased quite a bit over the last three years.

It would be good to move out of town. The city traffic is crazy now, Dad. The fumes can be suffocating at times. Yes, it would be nice to live where I can breathe fresh air, and there's good air and energy in Kerry, that's for sure.

It's a bit of a radical move though… To sell up and move to the other side of the country. Maybe I'd miss the city. I don't think that I'm ready to burn my bridges just yet.

But, hey, I've just had another brainwave!

If my apartment has increased in value, that may give me more leverage to borrow. If I can get a loan, I could buy myself time – six months or a year. Then I could rent out the apartment so that the mortgage payments are covered.

Yes, I like this idea. It gives me the finance and the freedom to roam and find out how I'd adapt to life outside the city.

I know it's a risk, Dad. But I see it as an investment. I'd be borrowing to invest in myself – my time, my energy and my creativity.

I fear that I may not survive the stress of the city if I wait to save up enough to escape.

Yes, the idea certainly has merit. I'll check out the details when I get home.

I'm so glad that I've got a home, Dad.

God help those poor people in North Carolina, their homes are really taking a pounding. Hurricane Bonnie has just hit, live on TV.

Thankfully, it's calm here. The weather forecaster says that it'll stay that way for the next few days. In some strange way, I feel calm, but it's like the calm in the eye of the storm. I know that the storm will hit again next Monday when I get back to the desk. Oh, change that thinking! I'm still on holiday until then and I've another full day left before my flight home on Friday.

So, what shall I do tomorrow?

Ken has recommended the Isle of Wight a few times via Portsmouth or Southampton. Although it has been on my mind a lot that maybe I should take the train over to visit Martin. I've tried to call, several times over the last few days, but I still haven't managed to get an answer since the last dropped call. Maybe he's away.

Oh, this is just too much, Dad!

My gaze drifted out the window a moment ago as I considered whether to just get the train over anyway. A little old grey-bearded man walked past the window with a walking stick and rucksack.

On the back of his rucksack, above the Nike symbol, a hand painted graffitti-style sign said, 'Just Do It!'

So perhaps I will… Tomorrow.

Brighton–Southampton Train

Thursday, 27ᵗʰ August '98

The Isle of Wight and Southampton surfaced again this morning on breakfast TV. As I emerged from the shower, the news reporter told of a tragedy:

'A computer programmer has died following an accident on his boat off the Isle of Wight, leaving a wife and four children. He had got tangled up in the ropes. His body was brought to Southampton General Hospital.'

How dreadful! His poor family must be devastated with no time to even say goodbye.

At breakfast, Barry was just back from visiting his family in Swansea and chirpy as ever. He was surprised that I was still here. No more than I am. I came for two days and now I've been here for ten. I guess Brighton is just that sort of place. But, I told him I'm definitely going home tomorrow. He said that he hoped I'd come back to visit again. I probably will.

I spent the morning wandering around some of my favourite haunts and dithered all day about taking the train, feeling edgy. Why? I'm still not entirely sure.

Nervous, I guess. But nervous about what?

Perhaps I was just apprehensive about Martin's reaction to me turning up unannounced. I see now that Chatterbox ruled the day, winning out over my intuition, which told me to 'Just do it!'

My decision was finally made in the Sanctuary Café. A stranger, Jimmy Linn, was the trigger. Mid-afternoon I took a break from my rambles there after another unanswered call. The waiter brought a big bowl of coffee over to my table by the window. But I barely noticed him set it down. I was gazing out into the sunshine, lost in my thoughts – so many of them. Then I heard a voice from a table behind mine. It was directed at me.

'Hey, sista! Why are you so intent? The sun's shining; you should lighten up!'

I knew he was right. Relax your mind and all will become clear in time. He offered to buy me a drink. I was about to decline, but when I looked down, the coffee bowl was empty. So I accepted his kind offer and invited him to join me at my table, glad of the distraction from my thoughts.

We chatted for a couple of hours. Jimmy was on his day off

from work. He told me of his job at another restaurant. But his real passion is to make music. I believe he will, when the time is right. His mother – the beautiful Katie Daly – was from Ireland. From his description of her, I could tell that he loved her very much. I felt the sadness of his loss. For a young guy, Jimmy is quite the philosopher, and very astute.

'There's something on your mind,' he remarked.

'Oh, there's a load of things on my mind,' I deflected.

'No, there's something in particular,' he insisted.

So I told him of my dilemma and my dithering.

'I'm trying to decide whether to get the train over toward Southampton to visit a friend who I haven't seen since last March. As coincidence would have it, I'm only an hour away. But I'm travelling home to Ireland tomorrow. I've been trying to phone him, but I can't get an answer...' I babbled.

Jimmy cut to the crux of the matter.

'So, do you love this guy?'

It's a funny thing, Dad, the way strangers can ask questions that we avoid asking ourselves. Jimmy's eyes looked straight through me and into my soul. I surprised myself with my lack of hesitation in answering. 'Yes. I guess I do.'

Then I babbled again. 'But there seems to be a lot of things in the way just now, apart from the lack of phone connection. He has a lot of challenges in his life, and he has his own path to follow. And I'm trying to find mine. Perhaps our paths will cross again, perhaps not; who knows?'

Yet again, Jimmy cut straight to the point. 'Will you regret it if you don't go?'

Inside my head, a voice said, 'Hell, yes!' And I knew that

I should go. Somehow, I sense that he is another piece of the jigsaw too.

I thanked Jimmy for his company and the conversation. After taking note of his address, I left with a promise that I'd keep in touch.

I can't regret the decisions that I make with conscious choice. But I know that I'd regret it if I didn't make the decision. Chatterbox would come back to haunt me, with questions: 'What if…?' 'Why didn't you go?'

So here I am on the train, Dad, wondering what's ahead. I barely got to the station in time and only caught the train because it was running late. When I asked the man at the ticket desk for a timetable, he said, 'That's your train at the platform; you'd better go now!'

I snatched the ticket and timetable and made a dash for the train.

After checking the timetable, I see that I'm not going to have a lot of time in Bursledon. The last train back is at five past ten. Even so, that still gives me a couple of hours. So if Martin's not there, I can go for another ramble by the Hamble before it gets dark, and then maybe a pint in the Jolly Sailor.

I'm enjoying the journey, Dad. The scenery is beautiful, as the sun mellows into early evening. We're passing by Arundel Castle, which the man from Milan mentioned. It looks impressive, crowning the fields of golden stubble that seem to glow in this light. Oh, there's a rabbit… and another… There's loads of them! It looks like something out of *Watership Down*. We're crossing a river now and there's a sort of peaty, low-tide smell coming in the window. Hold on… Which river? It surely couldn't be the Hamble yet! Time for a map check; I don't want to miss my stop.

No, I've another twenty or thirty minutes to go. But I think that I'll pack up my pen now, Dad, and relax into the scenery. In case I don't get a chance to write on my travels tomorrow, I'll fill you in on the end of my holiday when I get home. In fact, Dad, I'm really looking forward to getting home tomorrow; to sleeping in my own bed again and enjoying a weekend of peace before the mayhem starts again.

Time to sign off now…

Love,

Clodagh

Chapter 10

ACCENTUATE THE POSITIVE

The Waterside
Ringsend Road
Dublin 4

Tuesday, 1ˢᵗ September '98

Dear Dad,

I guess that my weekend of peace just wasn't to be. When I got home from England on Friday, there was a message on the answering machine from Brendan. As soon as I heard his voice, I knew that there was something wrong. Brendan doesn't usually ring for chit-chat.

'Hi, Clodagh, its Brendan. Would you give me a call when you get in. It's urgent.'

His voice was calm and reassuring, but grave. I got the sense that he had some serious news.

When I phoned back later, he told me that Mum had been in a bad car crash last Thursday. Brendan said that she was pretty bruised and battered and still in shock, but apart from that she was physically all right. Emotionally it was quite another story. Mum had been driving the car when the accident happened. Her friend, Betty, had been slightly injured. But her other friend, Sister Mercedes, had died from her injuries in the crash.

My plans for a chill-out weekend went out the window. On Saturday morning, I called over to see Brendan on my way down to Kilkenny to visit Mum. Fiona was there, packing the essentials that Mum would need for her stay in hospital. Brendan was coordinating. He asked me to drive down via Carlow and call in to the police station. The remains of the car had been brought there.

Mum wanted the cross that she had been holding up to Sister Mercedes as they waited for help to arrive. It was still in the car. Brendan said that I should also get the camera out of the glove compartment. Mum had taken some photos earlier on the day of the crash. He wanted to get them developed for her so that she would have them for comfort in hospital while the funeral was taking place on Sunday. But he said that the cross was more important. It was Mum's last connection with her friend.

At the station, I explained the situation to the policewoman behind the reception desk. She brought me out to the yard where they had taken the car. My heart lurched when I saw it. The front passenger side was completely mangled. Identifying the glove compartment proved to be a bit of a challenge. But then I spotted the edge of the camera, wedged in way back near the engine. My fingers couldn't quite reach it. So I borrowed a hefty crowbar. That did the trick and I ripped the remains of the glove compartment apart. By some miracle, the camera wasn't even scratched.

Next we searched the floor of the car for the cross. The policewoman told me to take care of my hand and knees as there were granules of broken glass all over the upholstery and the floor. I tried to shut my thoughts off while shifting the bloodstained tissues on the floor to look under the seats.

Then the policewoman raised her head and held out her hand to me between the front seats. 'Is this it?' she asked.

She held up a little black crucifix, attached to a single decade ring of rosary beads. I felt tears come to my eyes and an overwhelming flood of relief. I thanked her profusely and drove on to Kilkenny with the camera and the cross.

Fiona and Brendan were already at the hospital by the time I arrived. I produced the camera and the little crucifix. My heart sank when Mum said that it was the wrong one. There was another cross – a bigger one. (But I got it in the end, Dad. I drove back to Carlow on Sunday morning and found the right one, tucked in by the seat belt clasp. I brought it back to Mum in the hospital, before driving on to the funeral in Kilkenny.)

Mum seems to be bearing up well on the surface. She couldn't remember much of what happened just before the accident. I suppose it's only natural to block it out subconsciously.

Apparently, the three of them had been on a grand day out. Mum and Betty had driven down from Dublin to bring their former teacher out for a celebratory lunch. It was Sr. Mercedes' jubilee – fifty years of the religious life. That's a lot of years, Dad. That's a lifetime! Anyway, they were driving back to the convent so that Sr. Mercedes could rest for a while before the evening celebration with the rest of the nuns.

The car smashed with a truck at a country crossroads. It happened at a bad junction were the roadmarkings are faded to nothing and the approach signs are overgrown by the hedgerow. But it was an accident; nobody was to blame. These things happen. But why it happened to Mum is a mystery to me. She's such a careful driver.

Sr. Mercedes was in the front passenger seat and took the full force of the impact. The fire brigade had to cut her out of the car. Mercifully, she didn't regain consciousness before she died in the emergency room. Betty was thrown around in the back seat, but her wounds were seen to within a few hours and she was sent home. Mum will probably be kept in hospital for at least another week.

Mum told me that, on the night of the accident, she had been admitted to the ward just after 10 p.m. A while later, her blood pressure took a serious dive and she felt herself going. Then she heard your voice, Dad, telling her that it wasn't her time yet and that she had to fight. So she did. And she pulled through; though the doctor said that it was touch-and-go for a while. Physically, she's on the road to recovery now. But she'll be on an emotional see-saw for a while yet, with sorrow and grief over the loss of her friend. It'll take time for her spirit to heal.

Did you know Sr. Mercedes, Dad? I don't recall having met her myself. By all accounts, though, she was an amazing lady. Full of compassion and energy and drive at seventy-five. Somebody said that she would have hated to die from some debilitating illness where she would have suffered in confinement. But she died on the journey from one celebration to another – celebrations of her life. It was her time. And she left a wonderful legacy: an adult education centre, an old folks day care centre and pensioner pilgrimage groups, which she had conceived of and brought into being herself. They'll survive in memory of her years of hard work and dedication to the needs of others.

The nuns from the convent are wonderful. They have been

so supportive to Mum, through their own sorrow and loss of their sister. They really are very philosophical, Dad. And they have a marvellous perspective on life – finding the good in every situation, even in tragedy. One of the nuns I met at the funeral had such a positive outlook. She said to me, 'Wasn't it a miracle that your mother and Betty were spared.'

I knew she was right. After seeing the mangled wreck of the car, it was a miracle that anyone survived. If the truck had been coming from the opposite direction, it would have been Mum that was killed.

At the funeral Mass, I sat next to the nuns with Fiona, Niall and Bren. I recognised some of the nuns from school days so many years ago. They'd hardly aged a bit in twenty-odd years. There were others that I barely recognised. They look so different now that they've changed from the habits to wearing civvies.

What is it about funerals, Dad? I've been to so many that were attended by strained discomfort and a sense of anxiety. People don't know where to put their hands or rest their eyes. Sometimes, people have a sort of morbid fascination, yet a lack of words for expression of sympathy to the bereaved. Why have we become so uncomfortable with death? It's such a natural part of life.

Who was it that said, 'Life is like a twinkle of an eye in eternity'? Why do we think that death is the end? Maybe it's only the beginning… Or a new beginning in the great circle of life.

But this funeral wasn't like that. It was beautiful, Dad.

It was a true celebration of life.

The nuns brought gifts to the altar; symbols of Sr. Mercedes' contribution through her life: a camogie stick for her love of sports; a St Brigid's cross for her fifty years with the Brigidine Order; and a brightly coloured Fisher Price toy airplane for her organisation of pilgrimages abroad. That one brought a smile to many eyes.

One of the readings was from Ecclesiastes:

There is a season for everything, a time for every occupation under heaven:
A time for giving birth,
A time for dying,
A time for planting,
A time for uprooting what has been planted…
All that God does is apt for its time, but we cannot comprehend the work of God from beginning to end.

For Sr. Mercedes, the accident was her time to die. For Mum, it is a time to grieve; she's left to carry the weight of sorrow and pain. It must be so hard for her. She's had so many traumas over the last few years. But she says that she finds strength in her faith. I can't help but think that she must be very angry with God for dishing all those troubles onto her plate. I know that I would be, if I had her faith.

Some people really do get hit with more than their fair share of tragedy. But I believe that things happen for a reason – even if the reason is just that we find some meaning from the pain and loss. There's no way that we can go through life and avoid pain. But at least pain has some meaning if it helps us to appreciate the simple joys all the more.

I don't believe that God is vengeful. We weren't put here to suffer. We were put here to learn. To learn to find our own individual purpose in life; to find the best in ourselves and in others; to learn to love better and to evolve. And, in the process of learning, we must learn to embrace life and dance with the joy and with the pain.

The Waterside

Saturday, 12th September '98

The pace of life has stepped up again, Dad. And my dance with life is taking on the pace of a quickstep! But, before I get into that, I'll give you the update on Mum.

She came home from hospital last week. Physically, she's well on the mend, though she still needs a lot of rest. When she got home, there were so many friends calling to offer their sympathy and wish her well. But I think that all the visitors were draining her energy a bit. She's going over to the 'Wesht of Ireland', to stay with Aunt Kay for a while for a break. I think that a few days away, and more time on her own, will do her a lot of good and help her heart and her spirit to heal.

It's hard to believe that it's over two weeks since the accident – and two weeks since I got back from holidays. So much has happened since. But I never did finish telling you about my last holiday excursion, and I said that I would.

It was still bright when the train got in to the station at Bursledon. From there it was only ten-minute walk down to the boatyard. Dusk was starting to settle as I walked through the gates. There was a light on in the boat shed, but, just my luck, there was no one about. I climbed the steps to knock on the door of the cabin and called out, 'Hello! Anyone home?'

No answer.

From the top of the steps, I could see a tennis racquet and a tube of new tennis balls sitting on the stern. I thought, 'That's a positive sign – no broken bones then!'

The boat is in good shape and it looks like he's put a lot of work into it since last June. But it must have been a very challenging year for him – for one who loves the sea, to have the boat still out of water so late in the summer. That told me a lot.

There didn't seem to be much point in hanging about, so I scribbled a short note to say that I'd gone to the Jolly Sailor in case he got back while I was there. I only had a couple of hours before my deadline, for the 10.05 p.m. back to Brighton. But it was time enough for a sandwich and a beer, and to write a letter of my holiday detour from Greece, via Kent and Brighton, and some of my adventures en route. I slipped the letter into the card that I had bought in Brighton – the landscape of Brandon Creek. Then I sealed the envelope and wrote Martin's name on the front of it.

When I got back to the boat, there was no sign of his return. My note lay undisturbed. So I retrieved it and left the envelope in its place on top of the tennis racquet. Then I left to catch my train. I was disappointed that I didn't get a chance to meet Martin on my visit. But I was glad that I took the train. No regrets, thanks to Jimmy and his piercing questions.

It was sunny on the Friday that I was to leave Brighton, so I started the day by spending a few hours on the beach watching the waves and trying to piece things together in the jigsaw of my future. I still don't see the full picture. But I trust my intuition when it tells me to take action. And I've started to take action… A lot. Life has moved so fast over the last couple of weeks, I feel like I'm on one of those walking conveyors at Heathrow where you take one step forward and it carries you the same distance as four or five without any extra effort.

September is 'back to school' season, and I'm back to school too. The lectures for the business strategy course started up again last Friday and Saturday, so the reading is starting to pile up again. And we've been given another darn essay assignment as well.

Work is as manic as ever. But I'm trying to keep it in perspective. Whatever paperwork isn't done by the end of the day will just have to wait until the following morning. I'm not superhuman.

I had just about cleared the backlog, when I was off travelling again.

A colleague and I went over to Birmingham for a couple of days to visit a trade show at the NEC. I remember that you went to an exhibition there once, and you were amazed by how big the place was. You were right, Dad; it's huge. Two days was hardly enough to see all the exhibits at the Autumn Fair. The feet can only take so much of walking on concrete. Then the brain starts to dull. Even so, I gathered a lot of information for some of the companies that I deal with, as well as getting some good ideas for a business of my own, further down the Yellow Brick Road.

In fact, ideas have been surfacing fast and furious lately. My right brain seems to have gone into overdrive since I started making deep relaxation and visualisation a part of my daily routine. An idea for a book has been bubbling up as well, Dad. But I'm not letting my right brain get lazy. I'm putting it to use in taking action to follow up on my brainwaves. I'm employing your old friend, Logic, to support me in researching my ideas:

'What do I need to learn if I want to do that?

What obstacles might be in the way?

How do I get around that?'

But sometimes I have to employ my old friend, Intuition, to knock Logic back into his box. Especially when he starts to get uppity and self-righteous.

'Oh, you can't do that! That'll never work!' says Logic.

'Why the hell not?' says Intuition. 'Get back into your box until you come up with some more helpful questions or suggestions!'

There are so many people that are only too ready to pour cold water on my dreams. I don't need my Logic jumping on that bandwagon as well. In fact, Dad, I'm being very careful about who I share my dreams with. Some of them are too fragile to withstand a cold shower from people who'd like to put me in my box – as they see it.

But Uncle John is not like that. I invited him over for dinner last Thursday evening with the proviso that I wanted to pick his brains on the subject of writing. I gave him the low-down on what has been happening in my head over the last five months.

He gave me some very practical advice about writing and the business of publication. I hadn't even considered how much I needed to learn about the publishing business. But then again, the idea for the book has only evolved over the last few weeks.

Before that I had no idea of what I wanted to write.

I tossed my embryonic book concept into the conversation. Uncle J's comments were very insightful and helped me to develop the idea some more. He gave me some useful tips on writing for radio as well. And he should know about that, he's been producing *The Open Mind* programme for RTE radio for ten years now. I didn't realise that it had been running for so long. He's interviewed some very high calibre writers over the years. So I got some of the benefit of their experience as well. I hadn't thought of writing for radio, but I guess that's another avenue I could explore.

The conversation with Uncle J was thoroughly enjoyable. He really is a very lovely man. And I think that he enjoyed the dinner too. He certainly left me with plenty of food for thought.

Food is also an issue, Dad. Even writers have to eat. So that brings me back to finance and my shower brainwave in Brighton. I enquired about getting a loan at the building society and the bank. It seems that there are various options with different costs involved. I was told that approval shouldn't present a problem with the apartment as security for the loan; though I will need to get a revaluation. Now I need to sit down with a calculator and work out the cost of the various options in more detail. Those in the know expect that the interest rates will fall again before the end of the year. So I'll wait until they go down before making an official loan application.

Time has become another big issue for me. There are just not enough hours in the day. The reading is piling up now that the notes for the business strategy course have started to flow in again. The books that I brought home from holidays seem to be breeding – my unread library is screaming for my attention. I haven't even been able to find time to get out for a walk in daylight over the last few weeks. So, after due consideration, I've decided that something has to go, and that 'something' is the day job – it's getting in the way of all the things that I want to do.

I've decided to accelerate my plans to take time out. Why wait until April? The end of the year is as good a time as any other.

So I broke the news to my immediate boss yesterday morning, telling him that I intended to apply for a twelve-month career break. He was very concerned about me.

'Are you sure about this?'

'What if you change your mind after a couple of months?'

'How will you support yourself?'

'The organisation is changing. Where will you fit in when you get back?'

'What about the opportunities for promotion that you may miss?'

I appreciated his questions, as he played devil's advocate.

I'd answered most of them for myself even before he'd asked. That helped to strengthen my resolve.

But it took me a while to help him to understand that this isn't a career decision; it's a life decision. It's my life and I want it back.

Yesterday afternoon, I got to meet with the next boss up the hierarchical ladder. He didn't seem to be all that surprised by my news. Anyway, he said that he'd support my application, as long as I was sure of my decision.

I was. I am.

So, before I left the office yesterday, I drafted a memo to the personnel department. My boss signed his approval and I popped my career break application form into the post. The ball is rolling now, Dad. No looking back. And no regrets. I know that I've made the right choice.

The Waterside

Saturday, 19th September '98

Good news this week, Dad! My career break application was approved. Yippee! Full time freedom is on the horizon from January 1st for a whole year. A lot can happen in a year. Maybe thing will work out well… maybe not. But I have to give it a shot.

I know what'd happen if I don't – I'd probably crack up!

I felt such a sense of relief having told the boss of my intentions. It means that I can now share my ideas and plans with other colleagues without having to worry about the grapevine spreading the news before I do. It's not quite common knowledge yet, though I've told a few people that I trust. And, since I started doing that, things have started to snowball. Synchronicity is back in action again! People have been so generous to me with offers of help, advice, contacts and even the use of a house in the country.

On Wednesday, I phoned Dick Blake about a business plan that he had submitted on behalf of a client company. Dick is an independent consultant who seems to get through a phenomenal amount of work. A few months ago, I asked him how he managed his workload and how he found time to write up so many detailed business plans. I was so frustrated at the time, trying to write up a simple report amidst all the distractions of an open plan office.

Apparently, he has a 'rural retreat' – a holiday home in County Cork – where he finds peace and solitude to concentrate on writing when the workload starts to pile up. His family spends a lot of time there in the summer and on holiday weekends. But he had said that I was welcome to use the place in the winter if I wanted to get out of town for a quiet weekend. I thought that was very generous of him.

While I was on the phone to him this week, I told him of my decision to apply for a career break and my provisional plans to move out of the city to travel and write.

He said, 'Well, there's always the house in Courtmacsherry if you need some place with peace and quiet for writing.'

His family will be using the house over the Christmas break. But he offered me the use of the place from January right up until the Easter school holidays. I was overwhelmed by his generosity.

It's a funny thing, Dad… It was only last Monday evening when a thought struck me. I was watching a movie on TV, *Into the West* and one of the characters said,

'There's a traveller in all of us, but very few of us know where we're going.'

How true for me! I had applied for leave from the job and made initial enquiries about finance, but I hadn't a clue where I was going from the end of this year.

Well, now I do. It's County Cork – for the first three months anyway.

And, after that... Time will tell.

Thursday brought me a useful contact in the publishing business. I was on the phone to another work colleague, Richard Keegan, about a seminar he's organising. He's written a very good book on World Class Manufacturing, which certainly gave me a much better understanding of the subject. His writing style is very much like his manner – down-to-earth and no-nonsense. When I asked for his advice on writing a book, he gave me the name of his publisher and told me to give him a call. So that gives me a lead for my next stage of research into the publishing world.

There was another interesting development in work this week. But I'll get back to that tomorrow. Right now, we're having a bit of an Indian Summer. It may well be the last day for sunbathing this year. So I'm off to Mum's back garden now to catch a few rays and top up my Brighton tan. Talk to you tomorrow...

The Waterside

Sunday, 20th September '98

There'll be no sunbathing today, Dad. The clouds are back. So, what was I going to tell you after my sunshine break? Oh, yes! I remember now.

I was at a very interesting lunchtime workshop over in head office last Monday. It's the first of a series organised by the health and safety officer, under the title 'Caring for Yourself'. The notification memo said that over the next six weeks, the workshops will cover a range of topics on physical, mental and emotional well-being, with the objective of creating 'an awareness of our own responsibility for our lifestyles'. With so much stress in the workplace these days, there's definitely a demand for this sort of thing. When I arrived, there must have been over seventy people in the hall.

A lady named Catherine McCann presented the workshop. She told us of her background – thirty-seven years working in the health services – and of her experience as a physiotherapist and counsellor. For the last ten years, she has been giving workshops on Living Creatively, Stress Management and Caring for Others. The workshop on Monday was just an introduction to caring for personal health and well-being.

I liked the way she explained about well-being as being more than just a lack of illness or physical symptoms. She described a scale of wellness levels – from total lack of life at one extreme, to living with vitality and creative fulfilment at the other. 'Lack of symptoms' of illness was only at the mid-point of her scale. Judging by the number of nodding heads around the room, most of us were somewhere on the scale between feeling 'not great' and feeling 'not bad'.

Catherine certainly looks as if she is on the upper end of the scale. She's full of vitality and very alert. I'd say that she must feel creatively fulfilled too, as she has written several books. Who cares? No, I'm not being sarcastic, Dad. That's the name of one of her books – *Who Cares? A guide for all who care for others*.

Another one is called *Falling in Love with Life*. I like the sound of that. I felt that she might be able to offer me some advice about writing, so I introduced myself to her after the workshop. She was pushed for time last Monday, but I made an appointment to meet with her after the session tomorrow. I'm looking forward to it.

The subject of stress and well-being has been cropping up a lot over the last week. But as I started to doze off in the sunshine yesterday, all the work stresses floated away. I felt a great sense of well-being in the garden, just listening to the birds twittering, with the warmth of the sun on my skin. As I relaxed, the words of a song kept pushing their way into my head. The Manic Street Preachers have been on the radio quite often lately. Maybe that's why the song was on my mind. But there's wisdom in pop culture too, if you choose to listen to the words.

'And if you tolerate this, then your children will be next.'

You tolerated stress, Dad. And what did it do to you?

I don't want to be next!

Is that my legacy? Bottling up emotions and striving to achieve the punishing standards that I set for myself. I need to let them go.

The more I hear about stress, the more that I see how I live my life and how I react to life is my own responsibility.

Life is short. Quality of life is so important.

I don't want to live mine on a treadmill constantly trying to catch up with work.

But I can't blame the job. That was my choice. Now I've made another one…

I choose to take on less work and learn to live more.

I want to fall in love with life again.

I don't know where the next year will take me, but there has to be more to life than this constant chasing around like a hamster in a wheel. There has to be a more positive way to live. Oh dear, Dad, the negativity is starting to creep in to my thinking again. I must be getting tired. It's time for a rest.

The Waterside

Wednesday, 30ᵗʰ September '98

Life's treadmill has been keeping me busy again, Dad. I haven't found any time to write over the last ten days. So where should I start? Where I left off, I guess.

I had a very interesting conversation with Catherine McCann last week. She really is a very lovely person, full of compassion and caring for others. I felt that I was babbling a bit as I explained my situation to her. But she listened with patience. Then she gave me some advice from her own experience of writing and getting a book into publication.

The bottom line was: 'Follow your instincts.' And, 'Just write from your own heart.'

I've enjoyed her workshops and I'm looking forward to the next one. But, unfortunately, I'm going to miss the last two sessions as the dates clash with a couple of conferences that I'm due to attend.

Just a glance at the desk diary tells me that October is going to be a hyper-busy month. With several conferences on over the next few weeks, I'm going to lose a lot of time from office work.

But I think it's important to attend the relevant ones to keep in touch with what's happening out in the big wide world. Still, it means that my workload is going to be condensed into a fewer number of days. And it's not just the regular workload… I need to start sorting my files out, and updating file notes for whoever is taking over my work. Oh God, I can't think about that now! If I start thinking about all that I have to do before the end of the year, I'll be a basket case by then!

Back to the present, Dad... I'm chewing on some food for thought that I picked up yesterday at the National Business Development Conference. A variety of entrepreneurs and business specialists gave some very interesting presentations on the theme of 'The Bottom Line: How to Improve Profits'. One speaker in particular caught my attention. She presented a case study on how she went about setting up her business. It took her a whole year just to research the idea and determine whether it was commercially viable. That was very encouraging to me.

I still have that notion that there must be some way to use technology to help relieve some of the additional stress that it is causing. But is there a viable business in that idea? I know that there is an opportunity there, I just can't see the business yet. But if it's a good idea now, it'll still be a good idea a year from now. And it'll be a better idea with more research. There's no rush. I guess that a business idea is a bit like an idea for a book – it needs plenty of incubation time to evolve.

So I'll put the shape of the idea to the back of my mind and tune into my intuition antenna to pick up any information that might be somehow relevant.

I can work on the shape of the idea again when I have more time on my hands.

One of the conferences next month is all about the Internet and its impact on business. Maybe I'll absorb some inspiration there, as well as information. But enough of this business talk, Dad!

On the home front, Mum is back from her visit to her sister, Kay, in Galway.

She sounded well when she phoned me last week to remind me about the Memorial Mass for Sister Mercedes.

A whole month since the funeral… Gosh, where has the time gone?

We all went down to Tullow last Sunday for the Mass. The nuns invited us back to the convent afterwards for tea and sandwiches. Walking in the convent door, the smell of floor wax brought me straight back to school days. I started to feel like I was out of uniform. The nuns were like bees, buzzing around from one table to another, making sure that everyone was looked after. There must have been at least sixty people there, in for a cuppa. Talk about feeding the multitude… The nuns are masters of the art!

Time heals, but it can take more than a month. Mum is on the road to recovery, but she needs a lot more time yet for the emotional scars to heal. She was very upset when we went over to put flowers on her friend's grave. The soothing words of Sr. Mary helped to comfort her somewhat. A little wooden cross had been erected above the grave and there were plenty of flowers too. But the wound in the earth still looks very raw.

After a while I left the others and went to walk on my own among the rows of metal crosses that had settled with the years. Each black cross had a name, age and date written on it in pristine white paint. It's an old graveyard. The dates went all the way back to the 1800's.

Most of the ages were well over seventy, and ninety was not unusual. Nuns certainly don't die young. But there are exceptions to every rule. One nun died at twenty-four years of age. I couldn't help but wonder what had happened to her. However she died, I bet it wasn't stress related.

There was such a sense of peace in the nuns' graveyard and the convent grounds. It was lovely. So quiet... such peace, for reflection.

No traffic mayhem. Just the sound of the trees whispering in the wind and the song of birds.

A wholly stress-free zone.

Perhaps that's the secret of their longevity: living in peace. Peace of mind; peace at heart; peace of spirit; and a positive outlook on life.

There was another wonderful stress-free zone on the TV last night, Dad. The weekly boating programme has a feature on barge holidays on the Grand Canal. Now that really is a good way to slow down the pace of life and gain a different perspective. The presenter maintained that, 'You haven't seen Ireland, until you've seen it from the canal.'

I was reminded of Martin's Grand Canal plan. That's his big dream, Dad. He intends to sail the boat over to Dublin and bring her along the Grand Canal and the Shannon, and then sail her down to Dingle.

When he first told me about it, I couldn't really see it. Logic piped up: 'What about the mast? There are a lot of bridges along the canal!'

But it seems that the mast can be collapsed or dismantled. I guess there's a lot I don't know about boats.

I hope he realises his dream. Canal calm would be a tonic. He sounded pretty stressed-out with work the last time we spoke on the phone.

As for me, this evening my dream is for a good night's sleep. I've got four meetings scheduled for tomorrow – another busy day. And as the month starts, so will it continue... And the next... And the next.

It's no wonder I have been having so many zany anxiety dreams lately.

But... Positive Thinking! At least I can see my short-term vision on the horizon...

I see me and Betsy driving out of town under a cloud-free sky in freedom and peace.

So I'll keep that vision in mind to help me get through the next few manic months.

Goodnight, Dad. Sweet dreams.

Love,

Clodagh

Chapter 11

NETWORK NEWS

The Waterside
Dublin 4

Sunday, 11ᵗʰ October '98

Dear Dad,

Greetings from the hamster wheel! It's still whizzing around as I chase my tail trying to catch up. It's been three weeks since I've had a full day to myself. So much of my time and energy has been spent with other people. It's a rare luxury to have a whole day of solitude with time to relax and reflect. I was hoping to get out for a walk on the South Wall this morning, but the weather isn't very conducive to walking today. Maybe it'll improve later.

Betsy has been acting up a bit during the last week. The temperature light kept flashing red to tell me that the radiator was overheating. But I couldn't figure out why as there seemed to be plenty of water in the system. I rang Tony, the car doctor, for a telephone diagnosis. As the fan was working, he reckoned that the thermostat might be causing the problem. He recommended a more thorough examination. It's only a twenty-minute drive to his workshop, but it took me over an hour to get Betsy there. I had to stop three times to let her cool down.

It turned out that the thermostat was completely burned out.

So I left her with Tony overnight as he didn't have the spare part in stock. She's been running like a dream since her replacement operation. Maybe it was just her way of telling <u>me</u> to cool down!

I have been overdoing it a bit lately with so many ideas buzzing around my head. Somewhere among all the activity over the last few weeks, my deep relaxation routine seems to have fallen by the wayside. It's no wonder I've been so hyper. But since I became conscious of that, I've started back into regular practice of the Mindstore techniques. It only works, Dad. I've felt so much calmer over the last few days. It's like my own thermostat is back working again.

Speaking of Mindstore, I had a call earlier this week from Anne O'Neill, of Essential Training Ltd. Her company organises the Mindstore training courses in Ireland. I first met her at the course last June. She really is a wonderful person; so openhearted and caring. I believe that she has a genuine interest in helping people to improve their lives and achieve their dreams. It was Anne who introduced me to Paulette from the Life Foundation, which led to my heart-warming holiday in Wales. Which reminds me, Paulette is running a workshop in Dublin next Sunday on yoga and shiatsu. I'm really looking forward to that. I could well do with a day of fun yoga to rebalance and re-energise.

Oops, I got sidetracked there, Dad. Back to Anne's phone call. She rang to tell me that Network Ireland (the organisation for women in business) were holding their annual conference on Saturday. Her company had booked a table for the conference dinner on the Friday evening. I was delighted when she invited me to join them for dinner.

I didn't know much about the conference before her call. But Anne said that there would be an interesting line-up of speakers. Knowing of my plans for next year, she thought that some of them would be of particular interest to me. I phoned to get a brochure faxed over and discovered that the theme of the conference was Change (quel surprise!) with presentations on topics across a range of issues related to the changing nature of how we do business and work at all levels – global, organisational and personal. I was intrigued by the title: 'Do we want an economy or a society?' So I decided to invest my Saturday in listening to what the speakers had to say.

But first, let me tell you about the dinner on Friday night. I had a thoroughly enjoyable time. Anne had invited ten people from various walks of business and life. Around the table, we discovered that we all had one thing in common, everyone had attended one of Jack Black's Mindstore courses. It was fascinating to talk to other people who use his techniques and hear what a difference it has made in their lives. Some just practice deep relaxation to help balance and counteract stress, while others use creative visualisation to see their goals and dream big dreams. But everyone seemed to have a vision of where they were going in life; a sense of purpose and a confidence in the future.

The future was very much in focus during the conference on Saturday as well. The first presentation was about 'Our Global Future' and the changing role of business. Some of the background statistics were scary – like the rapid growth of the world's population and the changing distribution of wealth.

Did you know, Dad, that only fifteen per cent of the world's population <u>has</u> disposable income? We are so lucky. Yet we're consumed with consumption. We trade our lives working longer and longer hours to earn more and more. For what? Just to consume more? How many meals can one person eat in a day? How many cars can one person drive at one time? How many people could be fed for the price of a Rolls Royce? There is enough to go around; it is distribution that's the issue. But, it's still the same old story – the rich are getting richer and the poor are getting poorer. Where will it all end?

Then there's the issue of our environmental health. As we consume more and more, we generate more and more trash. Picture a beautiful forest, Dad, with beams of sunlight streaming through the trees giving life to pretty flowers on the forest floor and soft mosses beneath your feet as you walk to the sounds of birds singing in the trees.

Then – crash, creak, groan – you hear the noise of a grinding change of gears.

Imagine a giant waste disposal truck with wheels as tall as the trees. It groans as it dumps a monstrous load of putrid, stinking black plastic, suffocating the forest of your dreams. The trees scream and the birdsong dies, as the sunshine cries upon a cloud of acrid dust.

That's where we're at!

But there's even more scary stuff, Dad. Apparently the two most profitable businesses in the world today are drugs and weapons. They feed a need, or a desire, to overcome unhappiness and insecurity driven by our lack of self-esteem and fear. When will it stop?

There is no avoiding it, Dad. The whole world is connected

and not just by the Internet and Network News. But the technology does bring the reality home. There's no 'there' anymore. It's all one world; one global village broadcast right into the living room. And on your TV tonight, take your pick: famine, civil war or gangland drug battles, if you prefer. Somebody is making big money out of broadcasting bad news. But it's not the whole truth of reality, this doom and gloom and sensationalism that we're being force-fed. There are a lot of good things happening in the world as well. It's not the end of civilisation; it's just another transition to a new age.

Which brings me back to the first speaker at the network conference; a lady called Sabina Spencer. She had some very encouraging news from her experience as a consultant to multinational organisations. In that role, she advises them on strategic leadership and change management and she shared some of her insights into the transition that businesses and people are facing. It seems that we are going through another paradigm shift. First there was the Industrial Age, then the Information Age, but now we are moving into what she calls the Relationship Age.

I was glad to hear that the focus is shifting back to people and the connection between them. After all, Dad, that's what business is all about – people – it's not just machines, technology and figures.

I'll be glad to see the back of the Information Age too. In some ways, I think it was very overrated. Information is only of value if it can be put to good use.

I've seen people hoard information for their own prestige and power: 'Oh, yes, I have the latest report, but it's confidential, you know!'

Big boys playing little boys' games – 'I know a secret and I'm not telling you. Naah, naah, naah, naah!'

So the report sits on the shelf gathering dust; unread, unused.

What a ridiculous waste of resources – time, effort and paper.

But the electronic media have been helping to change all that – only now we've gone to the other extreme. We're swamped with an overload of information; it's become a commodity now. But we're still only learning the skills to distil all this data into useful knowledge.

There was an article in one of the Sunday supplements today that reminded me of that. The story was about an archaeologist who claims to have rediscovered the original Garden of Eden in a fertile valley along the Euphrates River, somewhere in Iran. (There's some sort of irony in the location. What went wrong?)

In the course of the story, the archaeologist told of a conversation that he had with his guide about the march of civilisation. The guide was a local man who lives a simple life; a man full of insight, none the less. He said, 'We used to have wisdom, then we had knowledge, now we have only information. Like a donkey carrying books.'

How true! Where has our ancient wisdom gone, Dad? Can we get it back?

Planet of the Apes is one thing… Planet of the Donkeys quite another!

Although things are changing for the better. As we move into this Relationship Age, the power is shifting from the bright boys at the top of the old pyramid structures to the men and women who are the foundations.

The people on the front line have the new power of information – direct knowledge of the consumer. The consumer has the ultimate power. The customer is king and this king has the power of individual choice and the wisdom to vote with their feet.

If this sounds like revolutionary talk, Dad, well, maybe it is. But it's a quiet revolution. Although the sound of many whispers can be louder than that of a single voice shouting. From what I heard at the conference, many of the captains of industry are waking up to the fact that their role is changing from 'the boss' to leaders who must guide their people through the shifting sands. They're listening to the whispers on the wind. Consumers have choices and so do employees.

Some old-style pharaohs will never listen, though. They'll sit on top of their pyramids while the sand shifts beneath them, impervious to change. All they'll have left will be the tip of the pyramid like an ancient monument to the arrogance of power-hungry men.

Politics is much the same. The power is shifting from governments to business.

I've heard it said that the new leaders in the new millennium will be the entrepreneurs – the people who look forward and see new possibilities, new opportunities. They're people who build and create new enterprises and new ways of doing business. The reign of the hierarchy preserver is gone.

But back to the individual. It seems that consumers and employees really have started voting with their feet. At the conference, two former staff journalists with the *Observer* newspaper gave a presentation on a new trend. They call it 'downshifting'.

No, Dad, this isn't the 'downsizing' of the 1980s where companies hacked off divisions and departments and 'rationalised' staff numbers with massive redundancies and little thought for people. Redundant! What a horrible word!

(I once met a guy who had been a fiberglass fitter. He was made redundant at the tender age of twenty. It was the only trade that he knew. Four years later, he still defined himself as a 'redundant fiberglass fitter'. Redundant! At twenty! What does that word do to your soul and your self-worth? If I ruled the world that word would be abolished for a start.) Oops, there I go, rambling again!

Anyway, Dad, this 'downshifting' is not about redundancy.

It's about people choosing to jump before they are pushed, directly or indirectly.

It's not about dropping out or copping out; it's about opting in to having a Life.

The trend started with individuals making a pre-emptive strike against the long-hours work culture and the career rat race. More and more people have been making a conscious decision to trade in part of their income for time; time to improve their quality of life, to start out on a new path, or to gain more control over their own working life.

The two presenters, Polly Ghazi and Judy Jones, spoke from their personal experience under the title, 'Now that I've got what I want, I don't think I want it.'

They started out researching an article on the trend of downshifting, which has been gaining momentum in the US over the last ten years or so. It's been happening in Britain and

Ireland too. As things turned out, the two reporters chose to downshift as well. Both are now working as self-employed journalists and writers. From what they said, they are both living much happier lives. They have written a book on downshifting from their research and their own personal experiences.

I must get my hands on a copy of that.

As I listened to their story of the pressures and stress that prompted their individual decisions, I came to realise that that is exactly what I am doing next year – downshifting.

I didn't have a name for it when I made the decision. I was just following my intuition. But their experience has given me some valuable guidance on what to expect and planning the transition to my new life. There will be ups and downs.

The downs may be managing on limited finance and missing the companionship of work colleagues. But one of the ups is definitely the choice and control over how I spend my time, working at times that suit me best and being able to go for a walk when the sun shines.

The sun has come out to play now, Dad, on my rare day of freedom. So I'm off for a walk on the South Wall. Talk to you later...

Sunday evening, 11ᵗʰ October '98

It started out as a wonderful walk in the afternoon sunshine. Then the sea breeze caught in my eye and tears started to fall. They weren't from the wind. They were from me. From some place deep inside; a place I hadn't been for a while. But where? I didn't know. So I played a game with myself – 'Name That Emotion'.

It was grief rising again. Grief for the loss of my father.

But why did it come back today, Dad?

The only trigger that I could think of was one of the speakers at the conference yesterday. A lady called Paula Downey spoke of 'The Power of One' and our personal responsibility for the lives that we lead.

We can't blame the system; we are the system, and what we cause, we can change.

She spoke of the purpose of work in our lives: to fulfil the self and add value to the world in a way that is meaningful to ourselves.

She also spoke of the lives that are given up to work. Her voice faltered slightly as she spoke of her father. Like many men, he had endured the nine-to-five penance – scheduling his life to the job, expecting to live out his life after his retirement. But his life didn't go according to his plan. He died before his retirement at fifty-one years of age. She spoke on the day of his anniversary.

It must have taken some courage to accept a speaking engagement on that day. I admired her strength and I felt for her loss. As she spoke of work 'eating souls to feed the belly', her words hit to my heart.

Would you still be with us now, Dad, if you hadn't let work eat away at your soul and into your body? 'We can't schedule Life'. How true! But old habits die hard. And my thoughts are now turning back toward my schedule for tomorrow and the rest of the next crazy week. I have enjoyed chatting to you again today, Dad, though the talk is a bit one-sided. I do miss our conversations… still.

Goodnight, Dad. I'll write again when I can find time.

The Waterside

Saturday, 17th October '98

Well the word seems to be out on the grapevine this week. On Thursday, I was at a seminar organised by one of the banks to raise awareness of the impact of our changeover to the new currency, the Euro. More change! Several work colleagues were there also, as it's a topic that's relevant to everyone. Cathy came over to me after the presentation. I hadn't seen her around the office in quite a while as we've all been so busy lately.

'Any truth in the rumour?' she asked.

I confirmed that my career break had been approved and that I'd be finishing up in the job at the end of the year. She was curious.

'What prompted you to make the decision?'

I explained about the stress and frustration being the initial trigger. But, at this stage, I just want a change and more control over my time – time to explore new things and find what is meaningful in my life. We chatted for a while about work, job satisfaction and dissatisfaction, and the urge to do work that in some way makes a contribution to the greater good.

Cathy has a dream too, to make her contribution back to life. She told me that she wants to spend a year doing voluntary work in Africa when her children are grown.

How little we know of the dreams and aspiration of the people with whom we work. It's a funny thing, Dad, but through that conversation, I got to know her better in fifteen minutes than I had over the last three years.

Why don't people talk about their dreams, Dad?

I guess that it's for fear of the cold water shower that some others are only too ready to deliver – the cynics.

A guy at the Network conference gave a good definition: 'A cynic is someone who pisses on an idea.'

Yet there are so many people out there willing to help – with ideas, guidance and advice. I've discovered that since I started sharing my dreams with others.

When I share my dreams, other people seem to be more open and share their dreams with me too. Once the conversation is open, I give my tuppence worth and they give me theirs. It's usually a fair exchange.

We tend to undervalue the knowledge and insight that we each have inside.

But it can be of tremendous value to others when shared. Over the last few weeks, so many people have offered me help in the learning that I'll need for my new path – 'Oh, I know somebody that works in that area. Perhaps they can help. Tell them that I told you to call.'

I guess that's what networking is all about. It's not about, 'Here's my business card; now, what can you do for me?' It's about sharing and trusting and giving with joy and without calculation.

Yet rewards come in their own time, in unexpected ways and from unexpected places. As the saying goes, 'You reap what you sow.' But you have to sow first.

At last, there has been some good news on the networks this week, Dad.

Yesterday it was announced that John Hume and David Trimble have been jointly awarded the Nobel Prize for Peace.

Well deserved, too! They've received global recognition for the seeds that they've sown toward lasting peace in the North.

I'm sure that they'll reap an even greater reward when their vision of peace becomes an enduring reality to the greater good of all.

Thinking of the North, but back on the local front… I saw your sister, Evelyn, in her car near my apartment block earlier this week. It was the first day in weeks that I had been able to find time to get home for lunch. It seemed a coincidence to see Evelyn driving past as I waited to cross the road. I thought it a bit strange that she was driving towards town on a workday. Maybe she was going in to do some lunchtime shopping. But she had a very serious look on her face.

Well that is strange indeed!

As I was thinking of Evelyn, the phone rang; it was her voice on the line.

She called to tell me that Granny has taken a bad turn. She's in hospital in Enniskillen.

Apparently, Granny had an operation on Thursday and seemed to be recovering well. But then, yesterday afternoon, suddenly her heart stopped.

As luck would have it, she was still in Intensive Care when the heart attack struck. The doctors resuscitated her heart, but she won't be out of the woods for a while yet.

Evelyn sounded exhausted. I'd say she hasn't had much sleep over the last few nights.

Got to go now, Dad. I want to ring Mum and Fiona to make some arrangements about going up North to see Granny while there's still time.

The Waterside

Tuesday, 20th October '98

Well, Dad, here's the latest news from the North. Mum phoned last night to say that she is up in Enniskillen with Granny and Evelyn. Granny's condition has stabilised, as they say in hospital-speak. She's still in Intensive Care and heavily sedated.

Mum said that there wasn't much point in the rest of us going up to visit just yet.

So I've made arrangements to drive up with Niall next Saturday. And I told my boss about the situation, in case I need to leave at short notice. The news about Granny has sure put work into perspective – there's nothing so urgent that it can't wait.

There are higher priorities in life.

The Waterside

Sunday, 25th October '98

Niall and I drove up to Enniskillen yesterday to see Granny. Out of habit, we planned to take the usual route through Lisnaskea. There had been torrential rain all Friday night and we passed some very bad flooding on the roads.

But before we got as far as Maguiresbridge, we came to a stretch that was completely blocked. The road had turned into a lake and detour signs had been set up. So we followed the signs.

It seemed that the only way through to Enniskillen was to go back to Belturbet and then all the way up the west side of Lough

Erne. I'd never been in that part of the country before, although I'm sure that you know it well from your youth. It really is a wild and beautiful part of the world. The road took us past pine forests and mountain bogland, with bracken in wonderful shades of autumn red and rust. The sun came out for a while and the bog blazed with colour in the light.

I was mesmerised by the landscape. Just as well that Niall was driving! We wouldn't have taken that route if it hadn't been for the floods. So I guess that those Friday night clouds did have a silver lining after all.

When we arrived in Enniskillen, we headed straight for the hospital. The journey from Dublin had taken almost four hours, instead of the usual two and a half. I thought that Mum would be worrying. When we finally got to the hospital, Mum said that Granny was sleeping. She's still in intensive care and still on the ventilator.

After being cooped up in the car for so long, Niall and I decided to go for a walk down to the town to stretch the legs.

The main street was buzzing with Saturday shoppers. Somehow, it felt sort of unreal – or was it the hospital that had felt unreal. There was such a sharp contrast between the hospital and the shops. Although I'm sure the shoppers of Enniskillen know that contrast only too well.

Back at the hospital, it struck me that it really has been a turbulent few months for Mum. She's still in the recovery process after the car crash and the loss of her friend. And now, life has thrown her back into the hospital scene again – in support mode this time. I hadn't seen her since she got back from Galway. She's looking well. Although she's lost some weight since the accident, she seems to have gained more life in her eyes. It makes her look ten years younger.

It's been a turbulent few years for Evelyn too, since you've gone. Granny has had several health scares and Evelyn is always on call. It must be very stressful for her. She looked distraught when we met outside the intensive care ward.

Although Evelyn didn't say so, I got the sense that she fears that this may be Granny's last health scare... And, Evelyn does love her so much.

I wish you were here for them both, Dad.

I had a bit of a scare myself, walking into the intensive care ward. It's all so high-tech. The buzz and hum of machines brought the reality home to me. I felt a lump come to my throat, seeing such an independent old lady wired up to so many tubes and monitors. But that's what is keeping her alive at the moment. Granny's face looked so pale and fragile against the snow-white sheets. But when she opened her eyes, I could see that her spirit was still there and fighting strong.

A brief look of alarm flashed in her eyes when she saw Niall and myself. It's usually only at Christmas that she sees all her grandchildren together. She's fully alert and knows exactly what's going on. We may not all be together again for Christmas this year.

Brendan and Fiona had been there for a while before Niall and I arrived. Fiona gave me her seat beside Granny's bed. But when I sat down, I wasn't too sure how to hold Granny's hand. I didn't want to lean on the bed, for fear of knocking some vital tube out of place. So I just rested my hand gently on hers over the monitor wire that was attached to her middle finger. Her hand felt warm.

I didn't know what to say at first. But I didn't want to alarm Granny with tears. So I just prattled on, as I do... About the drive up from Dublin, the floods on the roads, our wonderful detour, the brief shopping excursion and the bargains to be found down the town. I think the normality of conversation was some sort of comfort. She rested her eyelids and her face looked peaceful as she listened to my chatter. Then she shifted her hand slightly and squeezed mine.

I told her that we wouldn't stay very long. It gets dark so early these evenings, and we wanted to get on the road back to Dublin while there was still some light left. She nodded her head, and her eyes spoke – approving the prudence of the travelling plan. The lump came back to my throat as I said goodbye and told Granny that we'd see her again at Christmas, if not before then. Maybe we will. Maybe not. But Granny has had eighty-five years of strength and I believe that she has more in reserve to see her through this.

It could have been a sombre drive back to Dublin for Niall and myself. But we lightened it up by sharing stories and memories of the past... Of Granny and you. The tall tales of your fishing exploits surfaced again. Do you remember the one about the ginormous pike – the one that supposedly got away? Niall tells that story well.

But I have my doubts, Dad. I still think that you made that one up!

Well, that's all the news for this week, Dad. It's time to say goodnight and I hope that you find that mythical pike again in your dreams.

The Waterside

Sunday, 1ˢᵗ November '98

The news of Granny this week is a bit better than last. She seems to have rallied a bit, though she's still under close observation in the intensive care ward. Mum said that the doctors performed a tracheotomy operation earlier this week. So the tubes are going in through her neck now, instead of her mouth. That frees her to talk when she has the energy. I cringe at the thought of the tracheotomy. But, Mum says that Granny seems a lot more comfortable since.

Life in Dublin has been manic as usual. And Betsy has been acting up again. She wouldn't start for me when I was leaving the office last Tuesday. Battery trouble.

But I learned how to use jump leads. One of the lads from work had a set in his car, which got us back motoring again.

I think that she is protesting at all this city driving. She needs a good country run. And that's on the agenda too.

Dick suggested that I go down to visit the house in Courtmacsherry for a weekend before Christmas – a reconnaissance mission to see what I'll need to bring with me in January. So I'm hoping to do that later this month. I don't want Betsy to start acting up again on the journey miles from nowhere. So I've taken the precaution of booking her in for a complete overhaul with Tony the car doctor.

My own system has been acting up as well, Dad. I got a fit of the jitters during the week, which left me on edge for a couple of days. I think it was partly caused by having so many thoughts, ideas and plans buzzing around my head, draining my energy and upsetting my mental clarity. But another part of it was down to the fears creeping in again with the realisation, 'Oh, my God! I'm about to jump off a cliff at the end of the year!'

It's going to be such a big change, Dad, living on my own in the country, not knowing anybody. But I'm sure that I'll get to know some people on my reconnaissance weekend. And I'll still keep in contact with friends and workmates in Dublin.

You're never alone when there's a friend at the end of the phone.

When I realised that the root cause of my jitters was based on thoughts of uncertainties, I decide to pull back from those thoughts and focus on practicalities to ease my fears. First on the list was finance; the interest rates fell again this week, so I confirmed my application for a loan. I still haven't confirmed a tenant for my apartment yet, but I trust that I will in due course. Meanwhile, I'm working on logistics. I'm trying to tackle the clear-out of the apartment in stages – little and often. It's amazing how much stuff accumulates over just a few years. I think that I can get rid of a lot. Clothes were top of my clear-out list this week – office wear in particular. I found clothes that had been hiding at the back of the wardrobe which hadn't seen the light of day in years! That includes the dress that I wore to my twenty-first birthday party… It's definitely time for that to go!

Anyway, I now have a bonanza bagged and ready for the charity shop.

I'll be leaving most of the household stuff for the new tenant, whoever that may be. But I've realised that I'm still going to need some space for long-term storage. So I've been easing Mum around to the notion that I may be using her attic as a storage depot for a year or so. She claims there's no space. So I've volunteered to help her do a clear out of the attic as well. There's another weekend gone… and time marches on…

Last Friday, I took time out to attend a training course in the library at head office. It was all about Electronic Information Searches. They showed us how to use search engines and various other means of finding information on the Internet.

It's an amazing resource, Dad, and it would be very useful to me for the big project that I have to do for the business strategy course. The project doesn't have to be submitted until the start of next May. But it's worth thirty per cent of the final marks, so it's worth putting in a bit of effort.

Dick said that the house in Courtmacsherry has a phone line, but I'll need to get it reconnected. I will need a phone anyway, but the line could also give me access to the Internet… though I'll need a computer for that. But I'll need a computer in any case, for writing and typing up my project report. I'd better have a think about that. There's just no getting away from technology, Dad.

At the course on Friday, I met Jackie, who works in the technology division. She's doing the business strategy course too. We're in the same project group. Over the coffee break, we had a chat about the presentation our group will have to make at the next session. Shock, horror! The realisation dawned… that's on next weekend!

And we still have so much preparation to do. We're all going to be under a lot of time pressure next week. But there's some consolation at least – after that, there's only one more session of lectures before we break for the Christmas holidays.

After I gave Jackie the update on my January plans, the conversation wound around to the subject of stress. She cautioned me to look after my health, considering all the demands on my time and energy over the next couple of months.

'You don't want to give yourself a heart attack,' she warned.

'Too right!'

I told her that I had been making deep relaxation a part of my daily routine. Although sometimes it is a challenge to keep up the practice; especially since the word 'routine' can no longer be applied to my days.

Jackie told me about a colleague of hers who suffered a heart attack last year. He's quite a young man. Fortunately, he has recovered since. The doctors said that the heart attack was brought on by stress. Among other preventative measures, they prescribed twenty minutes of meditation twice a day, every day.

He follows their prescription with diligence and now has a clean bill of health.

Another colleague, she told me, had been diagnosed with cancer – stress-related.

He was also prescribed deep relaxation along with medication. But, tragically, for him it was too late. He died last year.

I took heed of her cautionary tale. Sometimes, in the whirl of activity, I lose sight of the big picture and the distinction between what is urgent and what is important.

But, right now, what is both important and urgent is making the most of the gap between the rain showers. So I'm off for a walk. Talk to you later...

Sunday evening, 1ˢᵗ November '98

Walking does work wonders. I feel so much better after the exercise and the fresh air. At this time of the year, I really start to feel the lack of daylight during the week – and working in a sick building doesn't help.

On these winter evenings, it gets dark so early that I don't get out for a walk on the South Wall after work. So I really only get my dose of fresh sea air at the weekends. Roll on January, when I can set my own walking routine unconstrained by office hours.

I didn't walk the South Wall today. I chose to walk on Sandymount Strand instead. With the realisation that I'm going to be walking into the great unknown in January, my mind took off on a flight of fancy. I found myself practicing walking blind.

Fixing my sights on a shore landmark, I'd make that my target. Then I'd close my eyes and keep walking along the strand. It felt strange at first. I may have veered a little off course, but each time I opened my eyes, I was still facing my target.

I guess that I was practicing trust – trusting myself and trusting my instincts and trusting my feet on automatic pilot. Once I know where I'm aiming for, my instincts will get me there – with an occasional check that I'm still on course.

The game was engaging on the walk out. But on the way back, my mind was engulfed with thoughts of my to-do list and all the steps that I have to take before January when I jump off the cliff. The list just keeps getting longer, and time is a limited resource, especially over the next couple of months.

So, in a round about way, what I'm trying to say is – I won't have much time to write to you for a while. I know that it's important to keep in touch, and I will. I'll fill you in on all the news when I can. But for now, I've got so much else on my plate that I need to take a break from writing for a few weeks.

I'm sure you understand.

Talk to you again later on this month, or next.

Goodnight, Dad.

Love,

Clodagh

Chapter 12

CELTIC CONNECTIONS

Courtmacsherry
West Cork

Saturday, 5ᵗʰ December '98

Dear Dad,

Greetings from Wonderful Wonderful Courtmacsherry! I took the day off work yesterday and drove down here for my 'reconnaissance' visit. I felt a real sense of indulgence driving out of the city on holidays… and on a workday. But that is one of the perks of working on flexitime. Perhaps I have been spoiled by it, or maybe I have just got too used to it, but I am really looking forward to total flexitime from January onwards.

It's a good road down from Dublin, but it is still a long drive – five hours in total, if you keep within the speed limit! I left Dublin early as I had arranged to break the journey in Fermoy to meet Mary Moss for lunch. Mary is an old friend from college days who lives in Cork now. I don't think that you would have met her before. Anyway, I haven't seen her in quite a few years as I'm not down this direction too often. But I should see her more often in the New Year. We'll be almost neighbours then as she only lives about an hour's drive away from Courtmacsherry.

We had a lot of catching up to do over lunch. But I think

that I may have blitzed her a little bit, filling her in on all that has been happening over the past year or so, and my change of outlook on life. And, boy, how it has changed!

When I got back on the road, past Cork City I was in new territory, as I don't know this part of the country at all well. It is really beautiful countryside, Dad. After Bandon, there was a magnificent stretch along a steep river valley covered in bare winter trees. Then the road into Timoleague curved onto a bridge with a spectacular view across the river where the ruins of an old abbey jumped out from the landscape. I could feel my heart quickening at the sight of a flock of birds rising from the mudflats. It was an awesome sight. Somehow, the light down here seems to add intensity to the colours, which you don't see so clearly through the city grime. Or maybe it was just me!

Driving on another 5km to Courtmacsherry, I eventually found Dick and Fionnula's house after a couple of false starts. I'm so grateful to them for letting me use it. They really are very generous people, and the house itself is just perfect.

I think that I was half expecting a little country cottage, but it is a bit more than that. It's a three-bedroom house on a bit of a hill overlooking the estuary. There are a few apple trees in the back garden and, further uphill, there's a forest. (I'm starting to feel a hill-walking, exploring urge coming on!)

At the front of the house, the living room has a big picture window that looks out over the water. I discovered that, if you sit at one side of the room, the window gives an amazing view of the sunset sky. The chair on the other side of the room gives a perfect aspect to gaze at the early evening moon – it was a big yellow moon last night, floating on wisps of silvery mist.

Beautiful!

The house hadn't been used in a while, so I turned on the heating to warm it up a bit. Then, as there was still a bit of daylight left, I went out in search of firelighters. I took a walk down to the shop by the pier and stocked up on provisions for the weekend. It turned cold after dark yesterday – the weather forecast said that it was due to hit zero to minus four degrees! Brr! But at least it was dry. In any case, the cold was a good excuse to check out a local hostelry on the way back from the shop.

I spotted a fire flickering through the window of the Pier Inn and went in for a 'hot one'. You'd love the place, Dad. It's your kind of pub. The locals are really friendly, but they allow you your own space as well. After a bit of chit-chat at the bar, I retired to a seat by the fire to thaw my hands out so that I could write a few postcards. At the same time, I was half-tuned to the conversation at the bar – there were some great stories being told.

When I'd finished writing and packed my cards and pen away, a few of the people that I'd been talking to earlier moved over from the bar to the fire. I have to say, Dad, the art of conversation is alive and well and living in Courtmacsherry!

The pub had a really cosy atmosphere and, with such good conversation, I could have stayed all night. But after the long drive, a walk and a couple of drinks, I felt the need for some food. So I came back to base to explore the kitchen and light the fire. A fireplace... Luxury, luxury! The lack of fireplace is certainly one of the drawbacks of apartment living. After all the hustle and bustle of the last few months, I thoroughly enjoyed a peaceful evening of reading and fire-gazing.

I must have been awake before the rest of the village today, and it was a bright crisp morning. So, as the tide was out, I went for an early walk along the strand. Further along, I found my path blocked by the incoming tide so I scrambled over some rocks to climb onto higher ground. Then I discovered a well-worn track for a walk through the woods. There is a real magical, mystical feel to the woods, with all those gnarly old trees covered in moss, and there are some real 'characters' down there – the trees, that is! It's a winter wood just now, but I can imagine it in the spring when the bluebells are in bloom and the wood turns into a million shades of green.

I think that I am going to enjoy living in the country. The nature walks are great for getting things in perspective and calming down after all the buzzy city energy. I'm beginning to see things that are hidden in the city… Like the sky. It was a clear sky last night, and the stars were spellbinding, Dad. I started to get a sense of just how vast the sky is. But in the city, the streetlights focus downward and my vision is limited to a small part of this huge universe. I'm so looking forward to escaping from the city and broadening my own horizons.

There I go, rambling off again! But back to practicalities, Dad. It's time to take a break from this letter as I've got a couple of boxes of Christmas cards to write! And then I want to go exploring Timoleague Abbey and the local 'metropolis', Clonakilty. But I'll fill you in on that tomorrow…

Courtmacsherry

Sunday, 6ᵗʰ December '98

I don't know if you have ever been there, Dad, but Clonakilty really is an excellent town. It has everything from traditional pubs, well-stocked library and a Natural Healing Centre to a mobile phone shop and a Compustore. The latter may well come in handy if I need technical backup for my new work tools.

Over the last couple of months, I have come to realise that I am going to need the modern tools of the trade for writing and staying in touch with friends while I'm travelling. Much as I love writing with a good pen, I'm going to need access to a word-processor and email. So I've decided that I'll have to invest in a laptop computer.

I've been doing a bit of research and asking around to try and find out what exactly it is that I am buying! The decision process is a bit like buying your first car:

'I want to buy a car!'

'And what type of car do you want to buy?'

'Well, I don't know really. One that I can drive and afford!'

But after making a fool of myself (several times) with idiot questions, I have learned a bit more about the technical jargon and I'm getting a better understanding of what type of computer I need. I've nearly decided on the one to buy, but I'll leave the final decision for another couple of weeks.

At the moment, I'm still grappling with the operations manual for my new 'techno toy' – a mobile phone. Yes, Dad, I'm afraid that I could put off the evil day no longer. I'm turning into a true phone-carrying yuppie. The only consolation is that

I'll be balancing it with less of the 'young' and 'urban'! It is a bit scary as the darn thing keeps beeping at me any time I hit one of the buttons. But I'm determined to get to grips with it, and I know that I'll get used to it… eventually.

Anyway, enough of the techno shopping, back to the Christmas shopping. It's hard to believe that it's only three weeks to Christmas. So much to do, so little time! At least I can cross the Christmas cards off my to-do list. I put them in the post when I was in Clonakilty yesterday, and – more progress – I managed to cross a few pressies off the list too.

I really enjoyed the afternoon rambling around the shops. And, true to form, I found myself in a bookshop for a couple of hours. It's a pretty good bookshop too, Dad. But what really struck me was the range of Celtic books that they have in stock: history, legend, folklore, spirituality, art, design, and even Celtic colouring books for children!

There seems to have been some sort of Celtic revival thing happening over the last few years. I think that it started with *Riverdance*. But I almost forgot, that would have been after your time, Dad. It was the interval act for the *Eurovision Song Contest*, which was on a few weeks after you died. A very 'non-traditional' traditional Irish dance routine. I didn't pay too much heed to it at the time as I was still feeling very distracted so soon after your death.

But, a few months later, the stage show came to the Point Depot in Dublin. Mum got us all a ticket as a Christmas pressie. There was amazing energy from the show, Dad. I never knew that music and dance could have such a powerful energy. At the end of the show, there was a sort of Mexican wave ripple effect as the audience jumped up to applaud. Despite her gammy knee, I think that Mum was probably the first to her feet! Her face was beaming. It was really great to see. I hadn't seen her face lit up like that in a long, long time.

This *Riverdance* 'phenomenon' (as they are now calling it) seems to have triggered an interest in all things Celtic, not just in Ireland, but all over the world. Celtic design jewellery is definitely doing a roaring trade. And the latest craze seems to be Celtic-style tattoos.

I bumped into Sue in town a while ago. You remember Sue, my old school mate, don't you, Dad? She's still as zany as ever – and still into the Irish music and the 'craic'. Anyway, herself and her friend had just come from getting tattooed – they're very discreet ones, mind you!

Sue's tattoo is that triple spiral design, like the one on the big stone at Newgrange. She says it's called a 'triskele'.

I like that word… triskele. It has a nice ring to it.

It's a funny thing, but I've been seeing those triple spirals all over the place lately – from tattoos and T-shirts to wall hangings and fabrics.

I wonder what the spirals mean?

I remember learning a little bit about the Celts in school, but it was only a couple of pages in the history book. That sketchy history was mostly about how people lived in the Iron Age: housing, clothing, food, hunting, feasting, tribal warfare etc. I don't remember learning too much about the Celtic psyche and their outlook on the world.

There were some really good books in the shop in Clonakilty. So I bought a few of the Celtic ones for Christmas presents. But I couldn't resist dipping into them myself last night. It is amazing how much reading you can get through with only the crackling of the fire for company. I'm almost finished one of them already.

It seems that the Celts lived across most of Europe at one stage. But they lived in clans or tribes, so there was no Celtic Empire as such. Perhaps that was because they were always fighting with the neighbouring tribes. Some things don't change! I guess that there must still be a lot of Celts around Europe, even now in this modern-day world. But the ancient Celts had a great respect for heroes and warriors – and there were women warriors too. It gives the 'battle of the sexes' a whole new meaning! I guess if they were fighting side by side, there was no cause for any 'battle between the sexes'. They sound like a pretty fearless bunch, Dad. I reckon they would have had no need for *Feel the Fear And Do It Anyway*!

But, apparently, the fierce side of their nature was balanced with a gentler, more artistic side. They loved poetry and music, and storytelling was a big part of their daily life. Well, there weren't many books around in the Iron Age, so I guess the storytelling was the equivalent of Iron Age Radio or TV. Maybe that's where the 'gift of the gab' came from.

Although life wasn't all about fighting and telling stories, Dad. There was a bit of planting and harvesting to be done too. They lived very close to the land and they lived in tune with nature and the cycle of the seasons. In fact, the earth was revered as the source of fertility and life. I'm sure they would be horrified at the way we treat the earth today – drowning it in plastic and polluting their life-giving water. I reckon we have a lot to learn from the Celts and their love of nature.

They had a healthy respect for nature and they recognised its dark side too – the menacing side of nature's mighty power. We had a touch of that dark side here this morning. The clouds unleashed a downpour and the wind whipped up the sea. It was wonderful to watch from the comfort of the sofa! Definitely a day to settle indoors.

But it's starting to brighten up outside now. So I think that I'll wrap up and go for another nature walk. I love the smell of the trees and hedges just after a downpour. Then I want to get on the road early to break the back of the journey before it gets too dark. I'm heading back to 'Stressville' this afternoon for work tomorrow. Yeugh! Into work in the dark, and back home in the dark. I really miss daylight at this time of year. Change that thinking! The sun is shining now. Fill you in later...

Back in 'Stressville'

Sunday Night

Well I'm back at base now, Dad, and the drive wasn't too bad. I would have liked to spend more time out walking, but I'll have plenty of time for that in January. The walk did set my mind to free-flow thinking, though, and then loads more thoughts popped up on the drive back. Good job that I didn't have too much traffic to contend with!

I recalled something that Mum said to me recently. It was shortly after I told her that I was taking a year out from the job and the city to explore other things. She passed a comment: 'Your father used to say that you work hard at being a rebel!'

Is that what you used to think, Dad? I don't, you know.

It's funny, really, because I always thought that it was the opposite case.

I thought that I worked hard to conform, not rebel – to conform to what was expected of me; to be who I was expected to be. Or maybe it was just my assumption of what was expected of me.

I lived my life to meet other people's expectations, as I perceived them to be.

But then, occasionally, something inside me would say, 'Stop! Be yourself! Do your own thing!'

It wasn't that I was working hard at being a rebel. I was just listening to my intuition.

Or maybe it's just the voice of the 'warrior Celt' in me!

On the drive home, I had a flashback to that time I was caught out mitching from Confession. Do you remember that incident, Dad?

I must have been about fourteen at the time. Saturday was the day for Confession. I had full intentions of going up to the church when I got on my bike. But when I got to the end of the road, I turned left instead of right and went for a cycle around the grounds of the university in Belfield.

It was a glorious day; the first sunny day in weeks. It seemed a sin not to be out in nature, appreciating the sunlight playing through the trees.

My mistake was to say 'Yes' when Mum asked if I had got Confession.

'Well how come your father didn't see you in the church, then?'

Oops! I should have known that I'd be caught out in the lie!

I couldn't think of an answer quick enough. My face probably gave me away, anyway. Mum's face turned stern. 'I'll have your father speak to you!'

Phew! 'I'm off the hook!' I thought.

Well, at least I knew that there wouldn't be a lecture, more of a discussion.

I remember our chat. You said that you had a lot of questions about religion too, when you were at my age. You said that you had done some 'searching' for answers, reading up on other religions and the philosophy behind them.

I remember your words. You said that, 'After you go through some of life's transitions, you eventually go back to the one you know.'

Maybe that is what I am doing now, Dad. Going back, but further back into the Celtic connections, to find the one I 'know'.

I still have too many questions about the religion I was born into. It still feels too dogmatic and intolerant; based on fear.

Fear stifles the spirit and I don't believe that the spirit is meant to be stifled.

It's a funny word that – 'spirit'. Some people hear it and think of ghosts and ghouls. Others hear it as liveliness, energy or courage – the exact opposite of fear.

Yet others hear it as life force, essence or soul.

Where is your spirit now, Dad?

The Waterside

Monday, 7th December '98

Well, I think I'm starting to find an answer with a bit of help from the ancient Celts and their view of life and death. When I got back from work this evening, I finished that book that I'd started over the weekend. It turns out that the Celts had a pretty imaginative way of seeing, feeling and sensing things. It sounds like they weren't so constrained by left-brain logic like we are today. In fact, it sounds as if they had a pretty good balance between the left brain and the intuitive right brain.

But what got me onto that train of thought? Oh yes... The Celts. They had a strong belief in the afterlife too. Not only that, they also believed that the past and present were intertwined. They didn't have our rigid linear view of time and space. And they believed that their ancestors were still present in the 'otherworld'. They felt that the otherworld was very close and that there were certain 'thin times' or 'thin places' when the boundaries blurred and the veil between the worlds became very thin.

I take comfort from that thought, Dad. That your spirit is still close in some shape or form, or energy. I feel your guidance at times and not just in things you might have said in the past. I feel your hand in some of the things that have been happening to smooth the path for me. That helps to ease my fears when I'm not quite sure which way to go.

I remember holding your hand on that last night in the hospital. And I realise what a privilege that was for me to be holding your hand when you died. Sometimes, I wonder if we could really have been of any help to you in facing your fears as you faced death. But I think that you have helped me find an answer to that question too.

I went on a holiday with Mum and Brendan six months after

you died. Mum was trying to read *Buddenbrooks* by Thomas Mann. I asked her if it was any good. She said that it wasn't really her type of book, but that you had asked her to read it and it was the last book that you had read before you died. So I asked her if I could borrow it.

It's not really my type of book either, and I found it a bit of a struggle to read. But, then I got to Chapter 5!

The words jumped out at me:

"For the truth was that Thomas Buddenbrook, at the age of forty-eight, began to feel that his days were numbered, and began to reckon with his own approaching death!"

He was a full ten years younger than you were, but it felt as if you were talking through him, telling me of your thoughts about facing death. Only I couldn't take it all in then.

I took a photocopy of that chapter. It's funny that, all these years later, I knew exactly where to lay my hands on that copy. I guess my mental filing system must be better than I thought!

I read that chapter again just now.

Words jumped out at me again, three passages this time:

"Where shall I be when I am dead? Ah, it is so brilliantly clear, so overwhelmingly simple! I shall be in all those who have ever, do ever, or shall ever say 'I' – especially, however, in all those who say it most fully, potently, and gladly!"

So that's where you are! Well it may be 'brilliantly clear' to you, but it is a little bit cryptic to me, Dad.

"And in so far as he could now understand and recognise – not in words and consecutive thoughts, but in sudden rapturous illuminations of his innermost being – he was already free, already actually released and free of all natural as well as artificial limitations."

I'm happy that you've found your freedom, Dad, and I hope you'll be glad that I'm finding my freedom, too, from my self-imposed limitations.

"He was no longer prevented from grasping eternity. Nothing began, nothing left off. There was only an endless present; and that power in him which loved life with a love so exquisitely sweet and yearning – the power of which his personality was only the unsuccessful expression – that power would always know how to find access to this present."

Well that's certainly a Celtic sort of outlook, Dad… Or is it a touch of Eastern philosophy?

Whichever, it gives me great comfort to know that you are free and present.

But, back to my present. It's late.

I'm afraid that I am not free of natural limitations yet, and my eyelids are insisting on rest. So I'll finish this letter later in the week.

Goodnight, Dad… wherever you are tonight.

The Waterside

Friday, 8ᵗʰ December

Life's gone a little bit crazy again, Dad. I'm trying to 'clear the decks' as much as possible in work, as I'll be finishing up on Christmas Eve. The round of Christmas social sessions seems to be starting early this year. My diary is choc-a-block. I have five business lunches pencilled in for next week and three evening functions as well. But there's no fear of my putting on weight as I have so much running around to do over the next week or two.

Quite apart from keeping up with the social whirl, I have to clear out my stuff from the apartment before the end of the month. And I've still got some Christmas shopping to do. Aargh! Enough!

My mind is in such a flurry, Dad, I almost forgot to tell you; synchronicity struck again this week, in a way that left me speechless – a rare occurrence, as you well know.

It happened at the seminar that Richard had organised on World Class Manufacturing. I had invited the managing directors of two of the more progressive companies that I have been working with, as the seminar seemed to be relevant to the next stage of their business development.

At the coffee break, I was chatting with Frank Carroll, the managing director of Alfrank Designs. We've worked together on various programmes over the last two years and he has taught me a hell of a lot about the furniture industry during that time.

Anyway, as I was giving Frank the update on my own personal change programme, I noticed a look of concern on his face. Then he asked, 'If you're going to be working away from the office, how will you manage without a PC?'

I explained about my decision to invest in a laptop computer, and my recent self-education on some of the technical aspects and the costs.

Frank interrupted my technical prattle. 'I'll tell you what, as you'll need the computer if you're going to write a book, Alfrank Designs will sponsor you for the use of one.'

It took a moment for his words to sink in. When they did, I was overwhelmed by his generosity. My mind went blank and I was so choked with emotion that I couldn't speak. As I grappled with words to express my gratitude, all that came out was one word… One heartfelt, 'Thanks.'

It seemed so inadequate.

I know that his company has sponsored awards for design students and other arts. But I hadn't considered that writing would fall within that category – a creative art.

It's all so new to me. When I managed to regain my composure enough to speak, I thanked him for the offer to sponsor the tools of my new writing trade, and also for the confidence in my capability that such a gesture demonstrates.

It means so much, to know that somebody else has faith in me.

But quite apart from that, Dad, on a practical level, the sponsorship will extend my budget by at least two months. That'll help to take the pressure off finance while I take time to learn more about the process and art of creative writing.

As I'm back on the subject of writing, I should let you know that I'm not going to have much time to write to you until January.

But then I'll have all the time in the world!

Oh, I am so looking forward to the freedom of total flexitime, away from city stresses. It's not like I am going to be twiddling my thumbs for the year. There's exams coming up in February, and then there is the project for the strategy course. That'll keep me well occupied up until May. After that, I'll start work on the book that is presently floating about in my head.

Yet, despite all my various projects, and perhaps more important, I want to spend more time just 'being' – and walking, and writing, and reading, and learning, and doing whatever 'catches my energy'.

In a way, I wish it were starting tomorrow. But what is the point in wishing my life away? So I've decided I'm going to enjoy the buzz over the next few busy weeks.

But, before I move on, there is something else that I want to share with you, Dad. I suppose it goes back to another part of the Celtic mindset. They had this tendency to wander, to roam, to go exploring.

Do you remember when I was a child, Dad?

That was one of my favourite pastimes – 'going exploring' – whether it was climbing the tree over the back wall, or wandering the paths through the trees in Belfield.

I loved going exploring. Everything was an adventure!

Life was an adventure!

Well I'm determined to get that sense of adventure back!

I've been reading this book on Celtic saints and their wandering off on pilgrimages. A lot of the saints in the book were just ordinary people, living good lives and doing what they should be doing. They didn't have to be qualified with a quota of miracles in those days. Life was a lot simpler then.

But, even way back then, ordinary people sometimes found that their lives were a bit out of balance – the body and soul were out of kilter.

So, at times like that, they'd take a break from ordinary life to reassess and reorient themselves. They'd go on an adventure – a journey or a pilgrimage.

I suppose that I'm on some sort of personal pilgrimage, Dad.

I guess I'm searching for something, like a lot of people these days.

But what is that something? Maybe it's meaning?

Not meaning like, 'What is the meaning of the Universe?' (*The Hitchhikers Guide to the Galaxy* answered that question – it's fifty-four and a half! Or was it eighty-four by a half?)

But joking aside, Dad, maybe I am looking for the meaning of my own life.

Viktor Frankl said, 'Man's search for meaning is the primary motivation in his life.' He claimed that, 'What man actually needs is not a tensionless state, but rather the striving and struggling for a worthwhile goal, a freely chosen task.'

So what's my goal? What task shall I choose? Pick a goal – any goal!

No, I think that what I'm really looking for is my reason for being here. I suppose I'm looking for what Deepak Chopra would call my Dharma – my Purpose in Life: 'Everyone has a purpose in life; a unique gift or special talent to give to others.'

I haven't figured out what my 'unique gift' is… yet. But I trust that Life will show me what it is if I take the time out to ask.

So it's time for me to go exploring again, Dad. To find out

where I am going in the next cycle of my life. Life moves on – as yours did, as mine is – and we all have to go through the big Cycle of Life and pass on to the next one.

There's no point in resisting it, so I might as well enjoy the journey and get back into the spirit of adventure!

On the subject of spirit, you'll be glad to hear that Granny still has her fighting spirit; it must be the 'warrior Celt' in her! She has had an amazing recovery.

After spending six weeks in intensive care at the hospital, she is well enough now to be moved on to the nursing home to recuperate. So she is back in Lisnaskea now.

But I think that it is a source of frustration to her, to be so near to home, and yet so far. Her mind is as sharp as ever, but she is not too keen on being stuck in the nursing home 'with all these auld ones', as she says. Her mission in life at the moment is to escape from the nursing home, despite what the doctors say.

She wants her freedom and independence back. I can understand that.

I have a vision of Granny masterminding a tunnel-building project, just like in the movie, *The Great Escape*. Joking aside, Dad, I wouldn't put it past her!

Mum and I are going up to visit her over the Christmas holidays – assuming she hasn't finished her tunnel before then!

So, I'll give you the update in January when I get back to writing.

Meanwhile, I'd better sign off now and put some more time into planning my own 'Great Escape' from the city.

Happy Christmas, Dad… wherever you are.

Love,

Clodagh

P.S.

I found out what the spirals mean! I thought that it was a Celtic design, but it's older than the Celts – the triple spirals go all the way back to the Stone Age. The archaeologists reckon that the carvings at Newgrange are over 5,000 years old.

One theory is that the spirals represent the balance of different energies – positive, negative and a neutral energy that keeps it all together – a bit like yin and yang in balance with the universal energy that connects us all.

But that is not the only similarity with Eastern philosophies, Dad. Apparently, the spirals were also part of the Old Irish language of Ogham.

That's pronounced as 'Ohm', and it's the same sound as the word 'Om', the mantra that the Eastern religions use in meditation – and meditation helps to bring balance too.

So maybe, with seeing all these spirals lately, it's life's way of telling me to get more balance in my own life. Well, that is my plan for January anyway, Dad. I'll keep you posted!

Chapter 13

VIEW FROM THE CLIFF

The Waterside

Wednesday, 30ᵗʰ December '98

Dear Dad,

I've done it now; I've really done it. I've jumped off the cliff… Well, metaphorically speaking. Or perhaps it would be more correct to say that I've taken the first step away from the job. At the moment, I feel like I am floating in mid-air, between Dublin and Cork. My mind certainly is. But I'll land in Cork early next month. I sure hope that it's not with a thud!

Technically speaking, my career break doesn't start until 1ˢᵗ January. But, with the holidays and all, my last working day was on Christmas Eve. The week before that was really crazy. My brain was on overdrive, trying to remember all that had to be done; tying up all the loose ends. Christmas Eve had crept up before I had a chance to start clearing out my desk. Although there were no phones ringing, there were plenty of distractions on the day – pleasant ones, I should add.

It's a long-standing tradition that people bring their children into the office for a few hours on Christmas Eve to see where the big people work. It's all ahead of them!

But the children are great entertainment. At first, the little ones are shy. Although it doesn't take long for them to adapt.

Within a half-hour their personalities start to come out, challenging the grown-ups set thinking with questions of:

'Why?'

'What's that for?'

'Why do you do that?'

Sometimes it's difficult to find a reasonable answer to their incisive questions. The world of the office must seem quite ridiculous to their innocent eyes. But, on Christmas Eve, the serious world of the office becomes more like a crèche. More human; more fun. The children are right; work should be fun. Why do we do it, if it's not fun anymore?

They have great fun with the computers. It never ceases to amaze me how kids take to computers like ducks to water. No fear. They just dive in and learn by playing with their techno toys. Never mind how it works; what can it do?

I think that I should adopt that approach too.

I collected my new laptop on Christmas Eve, thanks to Frank's benevolence. But I haven't had much time to play with it yet. Although I did bring it over to Mum's house on Christmas Day to get help from our Bren with setting it up and connecting to the Internet (more of that later, Dad).

Back to the desk... I was surprised to find that all my personal files and belongings fitted into two small boxes. Somehow, I had expected that clearing out the desk would be a mammoth task. But it wasn't at all. It only took me thirty minutes amid the happy distraction of children running about and asking questions.

While I was packing, Eoin, on a break from his own desk clearance, called down to say goodbye. He's taking a career break too, to start up a business. After thirteen years with the organisation, it's a big move for him. I really admire his courage.

I'm sure it will go well for him, but I'd say that he is also glad to have the employment safety net for a year or two.

My last week in work was a very emotional one, Dad. Although I'm glad to be moving on from the job, and feel exhilarated about making the big break, last week I felt quite sad saying goodbye to friends and colleagues who I have been working with for the last three years through various ups and downs. It was an emotional see-saw week. It felt like the end of an era. I suppose that it is, for me.

Everything seemed to just fall into place before Christmas.

My financial safety net was approved. I collected the loan cheque and cleared my Visa bill – at last! The funds left over should buy at least ten months of my time. But, if I don't make any money from writing, well, I'm not going to be destitute. When the funds run low, I can always fall back to my first trade for a while. That's the beauty of waitressing! It's a bit like riding a bike – once you learn the skill you never lose it. After seven years of waitressing through school and college days, I'm sure that I could do that job in my sleep. Anyway, in the current economic climate, there should be no problem picking up casual work.

Now that I think of it, Dad, waitressing would be very good for me – for balance when I get on to writing the book. Writing is such a solitary task.

We all need contact with people. A few waitressing shifts would fulfil more than my need for cash. It would also fulfil my need for company while I work on finding my voice of creative expression. But I trust that everything will fall into place in its own good time.

The other thing that fell into place last week was a tenant for my apartment. As coincidence would have it, Andrew phoned me to say that he had bumped into an old friend who was looking for a one-bedroom apartment to rent. The place where she was living had been burgled and she didn't feel safe there anymore. On the phone, she sounded very enthusiastic. But when she came over to view the apartment, she seemed more relieved that she'd found a safe haven for the next year. I am so glad that it meets her needs, and that the apartment is going to a friend of a friend. In a funny way, Dad, it feels like I have found a good home for my home.

Although, for me, it has become a concrete box, in a concrete block, in a concrete city, and there's a whole world outside, waiting to be explored.

Since I started packing up ornaments and taking pictures down from the walls, it doesn't feel like home anymore.

Maybe it will feel like home again some day.

But, at this particular moment, all the apartment means to me is just a series of tasks: packing, scrubbing, cleaning, transferring phone and electricity connections, evacuating! It'll be another week before I fly out of this cage. That's plenty of time to get all those tasks done. Then I'll be staying at Mum's for two or three days before I move down to Cork for three months.

After that, synchronicity seems to be moving me on to County Wexford. Last week, I had a phone call from Gerard Redmond, who I used to work with about five years ago. I had sent him a Christmas card, with a note to say that I'd be moving on from the job and gave him my new contact number. So he phoned me at work to find out what I was up to. When I explained that I was taking time out to find peace and quiet, and work on some writing projects, he told me that he had finished his own 'project' in Wexford building a holiday home and he said that I was welcome to use it anytime.

I was temporarily speechless again, Dad, as I was so bowled over by his thoughtfulness and generosity.

Anyway, I've arranged to visit Gerard and Joan, and their children in County Wexford for the Easter holiday weekend. I'm really looking forward to meeting his family. He spoke about them so much when we were working together, I feel as if I know them already. The whole family have been going to Curracloe, Co. Wexford for summer holidays for the last ten years, and the place sounds wonderful. It's only a fifteen-minute drive north of Wexford town and the house itself is only five minutes from the beach. Miles and miles of golden sand for walking and inspiration. There's a nature reserve nearby too, for a walk through the trees if it's too windy for the beach. Oh, I'm so looking forward to it, Dad. And Easter does seem to be a very appropriate time for another new beginning. The February exams will be just a memory by then, and moving again in April will give me a target to finish my project for the course well before the deadline at the start of May. Then I can pack away my course notes and move on to a new location and my own writing projects. To a clean sheet, so to speak.

I'll be staying in Curracloe for the month of April, and after that? Who knows? I'll wait to see what emerges from my creative right brain. Though I do fancy the notion of travelling further afield over the summer. Time will tell!

Speaking of travelling far afield, Fiona is spreading her wings too. That was the big news on Christmas Day. She's planning on going to India for a month from mid-January. Oh, I know she's been talking about if for years, Dad; it's her big dream! But this time, she's not just talking about it, she's got a plan and she's finally doing it. Work in the movie production business will be pretty thin on the ground over the next few months and she still has the cash from her last big contract. So it's a case of now or maybe never. She's grasping the opportunity while she can – and she's determined. Within the space of a week she got her shots, a travel visa, a copy of *The Rough Guide to India* and a return flight to Goa from London at an excellent rate. Isn't it great, Dad? I think she is so courageous, making the trip on her own. Although she says that she knows some other people from work who will be out there at the same time, so I'm sure she'll be fine.

Christmas Day was the regular melee over at Mum's with friends and relations visiting. Matty and Martien called over, as usual, with their three children. Uncle Noel announced the arrival of the Quinn clan with his annual 'Ho! Ho! Ho!' and the red Santa sack slung over his shoulder. But there were people missing this year. Evelyn stayed up in Lisnaskea to be with Granny as she's still in the nursing home (more of that later). We missed your presence, Dad. But you were there all the same in the memories exchanged among all the presents and chatter.

Much of the chatter was about Fiona's big travel plan. There was an enthusiastic reaction from everyone. Everyone, that is, except Mum. The look on her face said that she wasn't impressed; she looked anxious and concerned.

Out in the kitchen, I asked her what was wrong.

'India! Why does she have to go to India?'

'She doesn't have to; she wants to. It's not like she's going off to find a guru and never coming back. She's only going for a holiday for four weeks.'

'Well, if she's only going on holidays, what's wrong with Spain or the Canaries? They have sunshine and beaches there too!'

I had to concede that it isn't just a holiday for Fiona. It's an adventure; a challenge; a dream. Even so, Goa is a fairly touristy resort; it's not like she's heading off to camp out in the jungle.

Mum wasn't convinced. I could see that she was concerned for Fiona's welfare and her fears fuelled her worry. I think that she was afraid of getting another call from a hospital, but from the other side of the world. After all the hospital calls that Mum has had over the last year, I can understand that.

Then I had a brainwave!

'Hey, Bren, if I set up the laptop, any chance that you'd help us to get onto the Internet?'

The objective was to find pictures of Goa with palm trees and beaches.

Bren got us surfing. (So I'll forgive him for all those 'techno-peasant' comments about me!) And we sat with heads huddled around the kitchen table to see pictures of Fiona's exotic destination. But sometimes the Internet gives you more information than you want.

'Quick… skip over that stuff about scorpions and snakes. We're trying to put Mum's mind at ease, not freak her out!'

Mum and I had our own little 'adventure' on St Stephens

Day, or Boxing Day as they say up North. We drove up to visit Granny and Evelyn. After the drive, we stopped off at the house for a quick cup of tea with Evelyn. But we didn't delay long, as Evelyn said that Granny was expecting us at the nursing home.

By the time we got there, Granny had battled the other Zimmer-framers to stake her claim on the visitors' room.

'It'll give us a bit more privacy away from all the "auld ones,"' she explained.

Granny was talking about going home next week. Physically, she's not really up to it just yet. But you know Granny, when her mind is set, it's like telling a river to wait!

Shortly after lunch, the wind started to pick up, so we left early to make the most of the daylight for the journey back to Dublin. Within a half-hour we realised that we were driving into a storm. Or was it a hurricane, with winds of 100mph? Whichever, when we started to notice torn branches and fallen trees, the drive became a bit hair-raising.

A big tree had fallen down, blocking the road to Cavan, so we had to detour by Monaghan and Castleblaney. That put an extra half-hour onto the journey. But, on the way, I learned a lot about my relations in that part of the country.

Mum kept her mind busy by pointing out the local points of family interest and reminiscing about her youth. I could tell that she was nervous about driving in such dreadful weather conditions.

I had no fear. Mum has survived one car crash this year, and I didn't believe that she had been spared from that just to crash again in the storm. As for me, well I've experienced so much synchronicity this year, confirming that I'm on the right path, whatever that may be. I trusted that fate wasn't going to knock my plans on the head with a tree. Even so, it was a hazardous journey. I was glad that we were driving in Mum's car as it's a bit more solid than mine (no disrespect to Betsy!).

I reckon that Mum was saying her prayers while I trusted in providence, and we both let go of a sigh of relief when we got back to Dublin.

But you were looking out for us anyway, weren't you, Dad?

Well, that's enough chat for now. I've started to notice a few sighs of fatigue creeping out. So it's time for some sleep to refresh myself for another day of packing and scrubbing tomorrow.

Happy New Year!

Courtmacsherry

Sunday, 10th Jan '99

Finally, Dad, the logistics phase is over. I'm done with packing and scrubbing now – for a few months at least. My nomadic life started last Thursday when I handed over the keys of my apartment for a year. I've been staying at Mum's house for the last three nights, as I had lectures in Dublin on Friday and Saturday morning. Thankfully, there's only one more session of lectures before the final exams.

It felt a bit odd to be sleeping at the house in Clonskea again after so long. It was the first night that I had slept under that roof in over ten years. I stayed in my old room that I used to share with Fiona. For some reason, though, I chose not to sleep in my old bed. I'm not entirely sure why. Although I think that it may be something to do with moving backward – and I want to move forward now. Do you understand that, Dad? Anyway, I slept in Fiona's old bed instead of my own.

I slept very well there for the first two nights, thanks to a combination of physical and mental exhaustion. Then, last night, sleep eluded me. Oh, I was tired all right, but my spirit wouldn't settle. I was so excited about finally moving out of town in the morning. With the long journey ahead of me, I knew that I needed to rest. So I closed my eyes and thought myself into a deep relaxation, from head to toe, using the Mindstore techniques. Then I thought that I'd send my mind to find my imaginary landscape and my imaginary house, which represents the inner me. In that house, I have an imaginary room, which I've decorated in shades of calming lavender and lilac. It holds a deep, comfortable featherbed where my mind is guaranteed to relax into peaceful repose.

But a strange thing happened last night, Dad. When I steered my mind into my imaginary landscape, I found that my house had gone. In its place, I saw clearly in my mind's eye, a gypsy caravan with a green curved canvas roof. It was like the one that I'd seen on the pier in Brighton – the one owned by the fortune-telling Australian Gypsy Jim. Isn't that odd, Dad? I guess that it was just my subconscious confirming my new nomadic lifestyle with imagery. Another funny thing, Dad. After my mind remarked on the image, a great wave of peace washed over me. I must have dozed off then and I slept like a log.

Mum was up early this morning. I heard her moving about downstairs in the kitchen when I emerged from the shower. A wonderful smell wafted up the stairs. She had cooked a full Irish breakfast for me to send me off on my journey. It set me up for the day. After breakfast, I went to work, loading up the car. Mum was a bit dubious whether I'd be able to fit all my boxes and bags into Betsy. But my years of supervising the van-loading at the warehouse stood me in good stead, so loading a Renault 5 was no problem. I managed to fit everything in and still see out the back window.

The day had dawned cold and frosty. By the time I had finished loading Betsy, the sun had warmed the frost from the roads. I gave Mum a big hug and then set off on my journey to Cork.

Somewhere along the Naas bypass, the glare of the sun made me see that my vision had come to pass – my vision of me and Betsy driving out of town under a cloud-free sky in freedom and peace.

I revelled in the feeling – my dream had become a reality.

Unfortunately, Dad, the cloud-free sky didn't last very long; only as far as Kildare. Then we hit fog. The weather report on the radio warned that there was a bank of freezing fog lying right across the middle of the country and, in all probability, it would stay there for the rest of the day.

It certainly was freezing, and Betsy's heating system is not the most effective in the world. She wasn't designed for Arctic temperatures and neither was I! I pulled in to a petrol station to dress for Siberia and ended up driving with gloves on, three jackets and a rug across my lap. Even so, it wasn't long before my feet felt frozen from my toes to my knees.

It must have been the coldest day in the past year. I don't think that the temperature rose above zero all day. The fog bank didn't clear until we got past Fermoy. Although the weather improved for the drive across County Cork, there was no heat in the late afternoon sunshine. So when I arrived at Courtmacsherry, I got stuck straight into unloading Betsy and unpacking boxes. The priority being to keep moving for warmth until the central heating started to take effect.

I'm well ensconced in front of the fire now, Dad. But I still can't get the heat back into my feet. The water should be piping hot by now. So perhaps these two ice blocks will finally thaw out in a steaming bath. My muscles will be glad of a soak too, after all the exertion of lifting and loading. That should ease the shoulder tension of driving for hours in fog. So it's time for me to go pamper myself with a hot bath, some relaxing oils, a glass of wine and a good read by candlelight.

Goodnight, Dad.

Sea Road
Courtmacsherry

Sunday, 17th Jan '99

The weather has been clement this week. Though it is still very cold, the days have been clear, crisp and dry. So I have been out and about exploring the local countryside. I found an excellent book in the house, *The Walks of Courtmacsherry Bay*, which gives very good details of some local walking routes on and off the beaten track. So I have been out walking for hours most days this week. I just lose all track of time when I start exploring – rambling my way along through the woods; headland paths; wide, sandy coves; and the tree-lined country lanes. Invariably, though, my rumbling stomach reminds me to return to base.

I've been rediscovering the art of cooking too. You can't beat a hearty, home-made soup after a cold winter walk. I tried my hand at baking bread also. But I think that I'll need a lot more practice at that.

This week has been such a wonderful holiday; although I have had my ups and downs. I've designated the next two weeks as holidays also, before I start into studying for the exams. I've earned a break. Although I must say, it does feel very indulgent going out to enjoy the fresh country air in late morning or mid-afternoon while the office world is back in the throes of the January blues. I remember those days well. Although I didn't miss them at all this week, I expect that I may encounter an occasional fit of nostalgia.

On Tuesday, I took Betsy for a spin over to the Old Head of Kinsale and stretched my legs there, before driving on to the town of Kinsale. I'd never been there before, but I know that you had. It really is a pretty town, Dad. I'd say that it's wild in the summer, but at this time of year it's fairly quiet with few tourists about. I felt like a tourist myself as I walked around the headland to take a photo of Kinsale from James Fort. There's a better angle there to get a wide shot of the town as it climbs up behind the boats in the harbour. As I walked back along the south side of the headland, I watched the sails of four dinghies tacking around the outer harbour. In January! Hardy sailors, indeed. OK, so the sun was shining, but my toes were numb, despite walking in two pairs of thick socks and heavy boots. I could imagine how cold it must have been out there on the water. The boat people must have been freezing.

Mr Telecom looked cold too, on Thursday, when he climbed

down from the telephone pole with the good news that the reconnection had been successful. Yippee! I now have a landline again. Just as well, too. I was afraid that I would go bald from tearing my hair out trying to get access to my email using the mobile phone. I think that I am missing some crucial piece of software. But I'll try it again before I admit defeat and call in the cavalry – i.e. our Brendan.

I phoned Mum to give her my new number and test out the landline. She rang back again last night to say that she'd had a call from Fiona in India.

Don't worry, Dad. There's no big drama. Fiona just phoned to say that she had arrived in one piece, and to give Mum her temporary address in Goa.

Mum sounded pleased, and more than a little relieved. Although it sounds like Fiona has got more sun and heat than she expected – it was over ninety degrees there when she called. One thing is for sure, Dad, there's no fear of me doing any sunbathing over the next few weeks! But the cold does have its compensations – like curling up with a book beside a cosy fire. It'll be a long time before the novelty of that wears off. Time to go now. I've got a pressing engagement with (more) rest and relaxation!

I'm not gloating, Dad. In fact, I have to keep reminding myself that January is my chill-out month. I think that I'm still falling into the activity trap. Over the last week I've been fighting the feeling that I should be *doing* something!

But the city jitters have been creeping in less and less as the days pass. Cutting down my coffee consumption has helped too. In fact, I've cut it out completely; though I think that the withdrawal symptoms may have been another factor contributing to the jitters.

Well, that's enough activity for today! It's time for a soothing cup of chamomile tea and a spot of fire-gazing.

Goodnight, Dad.

Courtmacsherry

Thursday, 21st January '99

I may have got through the coffee withdrawal symptoms, but this week I discovered another potential addiction.

Since the telephone line has been connected, I'm back online with email. Over the last few days, I have noticed that I have been spending a hell of a lot of time typing emails and checking my incoming mailbox.

My excuse to myself was: 'I'm just catching up on correspondence'; or 'Just letting people know my new email address.'

But, really, with hindsight, I have been turning into a communications junkie. Even though I've been enjoying my solitude and my nature walks, I still need my fix of people. So when I got back online to people that I know, it was like, 'Please don't forget me guys!'

It's funny the insights that you get into yourself when you have the time to observe and think.

Yesterday, I thought that the techno-jinx was back – one incoming mail seemed to be taking forever to download. Curiosity prompted me to time it, but after ten minutes I wandered off to make a cup of tea. Twenty minutes later, the message was still downloading. I thought, 'Bloody Hell! This better be worth it!'

When I heard the phone disconnect with a ping, I moved back to the screen to see what had come in. I felt a wide grin spreading across my face. It certainly was worth the wait. There on the screen, in full colour, was a picture of Trish in a hospital bed in Australia holding her new baby son. Her husband Gene had emailed the photo to me. 'Announcing the birth of Anders Francis Alois Sikkora.' Trish looked radiant and Gene's words oozed with pride.

Isn't technology great, Dad? It allowed me to share in the joy of the birth of this child on the other side of the world within a few hours of the happy moment.

Anyway, that was the trigger for me to start writing a real letter to Trish.

I've had a few email conversations with her over the last few months, but when I did a scan of past Christmas cards, birthday cards and photos that I had been meaning to put in the post, I realised that it was winter '96 when I last wrote a real letter.

Two years! Yikes!

Last night, I settled down by the fire for a 'natter on paper' to Trish. Somehow, I managed to condense the events of the last year into eighteen pages without losing too much of the content. So now there is a mega-letter en route to Australia with some light entertainment for the new mom, between feeds.

Now that I think of it Dad, I really have been doing a lot of writing and typing this week. Perhaps I should take a complete break from that for a few days. Yes, it's time to give the pen and the keyboard a rest and spend more time on my nature walks instead.

Courtmacsherry

Sunday, 24ⁿᵈ January '99

Greetings from 'Wes Cark', Dad! See, I'm picking up the local accent already! It really is a beautiful accent and the local people use words in such a melodic way – ordinary conversation is almost poetic here. Perhaps that's a reflection of the more relaxed pace of life.

I'm enjoying life in the slow lane again, although it has taken me a while to settle down. The city jitters are a thing of the past now. My objective for the first few weeks here was to just chill out… and I've certainly achieved that. If I was any more relaxed I'd be comatose! But there's no fear of me turning into a couch potato.

I've discovered a new pastime – birdwatching. Can you believe it? Now, where did I put that anorak?! Joking aside, the birds are great amusement. I wake to the sound of blue tits chirping in the hedge outside my bedroom window. The lady next door feeds them, and those wily little guys sure know where their next meal is coming from. They call every morning for breakfast and it is lovely to wake up to the sound of their happy song. It's much more pleasant than the city noise of the cars revving up below my apartment window.

While I'm having my own breakfast, I watch the swans on the estuary at the end of the garden. The lady next door feeds them, too, and they seem to find plenty more food when the tide starts to fall. They hang about there for the best part of the day. Then, as the light starts to fade, they head back upstream to their base near Timoleague. I saw four of the swans in flight the other day… A majestic sight.

When the tide goes out, it exposes a sandbank in the middle of the estuary and hundreds of seagulls gather to munch on the shrimp that are stranded there. After their meal, they start to swarm and dance in the air like snowflakes practicing synchronised swimming. Their dance reminds me of the starlings over the West Pier in Brighton. I could watch them for hours, but they only keep up the dance for about thirty minutes before they disperse.

Down the far end of the village, there is a chart which gives details of the seasonal visitors to the bird sanctuary. I've been learning the names of the birds from that. At night, I hear the cry of the curlews calling out in the darkness. It's a lonely, haunting sound, but I don't feel lonely with the crackling fire, my music and books for company.

I recognise the oystercatchers too. I've seen them before from the South Wall in Dublin – though I never knew their name until now. On the cliffs, beyond Wood Point, I found a perfect perch for myself to sit and watch the oystercatchers on the rocks below. They're hilarious! They're so lazy once they get settled on a suitable rock. When a wave washes in they do this little skip-hop dance thing to get away from it. But it's only when a really big wave comes crashing that they'll make the effort to fly. When they do, they look like little black and white arrows zipping around. They really are great entertainment.

Lest you think that I am turning into a total recluse, Dad, I should tell you that I've met some very entertaining people here too. After my walk on Friday, I called in to the Anchor Bar for some mid-afternoon refreshment, and it was very refreshing indeed to meet such friendly people. I recognised one of the two men sitting beside the fire. I'd seem him a few times before on my walks over to Melmane and Broad Strand. He gave me a nod of acknowledgement as I walked towards the counter. Billy, the bearded barman, remarked on my Dublin accent with more than a hint of curiosity.

'We don't get too many tourists down here at this time of year.'

So I gave him the potted version of my story – escape from the city stresses, in search of peace and quiet, and time to write… etc.

The man by the fire passed comment on my brisk pace of walking and my apparent knowledge of local walking routes. I had to confess that my knowledge was limited to the routes that I had learned from the book and my Ordinance Survey map.

Then Billy volunteered advice on some alternative local routes. I had to consult the map to get a clear understanding as he rambled the routes in his mind's eye.

'…And then, before the road turns the corner, you go up a few fields, through a gap in the hedge, toward the top of the hill, and one of them has bull in it sometimes, but they say that he is chained up.'

Think I'll give that route a miss, thanks very much!

'Have you been over to Coolin yet?'

With pride he describes the cliffs at Coolin, claiming, 'They're the second highest cliffs in all Ireland, after the Cliffs of Moher.'

Old Tom, by the fire, remarked on the legend of the lady who jumped from the cliff after being chased by soldiers.

Billy fleshed out the story. 'And just below that flat rock, there's a bare patch of land. They say that no grass has grown on the spot where her feet last touched the ground since....'

The bar fell under a hush – a mark of respect for the art of the storyteller, and for the lady who jumped to protect her integrity.

To my embarrassment, the hush was broken by the sound of my stomach grumbling for food. So I left shortly after to quell its protest with a bowl of soup at home. But not before thanking the men for their wonderful stories and the advice on walking routes.

I haven't ventured over to Coolin yet, Dad, but I may do that tomorrow.

Although I have been back to visit the cliffs near Wood Point several times. I sat on my perch there for over an hour yesterday, letting the sun warm my face while I watched the waves.

There weren't any oystercatchers about yesterday, but I probably wouldn't have been able to watch them anyway as my view of the rocks was blinded by flashes of light – reflections from the mirror surface of the rock pools below me.

Oh, Dad, I felt such joy just sitting there on the cliff, bathed in light, gazing out across the Atlantic toward the wide horizon. Such joy and such peace.

In some flash of insight, I came to realise that is my deep driving desire: peace.

Not just the peace that I've found in this particular place and in watching the waves... I mean the peace of being in my place in the world, wherever that may be. Peace in weathering the storms, peace of mind, peace of heart, peace of soul.

Yesterday, I found all that in the one place, just sitting there on the cliff.

It was such a wonderful feeling; I'd love to share it with everyone in the world.

Mind you, if everything is connected as they say, then perhaps I did, in some way. Maybe I shared that feeling just by finding it in myself and letting it spread out like ripples on the rock pools or waves on the ocean.

A fanciful notion, perhaps, but it's one that I like.

I can't change the world, but I can change myself and my world.

Perhaps, if I keep dreaming and make my dreams happen, then the world will too.

So tonight, when I sleep, I'll dream of freedom and peace… and a world where everyone can realise their dreams too.

Goodnight, Dad.

Courtmacsherry

Monday, 25ᵗʰ January '99

Aren't dreams funny things, Dad? This morning I woke with a vague recollection of a dream within a dream. I should have written it down straightaway, as I usually do, but it had flown from my memory by the time I got out of the shower.

Over breakfast, I picked up one of the books that I'd borrowed last Saturday from the library in Clonakilty – a little anthology of poetry. I opened it at random and found myself reading William Cowper's poem, 'The Morning Dream':

"I dreamed that on ocean afloat,
Far hence to the westward I sailed,
While the billows high-lifted the boat,
And the fresh-blowing breeze never failed."

Then the postman called with postcards from the other side of the world. Fiona had sent me a card from her dream holiday in India. Karyn had sent three from various places on the last stage of her travel adventure – the overland journey from Perth back to Sydney.

The cards made me realise something, Dad.

I'm living my dream of peace and quiet with time to read and write – and that will continue for the next year.

But what's after that?

Oh, I see a book very clearly, and a business at some stage, although that's still a vague outline right now. Yet I feel that I need to find another big dream; a big adventure – something to look forward to and hope for the future. But what?

My big adventure for today is to trek across the hills to the cliffs at Coolin. So perhaps I'll let my thoughts go into free flow during the walk. And maybe the view from the cliff will give me some inspiration.

Talk to you later…

Monday evening, 25ᵗʰ January '99

What a wonderful walk!

It took longer than I had expected, and it was definitely more of a trek than a walk. Though the view from the cliffs was stupendous. The mighty Atlantic was rolling today under masses of grey cauliflower clouds, which let God light stream through, adding texture to the swell of the sea. It was like an oil painting in motion. I didn't stay to watch it for very long though, as I was conscious of time and the daylight fading during the two-hour trek back.

It was dark when I got back to Courtmacsherry; dark and cold. So I called in to the Anchor Bar to warm myself with a drink by the fire. When I stepped in the door, the bar seemed to be just as I'd left it on Friday with the same two men installed by the fire and Billy behind the bar. I told him of my excursion to Coolin while waiting for my Guinness to settle. Then another customer came in, drawing his attention to the far end of the bar.

When my pint was ready, I moved over to sit by the fire to chat with old Tom. I was hoping to hear some more of his stories of the old days on the lifeboats. But Billy was conducting conversation from behind the bar and he launched into full flight. I'm not joking, Dad, that guy could talk for Ireland, if there was such an Olympic sport – and he'd probably bring the gold medal home.

He started off talking about the price of barley thirty years ago and now, and how many pints that would buy you, then and now. After his demonstration of price inflation, the conversation moved on to drink-driving legislation, the judicial system, political corruption, government tribunals, local politics, the new pontoon mooring down at the pier, stories of visiting yachts, the nuances of negotiating the channel at half- or quarter-tide, 'rookie' skippers getting stuck on the sandbank, and the relative merits of tourism versus fishing for the local economy.

All that was discussed within a half-hour! I was spellbound by the way conversation was woven from the threads of each previous topic.

Billy's attention to the conversation was interrupted briefly as he was drawn back to work by another customer – a man with a Canadian accent. But he wasn't distracted for long. Soon, he picked up the thread of conversation again on the subject of fishing. That led on to EU fishing quotas, fish stocks, water shortages, tax rates, house prices, city traffic congestion… And he would have gone on.

But someone else mused, 'Where is it all going for the next millennium?'

The comment led to a lively debate on a contentious issue: When exactly does the next millennium start, in 2000 or 2001?

Billy was adamant. 'There was no year zero. So, technically speaking, 2000 is the last year of the second millennium and the third one doesn't start until 2001.'

And, do you know what, Dad? I reckon that he's dead right!

There is so much hype about the year 2000 that we seem to have lost track of the maths. Yes 2000 is the end of the era, not the beginning of the new one. Though I suppose that, for marketing purposes, 2000 has a better ring to it than 2001.

While the men in the bar carried on their heated debate, my mind drifted back to a conversation that I'd had with Martin shortly after I first met him, in the early hours of 1998.

'What are you doing for the Millennium New Year's Eve?' he asked.

'Well, we've been going to Roundstone in Connemara for the

last five years. But maybe we'll come back to Dingle again. Or maybe we'll just stay in Dublin. I haven't really thought that far ahead. Why? What are you doing yourself for the Millennium New Year?'

'Oh, some of the lads were talking about sailing down to the Azores. But I haven't decided yet.'

I thought to myself, now that's a plan and a half to mark a big event!

In fact, by coincidence, I was talking to him on the phone only just last night after I had laid my pen down to rest.

He still sees his Grand Canal Plan happening, though it may take a bit longer than he had originally expected. It seems that he's had a few setbacks.

The boat is still out of the water, but he's been putting in a lot of work to get her shipshape. It sounds like it has been an exceptionally challenging year for him, though he didn't go into detail and I didn't pry. I believe he'll make his Grand Canal Plan come true, as long as he keeps seeing his dream.

Then there was another coincidence in the Anchor Bar.

With all the talk of Millennium celebration plans, I mentioned Martin's notion of a voyage to the Azores to ring in the New Year. It turns out that the Canadian guy had been thinking of undertaking that voyage too, in a 20-foot boat. He reckons that it would take about a week or ten days to get there, depending on the weather and whether you'd stop over in Portugal en route.

Thoughts have been buzzing around in my mind ever since that conversation.

I have an idea surfacing. Another brainwave… And it's a big

one.

So I'm going to take a break from writing now to gaze at the fire and think it through.

Talk to you tomorrow...

Tuesday, 26ᵗʰ January '99

Oh, Dad, I've found my Millennium Dream... And it's a wonderful one.

I hardly got any sleep last night with so many exciting ideas running around in my head. But I have a mental picture of my dream now. I see it, believe it and know it will happen – as long as I keep playing that picture in my mind.

I see myself 'on ocean afloat, far hence to the westward' sailing into the Azores in plenty of time to ring in the new millennium on 1ˢᵗ January 2001.

It's a marvellous picture, Dad.

Don't ask me how I'm going to do it. There are quite a few things that I'll need to work out.

I don't have a boat. I've never really been 'on ocean afloat', well, apart from on a ferry, but I don't think that counts!

I don't even know much about the Azores, apart from the fact that they're islands in the middle of the Atlantic and some legend claims that they were the capital of Atlantis.

But the 'how' doesn't matter just now; I've got almost two years to learn and sort things out.

I may ask Martin if he is still planning on going the next time that I'm talking to him. It would be nice to make the voyage with someone that I know and trust. But if he's not going, I can find some other way.

Perhaps I could find a boating site on the Internet where I might find information and a place to ask for help. Whatever way it works out, I'll get there somehow. I expect that there'll be big challenges along the way, but I'll learn from them.

That's it, Dad! I've decided. I'm going – with Martin, or without him.

I'm sailing to the Azores to ring in the new millennium in 2001. That's my new dream! I see it… I believe it… It will happen.

You never know, Dad, if I enjoy the adventure, I may just keep going and sail all the way down to Australia to visit Trish and Gene before their new baby becomes a little man. Now, there's a notion!

I've been talking about visiting Australia for the last ten years. It's time that I did something about it, and wouldn't a 2001 odyssey be a wonderful way to go!

Oh dear, perhaps I should pull my imagination back from its flight of fancy before I see myself doing a full circumnavigation of the globe!

Though, everything is possible with the right attitude, Dad!

Back in my present reality, I promised myself three weeks chill-out time, and that time is nearly up. From Friday, I've only got another three weeks until the exams. So I'm going to start into a new routine of studying with plenty of walking, entertainment and yoga built into the schedule too.

But I lose all track of time when I write, so I'm going to stop for a while to focus on the exams and on finishing the project before Easter. Then, with my course commitments out of the way, I can get back to writing full-time on my own work.

Come to think of it, though, the exams are being held on 12th and 13th of February – the two days before your St Valentine's Day birthday. So I probably won't have much energy left over to write to you at that time, although I will be thinking of you on the day, as always.

So, before I go… I have a birthday present for you.

It's a gift of verse – words of wisdom from your old friend Omar Khayyam from *The Rubaiyat* for you to ponder on, wherever you are in this great continuum of time and space:

With them the Seeds of Wisdom did I sow,
And with my own hand labour'd it to grow:
And this was all the harvest that I reap'd –
I came like Water, and like Wind I go.

The Moving Finger writes; and, having writ,
Moves on: nor all thy Piety nor Wit
Shall lure it back to cancel half a Line,
Nor all Thy tears wash out a Word of it.

Happy Birthday, Dad!
And thanks for everything,
Love always,

Clodagh

~

Further Reading – List for Dad

CHAPTER 1 – IT'S BEEN A LONG TIME

It's been a long time since we had a chat about books. I've read quite a few more since we last spoke. Here's some that I'd recommend to you.

CHAPTER 2 – SWIMMING IN INFORMATION

Handy, Charles, *Beyond Certainty: The Changing Worlds of Organisations* (Arrow/Random House, London, 1996).
Handy, Charles, *The Hungry Spirit: Beyond Capitalism – A Quest for Purpose in the Modern World* (Hutchinson/Random House, London, 1997).
Kennedy, Angus J., *The Internet: The Rough Guide* (Penguin, London, 1998).
Shircore, Ian & Lander, Richard, *Mastering The Internet* (Orion Business Books, London, 1998).

CHAPTER 3 – CRYSTAL BALL

De Mello, Anthony, *Awareness* (HarperCollins, UK).

Hanh, Thich Nhat, *Peace Is Every Step* (Bantam/Random House, London, 1995).

Popcorn, Faith, *Clicking* (Thorsons, London, 1996).

Rinpoche, Sogyal *The Tibetan Book of Living and Dying* (Rider/ Random House, London, 1992).

CHAPTER 4 – SEA CHANGE

Black, Jack, *Mindstore For Personal Development* (Thorsons, London, 1996).

Driscoll, John, *Learn to Sail in a Weekend* (Dorling Kindersley, London, 1991).

Goleman, Daniel, *Emotional Intelligence* (Bloomsbury, London, 1996).

Jaworski, Joseph, *Synchronicity: The Inner Path of Leadership* (Berrett-Koeheler, 1996).

Jeffers, Susan, *Feel The Fear And Do It Anyway* (Arrow/Random House, London, 1987).

CHAPTER 5 – FREEDOM CALLS

Gawain, Shakti *Living in The Light* (Eden Grove Editions, Middlesex, 1986).

CHAPTER 6 – CONNECTIONS

Gawain, Shakti, *Creative Visualization* (New World Library, Ca, USA, 1995).

Hewitt, James, *The Complete Yoga Book* (Rider/Random House, London, 1987).

Kingston, Karen, *Creating Sacred Space with Feng Shui* (Piatkus, London, 1996).

MacRitchie, James, *Chi Kung: Cultivating Personal Energy* (Element Books Ltd, London, 1993).

Stone, Michael H., *Healing The Mind: A History of Psychiatry From Antiquity to the Present* (Pimlico/Random House, London, 1998).

Sivananda Yoga Vedanta Centre, *Yoga Mind & Body* (Dorling Kindersley, London, 1996).

Zukav, Gary, *The Dancing Wu Li Masters: An Overview of the New Physics* (Rider/Random House, London, 1991).

CHAPTER 7 - HEARTFELT

Carr, Alan, *Alan Carr's Easy Way To Stop Smoking* (Penguin Books, UK, 1987).

Barron, Philip, T*he Natural Way: Cancer* (Element Books Ltd, Dorset, 1996).

Grey, John, *Men are from Mars, Women are from Venus* (Thorsons, London, 1993).

Hay, Louse L., *You Can Heal Your Life (*Eden Grove Editions, Middlesex, 1988).

Mindell, Earl, *Earl Mindell's Food as Medicine* (Fireside/Simon & Schuster, New York, 1994).

Patel, Mansukh & Goswami, Rita, *The Dance Between Joy and Pain* (Life Foundation Publications, UK, 1995).

Weil, Andrew, *8 Weeks to Optimum Health* (Sphere/Little Brown, London, 1998).

CHAPTER 8 – MISSING CONNECTIONS

Davies, Dr Brenda, *The Rainbow Journey* (Coronet/Hodder & Stoughton, UK, 1998).

Myss, Caroline, *Anatomy of The Spirit* (Three Rivers Press, New York, 1996).

Shapiro, Debbie, *The Bodymind Workbook* (Element Books, UK, 1990).

Sherwood, Keith *The Art of Spiritual Healing* (Llwellyn Publications, Minn. USA, 1995).

CHAPTER 9 - JIGSAW PIECES

Bain, F. W., *In The Great God's Hair* (Parker & Co, London, 1905).

Brennan, Barbara Ann, *Hands of Light: A Guide To Healing Through The Human Energy Field* (Bantam, New York, USA, 1988).

Fairless, Michael, *The Roadmender* (Citadel Press, London, 1902).

CHAPTER 10 – ACCENTUATE THE POSITIVE

Carlson, Richard, *Don't Worry, Make Money* (Hodder & Stoughton, London, 1998).

Hill, Napoleon, *Napoleon Hill's Positive Action Plan* (Penguin, 1995).

McCann, Catherine, *Who Cares? A Guide For All Who Care For Others* (Eleona Books, Dublin, 1997).

Kennedy, Sr. Stanislaus, *Now Is The Time,* (Town House, Dublin, 1998).

CHAPTER 11 – NETWORK NEWS

Ghazi, Polly & Jones, Judy, *Downshifting: The Guide To Happier, Simpler Living* (Hodder & Stoughton, London, 1997).

CHAPTER 12 – CELTIC CONNECTIONS

Chopra, Deepak, *The Seven Spiritual Laws of Success* (Bantam Press, London, 1996).

O'Donoghue, John, *Anam Cara: Spiritual Wisdom from the Celtic World* (Bantam Press, London, 1997).

O'Donoghue, John, *Eternal Echoes: Exploring Our Hunger to Belong* (Bantam Press, London, 1998).

Frankl, Victor E., *Man's Search for Meaning* (Washington Square Press, New York, 1984).

Gill, Elaine & Everett, David, *Celtic Pilgrimages, Sites, Seasons and Saints: An Inspiration for Spiritual Journeys* (Blandford/ Cassell, London, 1997).

Joyce, Timothy, *Celtic Christianity: A Sacred Tradition, A Vision of Hope* (Orbis Books, New York, USA, 1998).

Mann, Thomas, *The Buddenbrooks* (Penguin, UK, 1924).

Poynder, Michael, *Pi In The Sky: A Revelation of the Ancient Wisdom Tradition* (Ryder/ Random House, London, 1992).

Squire, Charles, *Celtic Myths and Legends* (Parragon, Bristol, UK, 1998).

CHAPTER 13 – VIEW FROM THE CLIFF

Carey, Ken, *Starseed: The Third Millennium – Living in a Posthistoric World*, (Harper, San Francisco, USA, 1995).

Coelho, Paul, *By the River Piedra I Sat Down and Wept* (Thorsons, London, 1997).

Gaarder, Jostein, *Sophie's World* (Phoenix/Orion, London, 1995).

Gawain, Shakti, T*he Path of Transformation* (Nataraj Publishing, Ca, USA, 1993).

Redfield, James, *The Tenth Insight* (Bantam Books, 1996).

Sullivan, Edmund J and Fitzgerald, Edward, *Rubaiyat of Omar Khayyam* (Avenel Books,1988).

~

ACKNOWLEDGEMENTS – WITH GRATITUDE

Writing a book can be a daunting prospect and publishing it even more so. While the act of writing may be a solitary task the production of a book takes teamwork, and guidance in the ways of the publishing profession. It can be a steep learning curve. But, as with life, when the student is ready the teacher will appear.

I am hugely grateful to all the teachers I have encountered, who have helped to bring this book to life, particularly those who I have not even met.

My thanks to Mark Thomas (Coverness.com), for a stand out cover design, interior design, creative suggestions, professional insights and sound advice.

Thanks also to Gillian Holmes, copy editor extraordinaire, for her patience and painstaking professionalism in repairing my punctuation sins.

Thanks to www.reedsy.com for providing the platform for authors like me to find such high calibre professionals as Mark and Gillian.

A huge thanks to Vanessa Fox O'Loughlin, the Inkwell Group and all at www.writing.ie for providing invaluable information, advice and resources for writers on independent publishing.

My thanks also to Amazon and Kindle Direct Publishing for providing the platforms for independent publishers to reach a wide audience of readers.

On a personal note, my eternal gratitude to Dick Blake and Gerard Redmond for their generosity in offering me the use of creative space to write, back in the last millennium.

A big thanks also to Frank Carroll and Alfrank Designs for sponsoring my first laptop, back in the day, which afforded me the freedom to travel and the confidence to write.

Huge thanks also to Denise Moroney, Brand Dynamics, for introducing me to Jack Black and Mindstore. It only works! Changing my thinking and finding the Dream has literally changed my Life. Thanks Jack! (www.mindstore.com)

My eternal gratitude to Paulette Agnew and all the wonderful teachers at Dru Yoga, for sharing practical tools for keeping mind, body and soul in balance. Another lifesaver, on many different levels! (www.druyoga.com)

Thanks to all my family and friends, many of whom are mentioned in this book…and many of whom have moved onto another realm since it was written. Rest in peace there. For those of you who are not specifically mentioned, you know who you are.

I have met many people on the journey back to life, finding the dream and realising the dream of publishing this book. I am grateful to all those who I have met along the way who have enthused, inspired or enquired of things that have given me pause for thought, on the journey to put this book into your hands. I hope that you may find some inspiration from them also.

In the further reading section, I have shared the books that informed my thinking while writing this book. I have endeavoured to ensure that I have not infringed any copyright in the process. But if any infringement has occurred, the owners of such copyright are requested to contact me at:

clodaghwhelanone.com

~

AUTHOR PROFILE

Author, teacher and sailor, Clodagh is a multi-talented, capable, dynamic woman, with the courage of her convictions to live her life fully, realise her dreams and share her experiences, talents and life learning with others. She regularly reinvents herself and is constantly learning new skills for realising new dreams and living a life of passion and purpose.

Clodagh has been practicing Dru Yoga and Meditation since 1998. After several years of study she qualified as a registered Dru Yoga Teacher, in 2007, and a Dru Meditation Teacher, in 2011. Since 2010, she has been a senior support tutor on Dru Yoga and Meditation teacher Training Programmes in Ireland. In addition to seminars and workshops, Clodagh also teaches Dru Yoga in the workplace.

A late starter to sailing, Clodagh has been bitten by the offshore bug and has a deep love of the sea and the oceans. She has raced across several oceans, with the Clipper Round The World Yacht Race, including the North Atlantic, North Pacific and Southern Ocean, as well as other voyages at a more sedate pace. With over 40,000 sea miles logged to date Clodagh is also a certified RYA Coastal Yachtmaster.

Clodagh has a strong business background and over the course of her career has worked in many different roles; in Catering, Hospitality, Factory and Warehouse, in Small Business and Multinationals. With business qualifications in

Marketing, Finance, Business Strategy and MSc in Training and Performance Development, Clodagh is well qualified to understand the needs of business and people in businesses in the modern world. She currently lives in Dublin, Ireland... until the next voyage calls.

Back to Life... Finding the Dream is the first in a series of four books, which chart the highs and lows of Clodagh's adventures, at sea and ashore; discovering the joy and challenges of sailing, following the dream to sail to the Azores and on to racing across oceans with the Clipper Round the World Yacht Race.

For details of Clodagh's next book and publication dates visit her website at:

clodaghwhelanone.com

~

21811013R00188

Printed in Great Britain
by Amazon